D1824338

Visions of Judicial Review
A Comparative Examination of Courts and Policy in Democracies

Benjamin Bricker

First published by the ECPR Press in 2016

The ECPR Press is the publishing imprint of the European Consortium for Political Research
(ECPR), a scholarly association, which supports and encourages the training, research and
cross-national co-operation of political scientists in institutions throughout Europe and beyond.

ECPR Press
Harbour House
Hythe Quay
Colchester
CO2 8JF
United Kingdom

Typeset by Lapiz Digital Services

Printed and bound by Lightning Source

British Library Cataloguing in Publication Data

A catalogue record for this book is available from the British Library

ISBN: 978-1-785521-47-8
PDF ISBN: 978-1-785522-11-6
EPUB ISBN: 978-1-785522-12-3
KINDLE ISBN: 978-1-785522-13-0

www.ecpr.eu/ecprpress

If you are interested in judicial systems, you may like

Policy Making in an Independent Judiciary
Gunmar Grendstad, Eric N. Waltenburg and William R. Shaffer
How do the justices of a nation's highest court arrive at their decision? The authors show how an understanding of judicial behaviour developed and most fully tested in the American judicial system is transportable to the courts of other countries.
Paperback ISBN 9781785521300

More in the ECPR Press Monographs series

Consultative Committees in the European Union: No Vote – No Influence?
(ISBN: 9781910259429)
Diana Panke, Christoph Hönnige and Julia Gollub

Why Centralisation? Concept, Theory and Comparative Evidence from Sub-National Switzerland
(ISBN: 9781785521294)
Sean Mueller

Politicisation, Issue Salience and Consumer Policies of the European Commission
(ISBN: 9781785521270)
Christian Rauh

Democratic Reform and Consolidation: the Cases of Mexico and Turkey
(ISBN: 9781907301674)
Evren Celik Wiltse

Please visit http://www.ecpr.eu/ecprpress for information about new publications.

Table of Contents

List of Figures and Tables

List of Abbreviations

AWS – Solidarity Electoral Action (Akcja Wyborcza Solidarnosc)

CBOS – Center for Public Opinion Reearch (Centrum Badania Opinii Spolecznej)

DC – Christian Democratic Party (Centro Democratico)

EC – European Commission

ESM – European Stability Mechanism

EU – European Union

GSS – General social survey

IMF – International Monetary Fund

JL – New Era (Jaunais Laiks)

LC – Latvian Way (Latvijas Cels)

LDS – Liberal Democracy of Slovenia

MP – Member of parliament

MWC – Minimum winning coalition

OF – Civic Forum (Občanské Fórum)

PiS – Law and Justice (Prawo i Sprawiedliwość)

PR – Proportional Representation

PRI – Republican Party (Partito Repubblicano Italiano)

PSL – Polish Peasant Party (Polskie Stronnictwo Ludowe)

PZPR – Polish United Workers Party (Polska Zjednoczona Partia Robotnicza)

SDPL – Social Democracy of Poland (Socjaldemokracja Polska)

SLD –Democratic Left Alliance (Sojusz Lewicy Demokratycznej)

SMD – Single Member District

TP – People's Party

UP – Labour Union (Unia Pracy)

WJP – World Justice Project

ZZS – Greens and Farmers' Union (Zalo un Ziemnieku Savieniba)

ZZS-SDP – League of Communists-Party of Democratic Reform (Zveza Komunistov Slovenije-Stranka Demokratične Prenove)

Acknowledgements

This book reflects the belief that the study of courts and judicial systems works best when observed from a broad perspective. In completing this work, I have had the good fortune to have worked with many others who also adhere to this belief. I began this project as a graduate student in the political science department at Washington University in St Louis after a conversation with Matt Gabel. Matt has been a terrific source for advisement and encouragement in all aspects of work. He encouraged me to think broadly and expansively in my theoretic and empirical investigations, always ready with a pertinent analogy or thought exercise to push my thinking. Matt has pushed me to have an interesting theory and solid data, and that has made this project much stronger in the end. Thank you.

A great many people have provided support and encouragement to me during the process of writing. I want to thank Margit Tavits and James Spriggs at Washington University and Scott McClurg and Stephen Bloom, current colleagues at Southern Illinois University, for their many helpful comments and suggestions along the way. I also thank Guillermo Rosas, Cliff Carrubba, Brian Carpenter, Jonathan Kastellac, Christoph Honnige, Chris Hanretty, and Justin Fox for reading and commenting on sections of this work along the way. I also want to thank Amanda Driscoll, Joshua Potter, Jeremy Caddell, Christina Boyd, Connie Schibber, Morgan Hazelton, Susanne Schorpp, and Hadi Sahin for helpful comments on various parts of this project and good discussions on a wide variety of matters – political and otherwise. Finally, I want to thank two former law professors at the University of Illinois College of Law. Tom Ginsburg's courses at Illinois encouraged me to think about law broadly and comparatively. William Davey's course on European law gave me a terrific insight into the operation of courts outside the United States. Professors and colleagues at the Universidade Catolica Portuguesa LLM program and the University of Mannheim's political science and law programs also opened my eyes to the possibilities of law and political science comparatively.

Several organisations have provided financial support that helped me to complete my research. I gratefully acknowledge the support of Ari Stern-Gottschalk, Indiana University, and the US Department of State Title VIII program for Eastern Europe and Eurasia for giving me the opportunity to improve my language capabilities. My own academic institution, Southern Illinois University, has provided me with critical funds to finish and improve this project.

Jakub Wondreys and Kim Turner both provided excellent research assistance. Whether they knew it or not, students in my fall 2013 course on administrative law and spring 2015 senior seminar on comparative law have also helped to test and refine my ideas. My students have often helped me more than they know, and I hope I have reciprocated.

I also want to thank Peter Kennealy and the editorial team at ECPR Press. During the process of completing the manuscript, Kate Hawkins and Laura Pugh at ECPR Press were always there to help me out. Simon Ward has helped me invaluably during the final stages of the project, and I thank all of them directly.

Finally, I want to thank my family. My brother Jesse has commented on ideas throughout the writing process. My parents have provided invaluable support along the way, often in ways that have nothing to do with academics. My wife Mary has helped me in so many ways during this project, listening to my ideas and providing all the support I could ask for. Thank you.

Chapter One

Introduction: Constitutional Review in Democratic Government

When Lech Kaczynski, mayor of Warsaw, received the application for a permit to allow a gay rights demonstration, the Equality Parade, through the city in 2005, he denied the request – just as he had the year before. Homosexuality, he reasoned, goes against the moral order in Poland, a Catholic nation of traditional values. To allow such a gathering would be tantamount to promoting a 'homosexual lifestyle' in the city (BBC 2005a).

In the traditional model of parliamentary democracy dominant in Europe for much of the nineteenth and twentieth centuries, the parade organisers may have had limited options to contest such decisions. They could appeal to their local member of parliament, or perhaps their local legislators, to try to get the city to reconsider. Options would have been even more limited in the old communist regime that ruled Poland for much of the latter half of the twentieth century. An executive order from the mayor of Warsaw, the capital city, would only be subject to repeal by even more powerful leaders at the highest levels of government.

Yet Poland's post-communist democratic constitution was created in a different mould. The constitution not only created positive rights for its citizens, it also established judicial review of legislation and executive acts to ensure that government would not intrude on the new individual rights within the constitution. The ability to take a social conflict to court – to judicialise conflicts over public policy – has fundamentally transformed the European political landscape, reshaping the way citizens view and interact with governments, legislatures and, perhaps most important, the judiciary (Stone Sweet 2000). The establishment of judicial review certainly guided the actions of the parade's organisers. They filed a complaint with the Polish Ombudsman, who then filed a referral to the Constitutional Tribunal requesting the law the mayor used to make his decision be overturned. In early 2006, the Tribunal's judges overturned the decision of (then) Mayor Kaczynski, finding that any ostensible traffic problems the parade might have caused were not sufficient to limit the fundamental rights of these citizens to freely and peaceably assemble, particularly given that the mayor granted gay rights opponents a permit to demonstrate just days later. Warsaw's Equality Parade has subsequently become a widely attended, and widely covered, annual event in Poland (Kulish 2010).

This use of judicial review described above is emblematic of a larger change: that courts and judicial review are increasingly fundamental to democracy, and to considerations of how well democracies perform. A basic tenet of democratic rule, from Plato to Rousseau and Madison, has been some form of majority decision-making process, either to make decisions directly or to elect leaders to make decisions. Yet modern constitutional democracies are, almost by definition, limited governments – with these governments limited in their permissible actions by the very constitutions that establish the democratic order. Around the modern world, constitutions not only establish the functions of government, they also set up important protections for individuals living within those societies.

In the United States, courts have long been perceived to protect, in the words of Justice Harlan Fiske Stone, the rights of 'discrete and insular minorities' from harm by government actions (*US v Carolene Products Co.* (1938)). Yet, the idea that courts could sit in judgment of legislation passed by parliament was for many years anathema in Europe, where parliamentary supremacy stood as a 'constitutive principle of European politics' and courts were a subservient branch of government (Stone Sweet 2000: 1). As seen in the example above, these days are now gone. Parliaments of the people's elected representatives, as well as local and national executive leaders, now must ensure their actions conform to the constitution, as interpreted by the constitutional courts. Judicial decisions by these courts, then, provide binding legal interpretations of the constitution's text that shape the parameters of legitimate social behaviour. Yet the constitutional court is not simply a legal institution. These courts also have the capacity to shape public policy – to define which policies can be implemented, which policies must be changed, and increasingly how they must be changed. In this sense, they have become true policy makers in the democratic system.

The role of judges as policy makers brings up questions of how courts fit into democratic government, and how the institution of judicial review affects the performance of modern democracies. We expect well-performing democracies to provide for representation of citizen interests, but to do so within an atmosphere that also provides for accountability, equality, and participation (Lijphart 1991). Judges are unelected actors, yet through judicial review they are able to examine and potentially overturn the work of the popularly-elected legislative and executive branches. This distinctly 'counter-majoritarian' function of courts has led some to question the legitimacy of judicial review in a democratic system of government (Waldron 2006; Sunstein 1999; Tushnet 1999).

There are many arguments to be made in favour of judicial review in democratic society. To some, judicial review serves to protect important democratic principles – the rule of law, equality, separation of powers – from majority overreach (Guarnieri and Pederzoli 2002; Scalia 1989a). Others focus on the ability of judicial review by courts to enforce ongoing political bargains, both constitutional and legislative (Landes and Posner 1975). Increasingly, judicial review is thought to protect important liberal democratic principles – notably, the protection of individual and minority rights against majority overreach (Ely 1980). Finally, an increasing number of scholars question whether judicial review truly is 'counter-majoritarian', instead focusing on the potential majority-enhancing aspects of judicial review (Dahl 1957; Whittington 2007). All of these rationales ultimately invoke a critical, perhaps the critical, question for modern democracies: does judicial review by courts improve the performance of modern democratic governance – that is, does the institution of judicial review advance key normative goals of democracy?

In this work, I develop a comprehensive examination of the use of judicial review in democratic government. Building from existing theory on judicial motivations, jurisprudence, and strategic court interactions, I develop several larger 'visions' for judicial review in democratic government. These visions for how judicial review should operate are then tested using cross-national empirical evidence from court opinions from democracies in Central and Eastern Europe. Some hypotheses test general relationships between courts and the elected branches, while others relate to broader judicial behaviour in democracies. Overall, this study examines the motivations for the practice of judicial review, how democratic actors can limit court powers, and how judicial review can be used to develop judicial power and shape law and policy.

The rise of the constitutional courts

The fall of parliamentary sovereignty is perhaps the most significant political trend of the twentieth century (Ginsburg 2003; Hirschl 2004). In both England and France, countries whose respective legal systems became models around the world for the common law and civil law traditions, judges long lacked the ability to overturn acts of parliament. In England, this limitation existed even after the increased independence from the king given to common law courts following the Glorious Revolution of 1688 (North and Weingast 1989). Shapiro (1981: 100) remarks that the Glorious Revolution simply 'transfer[ed] the courts from one master to another, from the king to the Parliament'. Though free from arbitrary dismissal by the king, and with increased authority to develop the common law, English judges could not question the correctness of the parliament's legislation. Final judicial appeals were held in the House of Lords, the upper house of parliament.[1]

By the eighteenth century, French judges had developed great power in France. They presided over court cases, but their office also held power over government administration and even law making (Mahoney 2001). But great power over outcomes often fed great corruption within the French legal system (Cappelletti and Adams 1966). Following the French Revolution of 1789, the role of judges in France, and later all of continental European government, became increasingly limited and circumscribed.

The post-Revolution Napoleonic Code was in many ways a response to this past history of judicial corruption and avarice. After the Revolution a parliament of popularly elected legislators stood as the ultimate embodiment of the public will. Judges would no longer have discretion to create, interpret, or modify existing law. Instead, judges were constrained to follow the legislatively established civil code (the Napoleonic Code), with no ability to interpret, modify, or develop unique strands of law (Cappelletti and Adams 1966).

---

1. As of 2009, the new UK Supreme Court hears final appeals. It does not have judicial review power over legislation.

Though this codification of law initially began in France, Napoleonic conquests gradually spread the French-inspired civil code to most of continental Europe, which brought increased legislative control and a concomitant decrease in judicial discretion throughout much of the continent. Thus, for many years the idea of parliamentary sovereignty prevailed throughout much of continental Europe, with parliaments holding an absolute monopoly on the legitimate law-making power within society.

In fact, during much of nineteenth and twentieth century Europe the idea of a 'separation of powers' meant, along the lines of Montesquieu, that the parliament held the power to create laws, the executive held the power to enforce the law, while the judiciary was responsible for applying the laws to resolve any potential legal conflicts (Stone 1992). Judicial decisions only applied to the parties in the case; unlike the English common law system, civil law judicial opinions could not establish precedent (Lasser 2004). This practice, of course, only served to reinforce the subordination of the judiciary to the legislative branch. In fact, during this time the judiciary became part of a larger career-based government civil service, with initial employment determined by a series of tests, often run by the government justice ministry. Advancement up the ranks of the judicial bureaucracy was (and generally still is) determined either by the justice ministry or by a senior judicial panel, which in many cases is appointed by the justice ministry (Piana 2010; Guarnieri and Pederzoli 2002).

As parliaments were both the voice and the expressed will of the people, the predominant political view held that parliament's legislative enactments should not be called into question, much less overturned, by judges. Instead, judges were to be simply 'the mouth of the law', applying a formalist and scientific method of 'legal science' to create discrete solutions within the Code's strictures (Cappelletti 1981: 21). Within this framework, legislatures ultimately controlled the maintenance and revision of democratic constitutions. Legislative supremacy entailed that 'conflicts between a statute and a constitutional norm were either ignored by judges, or resolved in favor of the former' (Stone Sweet 2000: 31).[2]

However, in the 1920s and 1930s the breakdown of democratic governments in Germany, Austria, Spain, Portugal, and Italy and the subsequent rise of authoritarian regimes throughout Europe challenged the idea that the legislature is the best guarantor of democratic principles. Parliamentary sovereignty and majority rule had been formulated as democratic devices, yet the European experience in the first half of the twentieth century showed that both could be used to limit or deny basic social and political rights to citizens. The robust constitutional rights created in post-war constitutions thus required some type of institution to protect them from

---

2. Judicial review was not totally absent in nineteenth century Europe. Greece adopted judicial review in its 1864 constitution (Spilitopolous 1983), the Dutch had some form of judicial review in the early nineteenth century (Ginsburg and Versteeg 2014), and Denmark's Supreme Court claimed for itself the right of judicial review in 1921. The Danish court has reviewed statues for constitutional conformity on only a handful of occasions, and only once (in 1999) used that power to overturn a statute (Rytter and Wind 2011: 474).

legislative or executive encroachment. Yet, the civil code system was designed to prevent the ability of judges to impede the general will as expressed through the legislature – to avoid the creation of a 'government of judges'. In post-World War II Western Europe, this problem led to the gradual adoption of Austrian jurist Hans Kelsen's constitutional court, an idea that was later replicated in Spain and Portugal during the 1970s and in Eastern Europe in the early 1990s after the fall of the Communist governments and subsequent establishment of constitutional democracies.

As they operate today, constitutional courts are essentially single, centralised bodies designed to perform constitutional judicial review. Table 1.1 provides an overview of standing and jurisdiction in European constitutional courts. Nearly all European countries now allow individuals the right to petition the constitutional court directly. Additionally, nearly all provide the ordinary courts the ability to directly refer concrete constitutional questions to the constitutional courts, though several countries limit court access to the supreme courts (both civil and administrative). Perhaps the most notable difference between the constitutional court system and the decentralised judicial review system seen in many common law countries is the ability of institutional actors to directly challenge the constitutionality of laws. Members of parliament (MPs), presidents, ombudsmen, audit agencies, and even unions in various countries have the capacity to refer laws directly to the court for judicial review.

Though constitutional courts engage in judicial review in the same manner as the US Supreme Court, constitutional courts are different, socially and institutionally, from US-style courts in important ways. For one, constitutional courts have limited jurisdictional mandates. They only review questions of constitutional law. Many courts review only the constitutionality of statutes, legislative acts, and treaties. Some courts, notably the Czech Constitutional Court, can also review the procedures followed in lower court cases for potential constitutional violations. A few other courts also are empowered to consider the validity of elections and the operation of political parties, yet even this jurisdictional grant is based on the need to ensure that elections have been held in conformity with the constitution[3] and that political parties conform to the mandates of the constitution.[4]

Yet in other ways constitutional court procedures allow for a much more expansive institutional role than that given to US courts. Notably, constitutional courts are not limited by a 'case or controversy' requirement: as noted above, specified actors are able to challenge the constitutionality of laws without a requirement that the law harm them directly. Instead, most courts operate based on three different types of review. The first is 'abstract review', in which specified institutional (generally governmental) actors are given the authority to challenge the constitutionality of laws without the need to establish a concrete

---

3.   See Slovakia Constitution, Article 129; Czech Republic Constitution, Article 87.
4.   German Federal Constitutional Court Act, Article 43.

Table 1.1: European constitutional court jurisdiction

Country	Individual complaint	Court referral	Legislative access	Other institutional actors	Local government
Albania	Yes	Yes	Yes	Yes (Omb, Audit, PM, Religious)	Yes
Armenia	Yes	Yes	Yes	Yes (Omb, PG, Govt)	Yes
Belgium	Yes	Yes	Yes (2/3 MPs)	Yes (Fed Govt)	Yes
Bulgaria	No	Yes (Sup. Ct. and Sup. Admin Ct.)	Yes (1/5 MPs)	Yes (Pres, PG)	Yes
Croatia	Yes	Yes (Sup. Ct.)	Yes (1/5 MPs)	Yes (Pres, Omb, Govt)	Yes
Czech Republic	Yes	Yes	Yes (25 MPs)	Yes (Omb, Interior Minister)	Yes
France	No	Yes (Sup. Ct.)	Yes (60 MPs)	Yes (Pres)	No
Georgia	Yes	No	Yes	Yes (Omb)	Yes*
Germany	Yes	Yes	Yes (1/4 Parl.)	Yes (Fed Govt)	Yes
Hungary	Yes	Yes	Yes (1/4 MPs)	Yes (Omb)	No
Italy	No	Yes	Yes	Yes	Yes
Latvia	Yes	Yes	Yes (20 MPs)	Yes (Cabinet, Pres, Omb)	No
Lithuania	No	Yes	Yes (1/5 MPs)	Yes (Pres)	No
Macedonia	Yes	Yes	Yes	Yes (Parties; Unions)	n/a
Moldova	No	Yes (Sup. Ct.)	Yes	Yes (Pres, Omb, AG, Justice Min)	No
Montenegro	Yes	Yes	Yes (5 MPs)	Yes (Pres)	Yes
Poland	Yes	Yes	Yes (60 MPs)	Yes (Omb, Pres, Audit, Unions, Religious)	Yes
Portugal	Yes	Yes	Yes	Yes (Omb)	Yes
Romania	No	Yes (Sup. Ct.)	Yes (50 MPs)	Yes (Pres, Omb, Parties)	Yes
Russia	Yes	Yes	Yes (1/5 MPs)	Yes (Pres)	Yes
Slovakia	Yes	Yes	Yes (1/5 MPs)	Yes (Pres, PG)	No
Slovenia	Yes	Yes	Yes (1/3 MPs)	Yes (Omb, Pres, Audit, Union)	Yes
Spain	Yes	Yes	Yes (50 MPs)	Yes (Pres, Omb)	Yes

* Two autonomous republics can submit claims to the court.

Note: Omb = Ombudsman; Pres = President; Parties = Political Parties; Audit = Audit Agency; PG = Prosecutor General; Sup. Ct. = Supreme Court case or controversy – that is, in the abstract. Specific political actors are generally given this abstract standing to initiate judicial review, though some countries give private actors and institutions similar powers.[5] It is typical for the president, local governments, the ombudsman or citizens' rights protector, the attorney general or procurator general, and, perhaps most important, legislative opposition groups to be given the power to initiate abstract review. In many ways, this system of standing provides the best opportunity for interested and knowledgeable parties to quickly utilise the judicial process and resolve constitutional issues. For example, a president can submit a referral immediately after the passage of a bill and obtain a final resolution from the court regarding the bill's constitutionality. At the same time, these challenges bring up unique political questions between warring parties that potentially compromise the constitutional court as a neutral legal actor. Despite the reputation for abstract review to take place before a promulgated law has ever been enacted, in many countries abstract review can be both *a priori* and *a posteriori*.

Lower court judges can also refer constitutional questions that arise in the course of litigation through a second form of review – 'concrete review'. Constitutional courts resolve the constitutional matter for the lower court in an advisory opinion, which the lower court then implements. As seen in Table 1.1, nearly all countries have adopted this method of referral. As of 2008, even France, which long limited the jurisdiction of its constitutional court to abstract referrals presented by political actors, now allows ordinary courts to propose constitutional questions that arise during litigation.[6] Finally, a third form of review is the individual 'constitutional complaint'. Many countries allow individuals to directly petition the court alleging specific types of constitutional violations. Most require individuals to have exhausted their claims in the ordinary court system before initiating an individual constitutional complaint. Thus, constitutional courts have three potential avenues to receive cases: policy questions from institutional or political actors; concrete constitutional questions from judges; and cases of constitutional rights violations presented by citizens.

Judicial review and democratic performance

From parliamentary sovereignty and a distrust of a 'government of judges', the opportunities for private citizens and public bodies alike to exercise judicial review are potentially transformative for democratic governance in Europe and elsewhere. But to what end? Does judicial review advance liberal democracy? A long line of research has addressed how specific institutional features have influenced the performance of democracy normatively (Powell 2000, 1982; Lijphart 1999, 1991). Lijphart focuses on electoral rules and parliamentary institutions as primary

---

5. In Poland and Slovenia, for example, unions have limited abstract review power, and religious organisations in Poland have the same limited abstract power to refer laws affecting religion to the court.

6. French Constitutional Court Law of 23 July 2008, Article 61.

contributors towards differences between majoritarian and consensus democracies and ultimately good democratic performance. Yet rarely do these works examine the role of the judiciary. Those that do consider the judiciary (e.g., Lijphart 1999) generally treat judicial review in a very abstract fashion, ignoring the considerable variation in institutional features that distinguish the practice of judicial review around the world.

With the growing importance of judicial review to policy outcomes (Stone Sweet 2000; Vanberg 2005; Staton 2006; Amaral Garcia *et al.* 2009), and the near universality of judicial review in some form across countries today, it is all the more important to understand how judicial review affects the performance of democratic government. Examining empirically whether and how the practice of judicial review affects normative concerns of democratic government requires preliminary attention to several definitional and conceptual issues. First, we need to identify the normative goals to which the practice of judicial review is potentially relevant. The value, and thus the desirability, of democratic government is premised on the realisation of certain goals that are generally viewed as beneficial to both society at large and the individuals that comprise society. Accordingly, the potential value of judicial review to democracy must be clarified. I do this by describing several distinct visions, or arguments, in favour of judicial review in democracy. Second, we would then need to specify the empirical implications of these normative visions.

Democratic performance

Democracy entails some form of majority rule, of government 'by the people' and 'for the people', in Abraham Lincoln's words. More specifically, democracy involves some form of group decision-making characterised by relative equality between participants. Powell (2004) defines a democracy as a society that chooses policy makers based on competitive elections, under conditions that allow for free suffrage, open information sources, and civil and political rights. This definition largely overlaps with the basic conception of modern liberal democracy – a democratic regime in which government is based on free and fair elections, and individuals hold personal rights and freedoms that cannot be violated by government.

The notion of democracy, particularly liberal democracy, as defined above, is justified on specific normative grounds. One is based on the fundamental equality of all citizens. Given this inherent equality, democracy provides the most legitimate method for the people to participate in decision-making processes. Democracy also offers, through elections or direct participation of the people, the most suitable processes for citizens to both create and exercise control over policy outcomes – that is, to have their views represented in government (Dahl 1989: 83). In short, democracy is normatively valued because it should lead to government policies and actions that comport with the interests of the majority of citizens. At the same time, modern liberal democracy is also valued because it provides to all citizens fundamental rights against which government actions cannot intrude.

A limited government that respects fundamental individual rights is secured through adherence to the 'rule of law' – a system in which the laws are publicly known and are applied neutrally and equally to everyone in society (Carothers 1998). This respect for the rule of law is critical for the performance of modern democracies, as the rule of law ensures – generally through court actions and judicial decisions – that individual rights are protected and government limitations respected. It is important to note, as Shapiro (2008) does, that adherence to the rule of law does not necessarily imply good democratic governance. Indeed, autocrats can enforce unfair or irrational rules on all in society and still fall within the basic stricture of the rule of law. Singapore arguably provides very strong 'rule of law' protections for economic rights, but less robust protection of individual civil rights. Yet, liberal democracies must adhere to the rule of law within society to ensure the goals of citizen equality, limited government, and majority processes.[7]

Scholars recognise that actual democracies vary in the ability to realise these normative goals of equality, participation, majority rule, and adherence to the rule of law in practice. This variation can occur, for example, as a result of the choice of institutions that connect voters to policy makers (Powell 2004; Lijphart 1999). The differences countries have faced in realising these normative goals has motivated a large body of research that empirically examines whether and to what extent certain democratic institutions can improve democratic performance and democratic outcomes (Lijphart 1999; Anderson and Paskeviciute 2006; Tsebelis 2002; Schmidt 1996; Powell 1982). Powell (1982), for example, investigates how institutional variation can affect the stability of democracy, the ability of citizens to participate in government, and the ability of democratic government to prevent violence. Lijphart (1991) discusses how institutional frameworks can influence democratic performance, specifically, the degree to which political systems meet democratic norms of (a) representativeness, (b) accountability, (c) equality, and (d) participation.

In a broad sense, I take this same approach to study the effect of judicial review in democratic government. Below, I identify normative goals of democratic government for which judicial review is potentially relevant. Then I examine how variation in the institution of judicial review should lead to differences in the quality of democratic performance. Finally, I test whether in fact these claims hold. Below I trace the outlines of these arguments, which will be discussed in greater detail in Chapter Two.

Visions of judicial review

Why give courts in democratic regimes the power of judicial review? In *Marbury v Madison*, Chief Justice John Marshall deftly sidestepped this crucial question, instead framing the primary issue as whether Congress can pass laws contrary to the constitution (Bickel 1962). So, why give courts the power to review and

---

7. The rule of law is, then, a necessary but not sufficient condition for democratic rule.

overturn legislation duly created and enacted by the people's representatives in the legislature? There certainly are other possibilities: notably, leaving constitutional revision to the people, either directly through a popular vote or indirectly through elections in which they can vote out lawmakers supporting unconstitutional acts. This, in many ways, is the practice in the United Kingdom and the Netherlands.

Given the ever-increasing aura of power placed around the institution of judicial review, and the unelected nature of the judicial branch, it is necessary to inquire how judicial review contributes to normative goals of democracy and democratic performance. The arguments, or visions, for judicial review are multi-faceted, yet in their own way all seek to explain whether and how judges are able to create representative rulings that deliver in practical ways the abstract benefits of democratic rule.

One vision for judicial review focuses on the ability of judges engaging in judicial review to find the 'right' answer to constitutional questions, based on legal doctrine and jurisprudential principles. This 'legalistic' view fits within a larger rule of a law-based vision of democracy, in which the purpose of democratic government is to ensure fair processes and orderly social outcomes within the constraints of the law. Judicial intervention and dispute resolution according to legal norms and doctrines, while maintaining subservience to the law, is an often-told story in democracies around the world – and is perhaps the most common justification for judicial review today (Guarnieri and Pederzoli 2002: 155). Judicial review, in this vision, is normatively desirable in that judges trained in methods of legal analysis and deduction will be able to apply these neutral principles – and the rules and insights from past cases – to reach the most appropriate legal outcome.

A second vision for judicial review focuses on the role of courts as protectors of constitutional rights, particularly the rights of individuals and of minority groups against majority tyranny. This vision for judicial review fits within a larger liberal rights-protecting view of modern democracy, in which the provision and protection of positive individual rights is of paramount concern. In many ways, this vision of democracy, and of judicial review, provides the archetype for modern democratic governance (Hague and Harrop 2010). The vision of democracy as rights-conferring and rights-protecting has been mirrored in the movement towards second and third generation constitutional rights – rights that not only protect individuals from government excesses, but also provide individuals with positive rights to certain procedures and to benefits, like health care and pensions. The movement towards individual rights and personal expression is perhaps best seen in the shift from materialist to post-materialist beliefs in many advanced democracies (Rogowski 1989).

Both the legalistic and the rights-protecting visions anticipate the possibility – even likelihood – of conflict between majority preferences and court outcomes. A third vision, one increasingly common in the political science literature, reaches the opposite conclusion: judicial review can actually be majority-enhancing. This majoritarian vision of judicial review argues that judicial review is valuable because it increases the correspondence between government policy and the preferences of the majority. In this majoritarian vision, courts of constitutional review advance majority interests by reviewing legislation to ensure it comports with contemporary majority preferences. If the preferences of the majority change over time, judicial review can allow opportunities to review and modernise legislation, thus bringing it in line with current preferences. This majoritarian vision of judicial review recognises that legislators may, for various reasons, have incentives to pass laws that diverge from the preferences of the broader public. Electoral laws, legislative procedures, and interest group influence all can create incentives for lawmakers to create policies that deviate from majority preferences (Klarman 1997). Judicial review of legislation can potentially shift policy away from these aberrant outcomes and towards the views of the majority.

A majoritarian vision of judicial review may be realised through several different paths. First, judges come to the bench with certain ideological beliefs. Rules in most countries place popularly elected leaders in charge of appointing judges to high courts. With these appointment rules, it is unlikely that court opinions will be far from the views of lawmaking majorities (Dahl 1957). Thus, judicial review largely serves to legitimate policies enacted by current elected leaders (Dahl 1957; Funston 1975), but may also be used to strike disfavoured policies (Whittington 2005, 2007; Rogers 2001). Second, courts may respond directly to public opinion, limiting or altering the exercise of judicial review in response to changes in public support for the judiciary (Clark 2011). Third, judges may respond to institutional incentives, like reappointment pressures, that encourage outcomes from judicial review consistent with majority preferences (Helmke 2002). A final argument for majoritarian judicial review focuses on the incentives courts have to gain compliance with their rulings from other political actors. Without the power of the purse or the sword, courts are dependent on the executive to enforce their judgments and the legislature to make necessary statutory changes. This separation of powers framework provides judges incentives to rule such that democratically elected actors will support and implement their rulings (see Carrubba *et al.* 2008). Of course, some of these mechanisms offer only limited incentives for constitutional review to correct counter-majoritarian legislation or administrative acts. I return to these issues in Chapter Two.

Application of the visions of judicial review

Each vision described above provides a distinct normative justification for judicial review in modern liberal democracy, whether it be a rights-protecting, a rule of law-process-oriented, or a majoritarian account. How well do these visions for judicial review translate into the real world of constitutional politics and adjudication? That is, does constitutional review actually advance any of these normative goals in practice? Returning to the Polish Equality Parade case mentioned earlier can provide some context. In that case, the court was asked to resolve whether the Road Safety Act of 1997, which requires non-religious organisations to obtain permission from public authorities before holding a demonstration, violated Article 57 of the constitution, which grants 'everyone' the right to 'freedom of peaceful assembly'. In legal terms, the question can be (and was) presented as an error of legal and constitutional process: specifically, whether local agents (such as city mayors) should be given the discretion to make procedural adjudications, given that the determinations of local agents might infringe on constitutional freedoms.

In overturning the law, the judges engaged in a wide-ranging investigation into the jurisprudence surrounding freedom of assembly, using the text of the constitution, precedent from Polish law, normative explanations on individual freedom and legal procedures from academics, and decisions from the European Court of Human Rights to reach and justify the ultimate outcome. Specifically, the judges decided that the law as applied gave too much discretion to implementing actors and thus failed to give the predictability and equality of outcomes required in a country governed by the rule of law.[8] Thus, the basic outline of the court's ruling appears to support the legalist vision mentioned above.

Though the court examined the case procedurally, focusing on past legal precedents and rule of law principles, the judges who decided the case ultimately went beyond the text of the law in reaching their decision. The judges also examined the meaning and purpose of democratic rule, particularly the importance of minority rights in a democratic Poland. Freedom of assembly, the court noted, is a fundamental part of democracy; extending this freedom to all groups, including minority groups, not only strengthens the democratic fabric, but also legitimises governmental decisions within democracy. Consequently, the court must protect the freedom of assembly for all citizens, 'regardless of the political views expressed by the holders of [political power]' (Case K 21/05, 3 (English translation)) in government. Such freedoms are inherent in the democratic order, and are not 'defined by the ... political majority in power at a certain moment in time'.[9] The political import of the case and the focus on gay rights also was apparent – the then-Marshal of the Sejm later described the case as 'the one on the homosexuals' right to demonstrate' (a case this MP thought the court got wrong) (Siedlecka 2008). Thus, we could also conclude from the court's opinion that the decision falls within the 'rights-protection' prism for judicial review, in that the judges deciding the case relied strongly on notions of fundamental rights and equal rights for all, apart from and in addition to any process-based jurisprudential arguments.

The rights-protecting vision for judicial review focuses on how courts can help democracies with important ideals of social equality and citizen participation, though it also acknowledges courts can be pitted against public opinion in the exercise of judicial review. Such a conflict appeared to exist at the time the decision was made. In August 2005, around the time the case was accepted for review, only 16 per cent of Poles believed homosexuals should be able to 'publicly display their lifestyle' (CBOS 2013).

Given public sentiment, could the court's outcome fall within majoritarian principles, as well? Yes, when we consider the parties and actors in power at the time. When the case was initially filed, the leftist Sojusz Lewicy Demokratycznej

---

8. Case K 21/05 (English translation).
9. Case K 21/05 (English translation).

(SLD) party held power in parliament. At the time, the SLD was the only major Polish party to actively promote minority rights (Volkens *et al.* 2011). The SLD also was active in the legislative arena. In 2003, an SLD Senator, Maria Szyszkowska, proposed legislation to create civil unions in Poland for gay and lesbian couples, and by 2005 the Senate had passed a civil unions bill. Prominent SLD politicians also were publicly critical of moves to ban such parades in Polish cities (PAP 2005; BBC 2005b). In the courtroom, the panel of judges that heard the case was predominantly appointed by the SLD, suggesting a link between majority parliamentary voting preferences and court decision-making. Thus, there is some evidence to conclude the outcome is majority enhancing, at least in the sense that political actors from the legislative majority are able to appoint judges to the bench, who then can legitimate the majority's favoured policies (Dahl 1957).

At the same time, an increasingly prevalent version of the majoritarian vision of judicial review holds that courts generally will align with the policies of the majority, due to the need to obtain compliance with their rulings (e.g., Vanberg 2005). At first look, the compliance rationale does not fit well with the Polish gay rights case. Lech Kaczynski, the man who rejected the parade petition, had moved from the Warsaw mayor's office to become President of Poland after the PiS electoral victory. Further, Lech's twin brother Jaroslaw Kaczynski led the PiS government as Prime Minister. In formulating their ruling, the court appears to have challenged the views of both the parliament and the new president whose decision led to the court case.

Yet, looking at compliance from a separation-of-powers perspective, the court arguably had little to fear from the PiS government. The PiS government, with only 33.7 per cent of seats in the new parliament seated shortly before the case was decided, was ultimately too weak to mount an effective challenge against or override the court's outcome – a fact borne out by Prime Minister Kaczynski's ineffective attempts to corral the constitutional court in 2005 and 2006 (Sadurski 2010). Thus, this case could present an instance of court activity in the face of government weakness. Further, the practical effect of the ruling bypassed parliament and the president altogether. For the purposes of the gay rights parade, the important implementing actor was not the national government but instead the interim mayor of Warsaw, Miroslaw Kochalski, who allowed the parade to proceed in 2006. Other than commanding the local government in Warsaw to disregard the constitutional court ruling, which would set up a constitutional crisis, the government was left (much like the Jefferson administration in *Marbury v Madison*) without a counter move after the decision was announced.[10]

A final version of the majoritarian vision of judicial review holds that judges should, in making decisions, generally stay within the bounds of popular opinion. As noted above, the Polish court's decision in the gay pride parade case seemed

---

10. Leading the legal challenge against the law was the Polish Ombudsman's office, an important and publicly popular oversight agency. In the end, the court's action could, in fact, be seen as the product of the preferences of the legislative majority in place when the case was filed – the same legislative majority that appointed the panel majority to the court.

to go against the prevailing popular opinion on gay rights. Yet in other cases, and other issues, the Polish court has seemed to engage in judicial contortions to stay within the bounds of public opinion. Poland is a Catholic country, one of the few European countries where most citizens still regularly attend church services (Manchin 2004). A 2007 poll by Polish polling firm CBOS reported that nearly half of Poles (48 per cent) believed politics should be based on religious values, and 61 per cent believed the Ten Commandments should be the basis for Polish law. Further, most respondents believed the Catholic Church should play a role in education. The Polish Constitution also guarantees impartiality on the part of public authorities regarding religious beliefs within the country.[11] The court was asked to address this neutrality clause in 2007 after the Sejm passed an education law creating a funding line for religious instruction in university education that appeared to benefit the Catholic Church.[12] Noting a line of case law balancing church interests against the need to ensure equality in society, the court found that parliament can, consistent with the constitution's neutrality clause, treat religious organisations differently if the law is rational, based on constitutional values, and advances the public interest more than it impedes the rights of other religious groups. Unlike the Equality Parade case, in this example the court seemed to go out of its way to allow an inequitable but popular law to remain in force.

Ultimately, one lesson from the examples above is that it is difficult to find descriptive evidence that distinguishes among these common visions of judicial review. In fact, descriptive evidence can be marshalled to support how all of these different visions of judicial review explain court outcomes and improve democratic performance. The muddled conclusions above show the importance of moving beyond the study of individual events and cases to find the larger causal factors in judicial decision-making.

To isolate these factors, we would need more specific empirical expectations about judicial behaviour and how it influences judicial review and, ultimately, democratic performance. I provide this analysis in later chapters by examining case outcomes from several Eastern European constitutional courts. Specifically, I am able to leverage information from differences in appointment and retention processes, panel compositions, differences in the actors who bring claims to the court, as well as the methods judges employ to justify and legitimate their outcomes to differentiate these goals. Yet before we move on to empirical matters, the second chapter frames the broader normative questions relating to judicial review, judicial power, and democratic performance. It is to these issues we now turn.

---

11. Polish Constitution, Article 25(2).
12. Polish Constitutional Tribunal, Case K 55/07, 14 January 2009.

Chapter Two

Majoritarian or Counter-Majoritarian? Visions for Judicial Review

The spread of judicial review was perhaps the most transformative institutional development of the twentieth century. At the beginning of the century, only the United States, Norway, Greece, and Switzerland (to a limited extent) allowed for the judicial review of government acts, yet by the end of the century, most democratic regimes had adopted some form of judicial review.[1]

Judicial review gives courts the power to examine and potentially overturn legislative and executive acts – a power that provides judges a crucial role in determining policy outcomes. Questions that formerly were decided by the legislature or the government are now decided within the judge's chambers. Providing judges these forums to determine policy questions establishes an important 'judicialisation' of government and policy – a judicialisation that, potentially, takes the views of political majorities out of the policy equation (Hirschl 2008; Stone Sweet 2000). For this reason, overturning an act of the legislature has been called 'the gravest and most delicate duty' that courts are called on to perform.[2]

The judicialisation of politics allows courts of constitutional review the potential to significantly shape the processes and outcomes of government. The ability to review and ultimately strike legislation also means that the court can direct the outcomes of the policy process. Moreover, the potential impact of constitutional review seems to induce legislatures – and even interest groups and voters – to behave differently (Stone Sweet 2000; Epp 1998). For example, through autolimitation, in which parliamentary majorities self-limit the content of the bills they produce to avoid a judicial veto, constitutional courts have been thought to directly alter the output of legislative majorities. These effects touch on central components of our normative goals and justifications for democracy. In particular, representative democracy is commonly espoused because it is expected to produce policy outcomes that reflect the will of the people – or at least get closer to that ideal than other institutional forms of governance (Dahl 1989). But, without a serious consideration of the role of judicial review in the policy process, we cannot

---

1. The Netherlands and the United Kingdom are two notable exceptions, though Ginsburg and Versteeg (2014) note a brief experiment with judicial review in the Netherlands from 1802 to 1805. In Switzerland, only cantonal laws can be overturned by the judiciary. Portugal adopted judicial review in 1911. Romania's courts adopted judicial review in 1912, which was ratified in the short-lived inter-war constitution (Sadurski 2005: 2).

2. *Blodgett v Holden*, 275 US 142, 142 (1927).

provide a comprehensive account of democracy in modern settings. The concern over judicial review is all the more important because, as many observers have noted, endowing typically unelected judges with policy making authority through judicial review has the appearance of undermining representative democracy (Waldron 2006). If this is the case, why have the institution of judicial review in modern democracy?

In this chapter, I set out an agenda to answer this question. I first provide several desirable normative goals of modern representative democracy and discuss how different 'visions' – or arguments – for judicial review could influence, and potentially enhance, representative democracy. Much like the comparative framework created by Damaska (1986), these visions represent stylised, ideal types of behaviour for judges exercising judicial review. Many existing theories of judicial review and judicial decision-making fit into these three visions, and I discuss these theories within whenever applicable. Second, I distinguish these rationales in terms of their empirical implications for the conduct of judicial review. These distinctions are critical to learning which (if any) of these rationales better describes outcomes in democratic society. Subsequent chapters will test these claims empirically to determine whether there is empirical support for any vision on a broad scale.

Vision 1: The majoritarian vision for judicial review

A primary goal of democracy focuses on the desirability of democratic institutions to produce policies that reflect the will of the people. This majoritarian goal of democracy fits well with a large and still developing literature that can be called the 'majoritarian vision' for judicial review. Encapsulated by President Abraham Lincoln's statement that democratic government is government 'for the people, by the people', majoritarian arguments for democracy focus on the inherent legitimacy of government based on the sovereignty of the people – specifically, the power of the majority of the people to produce, either directly or indirectly through elected representatives, policies and laws that guide society (Tocqueville [1838] 1966: 254). Legislatures elected by citizens through majority voting processes embody this democratic ideal, and their actions are imbued with democratic legitimacy precisely because they are the product of majority will. At first glance, judicial review of legislation and executive acts fits rather poorly into a majoritarian conception of democracy, as judicial review provides unelected judges the power to overturn the decisions of lawmaking majorities (Bickel 1962). Without constraints, the practice of judicial review may become, in the words of Justice Antonin Scalia, an 'assertion of judicial supremacy over *the people's Representatives* in Congress and the Executive'.[3] Or, in Edouard Lambert's classic phrase, judicial review raises the danger of a 'government of judges' unaccountable to the public.[4]

---

3. *US v Windsor*, 570 US __, 21 (2013) (J. Scalia dissent, italics added).

4. In fact, Lambert's 'government of judges' phrase was used to describe the behaviour of the US Supreme Court in the early 1900s.

Scalia and Lambert's concern illustrates the counter-majoritarian difficulty—the practical democratic problem that arises when judges review popularly created laws. The counter-majoritarian difficulty has motivated a large body of theory that examines whether judicial review can be normatively desirable from a democratic perspective (see, e.g., Bickel 1962; Cappelletti 1989: 117–149). Even with the influence in the early 1900s of the American and Scandinavian legal realists and the German free law theorists, who sought to legitimate judicial decision-making as an instrument for resolving social problems, this counter-majoritarian concern is all the more true in continental Europe, which, as mentioned in Chapter One, has a deep tradition of political power maintaining accountability to the popular will through parliamentary government. Even in the Nordic countries of Denmark and Norway, which have had judicial review for nearly a century, judges are strongly guided by a norm of judicial self-restraint, which provides wide latitude to the majoritarian and democratically legitimate parliament to create policy (Rytter and Wind 2011).

Despite the prevalence of the counter-majoritarian dilemma in popular thinking, many judicial scholars have begun confronting the notion that judicial review is, by definition, anti-majoritarian (see Hall 2012). Instead, driven by an empirical literature that has often failed to confirm the counter-majoritarian nature of judicial decision-making, an increasingly prevalent view – at least among American judicial politics scholars – holds that judicial review has the capacity to increase the correspondence between government policy and the preferences of the majority, and thus can be majoritarian or majority-enhancing in practice.

There are good reasons to question the validity of the counter-majoritarian difficulty. Some scholars take issue with the notion that legislative policy always realises the majority will. Instead, institutional features of the democratic system can inhibit the realisation of popular preferences. In presidential systems, executives can veto legislation, and bicameral legislatures can create blockages or veto points for majority-backed legislation to clear. These institutions can create policy discongruity, in which actual policy ends up far from the median citizen's (or legislator's) preferred location. When policy becomes sufficiently extreme, judicial review can impose a new solution that moves policy from a relatively extreme location to a position closer to the median (Klarman 1997). Acting in this majoritarian fashion, judges can still exercise discretion, deferring to the will of representative institutions when legislation represents the popular will and striking down laws only when they fall outside the majority interests (Guarnieri and Pederzoli 2002). Thus, judicial review may actually be able to advance majority interests in practice. Judicial review also can serve majority citizen interests by serving as a focal point for public grievances, allowing citizens and groups to coalesce outside of the normal political channels to directly challenge government actions (Weingast 1997).

Thus, judicial review could, in theory, allow for majority outcomes to be expressed. Assuming the theoretical ability and desirability of judicial review to operate in a pro-majoritarian fashion, why would we also expect judges to perform majority-enhancing judicial review in practice? A number of competing, partially overlapping, answers have been offered.

a. The ruling regime thesis

It was Dahl (1957) who first noted the majoritarian aspect of the US Supreme Court's judicial review powers. Dahl's 'ruling regime' thesis begins with the observation that, despite the fundamentally legal nature of court cases, Supreme Court decisions rarely are out of step with majority political preferences. To Dahl, this is largely because justices are appointed to office by political actors who themselves are selected through majority voting procedures. The power political actors hold over appointments should result in inherently policy-based judicial review by the Court. But, the ideological connection between the justices and the ruling regime makes it 'unrealistic to suppose that ... Supreme Court justices would long hold to norms of Right or Justice substantially at odds with the rest of the political elite' (Dahl 1957: 291; Funston 1975). With the guardians of the constitution chosen by those whom they guard, we should not expect serious disagreement between the court and its electors. Instead, judicial review by courts largely acts to legitimise the policies created by the dominant political coalition. Judicial review serves as a necessary part of this legitimating function. As the eminent American law professor Charles Black noted back in 1960, the Supreme Court's primary role in society has been to validate policy, but without the power to overturn legislation the legitimating aspect for majority policy would be meaningless. By reinforcing the sense that the political leadership is acting in accordance with a common set of social and political norms, judicial review thus becomes critical to well-performing democracies.

Dahl's analysis focused (by necessity) on the US Supreme Court from the early 1900s through the early 1950s. During that time period, new spots on the bench opened up on average every twenty-two months. Over a two-term presidency, then, the ideological shape of the Supreme Court could be completely re-formed. This is no longer the case: from 1975 to 2004 (a period of thirty years), only eight new justices were appointed to the Court. And of the seven US presidents since 1975, only one – Reagan – was able to appoint more than two justices to the bench. Current work examining the outcomes of the Supreme Court finds little support for the 'ruling regime' thesis (Keck 2007).[5] Hall (2012), for example, finds the Court frequently invalidates statutes adopted by the current ruling regime. Similarly, Owens (2010) concludes that the preferences of the current legislature and executive are not strong influences in Supreme Court voting.

Few works have tested this concept outside of the United States. Examining the Portuguese Constitutional Court, Amaral Garcia et al. (2009) found party politics did influence some judges on the Portuguese Court. Specifically, judges appointed by left-wing parties adhered to this type of majoritarianism, ratifying left-wing legislative policy at a much higher rate when the parties of the left were in power. No effect of this kind was found for right-appointed judges, however. Thus, based on current US evidence and the small amount of existing comparative evidence,

---

5. The 'ruling regime' thesis can also be termed the 'regime politics' thesis, as in Keck (2007) and Pickerill and Clayton (2004: 236).

there appears to be some limited support, but not substantial support, for Dahl's theory of legitimating judicial review. With Dahl's proposed temporal mechanism linking court rulings to democratic legitimacy now uncertain, in what other ways might judicial review still be majoritarian, or majority-enhancing?

b. Cooperative (allied) judicial review

A variation of the majority-enhancing theory focuses on the idea that judicial review of legislation does not need to be inherently conflictual. Instead, it can be a cooperative venture of mutual benefit to the court and the legislature. In this cooperative effort, some scholars have posited that courts and legislatures can, in practice, coordinate actions, whether altruistically to obtain better policy outcomes for society, or more cynically to obtain more ideologically desirable outcomes.

In one iteration of what I term 'cooperative' review, judicial review improves democratic processes by providing informational benefits to legislative majorities, which could allow for the creation of better policy outcomes (Rogers 2001). Legislators create legislation under conditions of high uncertainty. Legislators seek to create laws that will achieve certain policy ends, but they are not able to look into the future and see the actual outcome of their legislation (Bickel 1962; Vermeule 2010). Laws passed today may have unintended consequences tomorrow; alternatively, social circumstances may change over time. When courts review legislation, they are able to examine not only the text of the act, but also the actual impact the law has had since it was adopted. Thus, courts have an information advantage over legislatures in terms of how laws are working in practice. They can, in Justice Harlan Fiske Stone's (1936) description, exercise a 'sober second thought' regarding the wisdom of laws made under pressures to obtain immediate results, removing altruistically both bad legislation and legislation that does not account for new or changed social circumstances. Examples of such behaviour can be seen in the real world of judging, including a 2000 sex discrimination case in which the Polish Constitutional Tribunal overturned a law amended in 1998 that set different retirement ages for male and female teachers. Women were given mandatory retirement at age 60, while men could work until 65. When challenged in the court by the Polish Ombudsman, the court overturned the act, but in doing so was aided by a brief from the parliament – the same parliamentary majority that passed the amended law – admitting that portion of the law was unconstitutional and should be overturned.[6]

Judges may adopt this altruistic 'error correction' mode of decision-making, though a second variation of the cooperative judicial review – what can be called the 'allied court' thesis – downplays the altruistic function of judicial review in favour of a judicial review model that systematically favours the policies of allied majorities. Whittington (2005; 2007) argues that political majorities can use friendly judicial review from ideologically 'allied' courts to strike down

---

6.   Case K 27/99, 28 March 2000.

legislation that is mutually disfavoured. In this view, political leaders are able to use the finality of judicial review and the relative political insulation of high courts to remove old policies that are, for various reasons, difficult to change through the legislative policy process. For example, federal systems often have dispersed power arrangements, such as bicameral legislative chambers, or a president elected separately from parliament. These arrangements are designed, in part, to serve as veto points that prevent majority tyranny. Yet Whittington explains that friendly judicial review can be used to bypass these roadblocks, as the Warren Court did to remove segregationist laws in the US South (2005: 592).

Similarly, when Harvey and Friedman (2006) examined the lifespan of all US laws passed between 1987 and 2000, they found the Supreme Court does exercise some type of 'allied' review. Specifically, the conservative Rehnquist Court was more likely to strike down laws after the Republican takeover of Congress in 1994. In subsequent work, Harvey (2013: 15) confirms this point, finding federal laws enacted by the Republican congresses of 1995 to 2004 much less likely to be struck down by the conservative Supreme Court than laws passed by previous liberal-Democratic congresses.

The allied court thesis provides an avenue for the realisation of majority policy outcomes, yet the parties the court chooses to ally with could result in a failure to promote the majority will. For example, the Supreme Court's Eleventh amendment state sovereign immunity doctrine from the late 1990s and 2000s follows the allied court thesis, yet arguably fails to meet majoritarian criteria. In these cases the Court allied with local attorneys general who were seeking to avoid federal regulations mandating that states provide overtime and minimum wages to state employees.[7] These decisions fed the growing conservative demand for greater state's rights, yet they also allowed states to avoid punishment for violating federal gambling, disability, and worker overtime laws – laws duly enacted by different coalitions of nationally elected leaders.

Similar to Dahl's earlier theory, the allied thesis assumes that judges exercising review both have identifiable policy preferences and should generally act to further those policies. Yet, rather than legitimating the current majority policy, judicial review will be used instead to actively strike down old legislation passed by former political majorities. Arguably, the mechanism behind the allied review model would work well in the streamlined parliamentary systems that dominate most of Europe. However, the nature of abstract judicial review, in which specific actors like presidents, local governments, and groups of legislators can directly challenge the constitutionality of legislation, could present possibilities for the allied model to undermine majoritarian outcomes. President Walesa's – or President Kaczynski's – frequent use of abstract review procedure in the Polish Constitutional Tribunal could be seen as a way to circumvent parliamentary opponents in the legislative majority. Similarly, minority party MPs can use the abstract review procedure to continue legislative battles in the courts, potentially using the constitutional courts

---

7.   *Alden v Maine*, 527 US 706 (1999); *Seminole Tribe of Florida v Florida*, 517 US 44 (1996).

as a forum to overturn majority policy. Stone Sweet (2000: 198) notes this feature can 'instantaneously' change the dynamic in parliament.

Finally, apart from the allied or altruistic review models, cooperative judicial review can be majority-enhancing in a third, quite distinct way: fractious political majorities that are unable to choose between competing policies may, at times, invite judicial review to help resolve issues they either cannot resolve or would rather not address. Graber (1993) notes the Supreme Court's *Dred Scott* decision as an example of this type of outcome: with the US increasingly split on the issue of slavery, the Missouri Compromise, many politicians were all too happy to have the Court determine the final outcome of Dred Scott's fate and provide a definitive answer to the question of slavery. Justice Antonin Scalia's comments during oral arguments in the *Shelby County v Holder* (2013) Voting Rights Act (VRA) case are reminiscent of both the Whittington and Graber theses. Noting the overwhelming support for the VRA in both the House and the Senate (there was 'not a single vote in the Senate against it'), and the re-election problems that would no doubt arise from any legislator who opposed voting rights for minorities, Scalia questioned during the oral arguments whether amending the VRA was something Congress should even be involved in – might the legislature impliedly be giving the Court the heavy job of overturning the law, or amending it to remove minority protections? Scalia proposed this might be so:

> Whenever a society adopts racial entitlements, it is very difficult to get out of them through the normal [majoritarian] political processes. I don't think there is anything to be gained by any Senator to vote against continuation of this act. And I am fairly confident it will be reenacted in perpetuity unless – unless a court can say it does not comport with the Constitution. (*Shelby County v Holder* Oral Arguments Transcript (2013))

By striking down the law, the Court then imposes a majority-favoured solution, one that is too risky for political actors to endeavour on their own through the normal legislative channels. It is, Scalia implies, only the courts that can take on such a fraught issue and impose majority-preferred solutions on society.

c. Public support thesis

The theories of judicial review presented above all are premised on the notion that courts, specifically the judges who exercise judicial review, respond to or articulate the majority will indirectly as channeled through the legislature or the executive. Another view of majority-enhancing judicial review examines the direct connection between judicial outcomes and public support for the judiciary (e.g., Clark 2011; Friedman 2009). Given that nearly all high court judges are appointed, not popularly elected actors it may seem paradoxical to examine whether courts respond to public pressures and public opinion. Yet, the idea that courts must seek out and maintain the public's trust has been suggested for centuries: Tocqueville wrote in 1838 of the significance for US court power that judges neither 'lag behind' nor 'outstrip' public opinion, and the overriding importance for judicial power that they 'understand the spirit of the age' (Tocqueville [1838] 1966: 83). More memorably, American political cartoonist Finley Peter Dunne's popular Mr Dooley character said in 1901, 'the Soopreme Court follows th' illiction returns'. The need for public trust in the judiciary is equally evident in Europe, where the spectre of a popularly unaccountable judiciary imposing its views on the public gave rise to strong limitations on judicial power in France and elsewhere (Mahoney 2001).

Evidence on the empirical question of whether the courts actually respond to public opinion is still contested, though there is a growing amount of support that voting behaviour, at least on the US Supreme Court, does shift with the public's mood (Casillas, Enns and Wohlfarth 2011; Friedman 2009; Durr, Martin and Wolbrecht 2001; Giles, Blackstone and Vining 2008). Much of the work on the direct relationship of courts to public opinion has focused on the United States, though Volcansek (2000: 149) also finds that public opinion has undoubtedly influenced Italian Constitutional Court decisions. Reasons why the courts might engage in such shifts are varied. Some scholars theorise that judges, as members of a larger public, simply are influenced by the same outside factors as other citizens, and so update their policy ideas along with the general public (Giles *et al.* 2008). Others find the need to preserve institutional legitimacy guides the court's movements with public opinion.

Most of the comparative theory within what can be called the public support thesis has not focused on a direct link between courts and citizen views, instead focusing on the macro question of public support for the courts vis-à-vis other institutional actors. Epstein, Knight, and Shvetsova wrote in 2001 that the Russian Constitutional Court, and other Eastern European constitutional courts, must exercise caution and deference when weighing important policy disputes because the low level of public support and legitimacy given to these courts by their respective publics made their verdicts susceptible to overturn or override. Vanberg's (2005) theory of judicial power focuses on the development of legitimacy, though he assumes for the purposes of empirical testing that the object of his inquiry, the German Constitutional Court, has public legitimacy. His testing, then, is focused on the conditions under which courts are able to use this support to achieve policy goals. Yet Vanberg, too, is more cautious when making judgments on the legitimacy and the use of power by the newer courts in Eastern Europe (2005: 173).

Judges do, in fact, have a strong interest in gaining and maintaining public support, as public support ultimately creates and maintains the court's institutional legitimacy (Gibson and Caldeira 2009). The legitimacy of the judiciary – and specifically the legitimacy of court rulings – matters to judges in large part because judges are unelected officials who nevertheless have the capacity to check majority policies. To successfully exercise judicial review within democratic norms, judges need the public to perceive the courts as neutral, non-political enforcers of the democratic constitutional order. Thus, judges must ultimately 'pay close attention to what will be deemed acceptable by the populace and sometimes yield ... to avoid overstepping the bounds imposed by perceptions of what is legitimate' (Clark 2011: 22). For Clark and others, the need to ensure public support for the court as an institution shapes the exercise of judicial review, with judges constraining their own interests to stay within the bounds of public support. Thus, contrary to those who fear the introduction of a 'government of judges', adherent of the public support thesis view judicial review in practice should generally adhere to majority societal preferences.

The continual stream of referrals to the German Constitutional Court regarding the constitutionality of German participation in the European Central Bank's European Stability Mechanism (ESM) fund can help illustrate the way high courts may consider public opinion within their own rulings. Heading into 2014, a strong majority of the German public disapproved of supplying more bailout money to struggling Eurozone members (Reuters 2013). The German Court's March 2014 ruling in the case – which was brought to the court by a diverse coalition of actors and parties from the far left Die Linke party to college professors to representatives of the centre-right Bavarian CSU – ratified parliament's ultimate authority over the bailout funds, but placed an important limitation on parliament's (and thus the government's) power: the amount of funds the Germans could contribute to the fund would be capped at the amount of Euros the German parliament had already committed, a cap that must stay unless the German parliament held a new vote to grant additional funds. With this ruling the court appeared to grant the German government the limited mandate the German public allowed: current monies could be allocated, but further bailout expenditures would require a new parliamentary vote, and thus an opportunity for greater public scrutiny and transparency in German ESM participation. The ruling also fit within the court's earlier ECB bailout rulings requiring that German government participation fall within the constitutional principle that parliament 'represent[s] the popular will' in budgetary and finance matters.[8]

Empirically, what judicial behaviours should we expect to see from the public support model? As in Dahl's 'ruling regime' thesis, the public support model for majoritarian judicial review works on the assumption that judges hold preferences over policy outcomes. Yet, unlike the 'ruling regime' or 'allied' review theses, the public support theory does not anticipate significant inter-judge variation in decision-making based on policy preferences: to gain or maintain public support, judges as a group will generally accede to policy the public desires, even if this means limiting the fulfillment of their own policy preferences when the two clash.[9] Judicial behaviour can thus be markedly different under these different iterations of majoritarian review.

Additionally, unlike the 'ruling regime' thesis the public support model expects some amount of policy divergence between the court and the elected branches,

---

8. German Constitutional Court, 2 BVR 987/10, 7 September 2011, 129 BVERFGE 124.

9. However, those who believe the court is influenced by the same outside effects that influence all other citizens would likely dispute the severity of this self-limitation (see Giles *et al.* 2008).

specifically the legislature. In Clark's (2011) theory of judicial review, the Court's own outlook regarding its level of public support can influence the exercise of judicial review. Much (though not all) of this evidence comes from legislative attacks on the court in the form of court curbing bills from the legislature, which send signals to judges about the courts' own standing with the public. When the justices perceive a loss of public support, they respond by adopting more deferential review.[10] I investigate further the implications of public support in Chapter Five.

An important assumption in the public support model for the majoritarian vision of judicial review is that the legislature is able to channel the public's mood. Because the legislature is able to channel the public mood, it can provide the threats needed to ensure majoritarian preferences generally prevail in high court decisions. It is questionable whether these assumptions always hold true. Specifically, is it appropriate to assume the legislature is always able to channel to majority will? Leaving the specialised case of the United States and its solid two party system, it is questionable whether this assumption remains valid in all environments. For example, with the minority governments and oversized governmental coalitions that frequently appear in parliamentary systems, it is not clear we can assume a strong connection between the public will and the government's policies in all cases. I discuss this further in Chapter Five.

There are other reasons to question the broad applicability of the public support model. Apart from congruence concerns, Klarman (1997) notes that legislatures might be beholden to special interests within the polity, with the result that legislative policy moves away from both the median voter and publicly-desired outcomes. In these cases, the legislature may not be acting as the faithful agent of the public. Thus, in some cases, the court may need to rein in the legislature to ensure it does fulfill the majority's preferences.

Attempting to answer this latter charge, other scholars theorise that public support for legislative action is not a constant, but rather a variable factor (Stephenson 2004). Thus, judicial opposition to legislative policy can attract popular support if the court can express that its own announced policy is more in line with the public's interest than the policy adopted by the legislature. Vanberg's (2001, 2005) court-legislative interactions theory proposes that when courts obtain legitimacy from the public, judges can then count on the public to act as a

---

10. One issue with the 'public support' thesis is that for these bills to be effective constraints we must assume that judges take these court-curbing bills as credible signals of general public disapproval with the court. This is questionable: in the US House, such bills generally come from the more extreme elements of the legislature, and few make it out of committee or gain many sponsors. From 2005 through 2007, Reps. Ron Paul (R-TX) and Todd Akin (R-MO) submitted the largest number of court curbing bills. Both legislators were conservative outliers with little support even within their own party. Thus, there is the potential for judges to discount the messages sent by the legislature, which could result in the judiciary applying non-majoritarian judicial review. Or, courts could, in effect, listen to the wrong type of message from these extreme elements and withhold active review of radical, non-majoritarian policy on the mistaken belief that the general public supports these legislative efforts to reign in the court.

compliance monitor for their policy. In the end, public support helps the courts by ensuring that the government faithfully implements court rulings. Therefore, when the public is able to monitor the response of legislators to court judgments, judges should engage in active review of legislation. Staton (2006, 2010) argues the judiciary can selectively publicise certain rulings, thus better ensuring the public knows what policy the judiciary has pronounced. As in Vanberg's theory, the public would then act as a monitor for the implementation of court policy. Implicitly, both theories assume the court can, in many cases, deliver policies the public prefers; when this occurs, courts essentially behave as legitimate majoritarian actors in the policy world. If this Vanberg-Staton theory is correct, judges have incentives to create publicly popular rulings, similar to Clark's theory of judicial behaviour.

d. Institutional incentives, compliance, and judicial review

Majoritarian judicial review need not arise solely from replacement, court-parliament partnerships, or public pressures. Other scholars propose a separate, more indirect but potentially more powerful linkage between judges and majority preferences. Specifically, judges can respond to institutional incentives that connect the court to the legislature – and indirectly to the will of the people – to provide majority-enhancing judicial review. Such incentives can come from many sources, notably the desire to gain or maintain judicial careers. Yet whatever the inducement, institutional incentives all seek to enhance the accountability of judges exercising judicial review to the public will.

Under one variation of the 'institutional incentives' linkage, judges have ideological preferences but are primarily career-oriented. Hilbink (2008), for example, notes the intense pressure Chilean judges felt during the 1970s (and to an extent still feel) to either conform their decision-making to established interests or else lose their jobs. Perez-Liñan et al. (2003) find similar pressures occur in Bolivia, while Grijalva (2010) also shows that the reappointment process on the Ecuadorian constitutional tribunal can influence incentives for judicial outcomes on that court. Rasmussen and Ramseyer (2001) similarly describe how for years Japanese judges ruled conservatively to win favour with the ruling Liberal Democratic Party (LDP), which could advance or hinder careers within the Japanese judiciary. Judges who ruled against the LDP were less likely to obtain favourable posts, and earned lower salaries over their careers than those who deferred to the LDP.

Career-based institutional rules, then, help to motivate judicial outcomes and can steer judges towards rulings favoured by the parties or actors currently in power. One key institutional rule is the ability of political actors to appoint and reappoint constitutional court judges (Guarnieri and Pederzoli 2002). A reappointment incentive can align career-oriented judges with the policies of the current majority, or the current reappointing agent. Mary Vocansek (2000: 24), for example, describes the large number of judges on the Italian Constitutional Court who move into political positions at the end of their terms on the bench. With such incentives, judicial review can then be majority-enhancing, as long as the legislature is truly pursuing policies supported by the majority, and as long as the current governing majority is also the reappointing agent. Despite the importance of institutional incentives to broader theories of judicial review, most evidence comes from studies of US state court judges who face reelection. Within this subset of judges, the results are clear: judges facing reelection or reappointment tend to favour majority interests (e.g., Shepherd 2009; Hall 2001). A similar career-based incentive also has been found in US federal court judges seeking promotion (Epstein, Posner and Landes 2013).

Evidence of such decision-making behaviour by judges could indicate that majority preferences are respected and affirmed within the judiciary, which would make judicial review a positive factor for ensuring good democratic performance. Yet it could be troubling for democracy in other ways. Ideally, well-performing liberal democracies also protect individual (including minority) rights and promote the rule of law. Many of the arguments made by recent democratic protestors from Egypt to Turkey and Bulgaria to Brazil centre on the need for democratic governments to listen to and respect minority voices – both political and ethnic (Faiola and Moura 2013). Unfortunately, changes in judicial behaviour based on career inducements from politicians suggests neither a system based on the rule of law, nor a system in which the individual rights of all citizens are faithfully protected. Instead, when judicial behaviour is aligned with current majorities only based on personal benefits and career perks, the long-term health of liberal democracy could be weakened.

A different variation of the institutional incentives version of majoritarian judicial review also recognises that judges hold ideological preferences, but emphasises that judges are strategic actors concerned with avoiding override and ensuring compliance with their decisions (Vanberg 2005). In a separation of powers environment, judges should take care to ensure their rulings fall within a zone of compliance in which implementing actors will actually adhere to the court's rulings (Epstein and Knight 1998; Epstein *et al*. 2001; Carrubba *et al*. 2008). This 'compliance-based' view of judicial review is majoritarian in that it focuses on the concern judges have to ensure that other elected actors respect their decisions. Judges, it is often said, hold neither the power of the purse nor the sword. Instead, the judiciary is dependent on the wisdom of their judgments to gain compliance for their decisions (Hamilton *et al*. [1789] 1966). Without compliance, courts can neither gain nor maintain power within the system of government – that is, if other political actors ignore court opinions, then judicial power is critically weakened.

The concern with obtaining compliance should provide incentives for judges to vote in line with democratic majorities in the legislature. As with the 'public support' model, compliance-based review does not anticipate real inter-judge variation in decision-making. That is, judges, regardless of personal preferences, should maintain an overriding concern with ensuring their decisions are implemented. Though individual judges still hold policy preferences, the need to consider these strategic concerns should lead, among other things, to a smaller role for personal views to intrude into decision-making. Yet, the ability of compliance-based review to contribute to the majoritarian vision of democracy, and ultimately to the performance of democracy, depends crucially on the extent to which legislative majorities truly reflect majority preferences. If there is disconnect between the legislature and the public, then deferential courts are deferential to non-majoritarian policies. This concern should be all the more true in the developing political and party systems of Eastern Europe.

Of course, one way to ensure compliance with rulings is to consider the views of the legislature or government. As discussed in Chapter Five, many European constitutional courts benefit from receiving briefs that legislatures and governments send to the court explaining the outcome they seek from the constitutional case. Another way to ensure compliance is to maintain the support of the public, as noted above in section (c). In addition, courts may be able to rely on outside actors, including bureaucratic and non-governmental actors, to help ensure compliance (Spriggs 1996; Epp 1998). In many countries in Eastern Europe, institutions of government oversight, such as ombudsmen and national auditing agencies, have become important repeat players in the constitutional courts, with the capacity in their oversight role to ensure that legislature implements court rulings. These actors are examined in Chapter Four.

Vision 2: The liberal rights-protecting vision of judicial review

A second democratic vision – one increasingly popular in the modern era – projects a liberal view of democracy that both ensures protection of individual rights from government encroachment and offers protection of minority rights from majority tyranny. Within the 'liberal' vision, personal liberty and equality are paramount goals in democratic society, yet they are also goals potentially under peril. Constitutional rights to free speech and free expression, for example, are commonly threatened with limitation by dominant majorities – particularly those beliefs and expressions that do not fit with the dominant moral or social paradigm.

The Cincinnati city government's attempt to criminalise Robert Mapplethorpe's 1990 art exhibition demonstrates the pressures that can be put on unpopular expression even in relatively open societies – as does the 2005 refusal to authorise a permit to allow the Equality Parade in Warsaw mentioned in Chapter One. In fact, across Europe efforts to limit speech, expression, and media rights continue.[11] Then-Prime Minister Racep Tayyip Erdogan's tax ministry fined a prominent Turkish media group critical of Erdogan's government nearly $2.5 billion in 2009, a fine roughly equal to the capitalisation of the company (Arsu and Tavernise 2009). Similarly, shortly after gaining a parliamentary supermajority in

---

11. Of course, in making this point it must be recognised that legitimate differences exist between the more open speech rules developed in the United States through *Brandenburg v Ohio* (1969), *RAV v St Paul* (1992) and *Snyder v Phelps* (2011) and the greater limitations placed on *types* of speech – for example, hate speech rules and limits on the association rights of extremist groups – that exist in many European countries (see Bleich 2011).

the 2010 elections Hungarian Prime Minster Viktor Orban's government created a new Office of the Commissioner for Media and Communications, which was given powers to sanction the Hungarian media based on the content of their reporting (Sobczyk 2010). Likewise, Argentina's government in 2009 enacted anti-monopoly legislation to break up Grupo Clarin, a large media conglomerate that also became a frequent critic of the Fernandez de Kirchner government (Economist 2012). Basic equality rights, too, often are in peril even in modern democracies. The Equality Parade case, for example, involved limits on one specific minority group – homosexuals (and their allies) – to demonstrate.

In the liberal vision, it is the role of the courts to protect and defend the rights of citizens against political majorities by reviewing government actions for conformity with the constitution. The role of judicial review is particularly important for protecting broader rights to equality within the democratic system. As US Supreme Court Justice William Brennan said in 1985, 'the majoritarian process cannot be expected to rectify claims of minority right', particularly when those claims arise due to the very failures of the majoritarian process (Brennan 2008: 252). Writing in the context of Canada's Charter of Rights and Freedoms, Waluchow (2007) similarly argues judges have a duty to advance fundamental beliefs and values within the community, even if that means applying those values to a policy area (like gay marriage) the majority of the community is not willing to recognise. In the Hungarian and Polish cases mentioned above, the constitutional courts did act to strike down important limitations on speech rights imposed by the government. In fact, Ferreres Comella (2009: 35) argues the vision of constitutional courts as rights protectors is one that unites many European scholars behind the practice of judicial review, even those who are otherwise sceptical of strong court powers.

The need to protect individual liberty was at the core of changes in the way European societies were organised post-World War II. In place of parliamentary supremacy, the designers of new constitutions in postwar Western Europe created strong and extensive individual constitutional rights, with the requirement that parliamentary legislation conform to the constitution. Similarly, rights protection has became a powerful motivator for most subsequent democratising societies around the world, from Eastern Europe to North Africa. Today, this 'constitutionalism' is at the core of modern liberal democracy. Constitutionalism is based on the idea that government acts or laws are limited by a higher set of norms established through a written constitution, and is 'designed to limit the arbitrary exercise of power and make [power] legally accountable' (Sartori 1990: 19). Elected leaders are chosen by the people, but are limited in their official actions by 'higher law' constitutional norms. The judiciary serves a very powerful role within modern liberal democracy, in that courts with the power of judicial review are the ultimate arbiters of constitutionalism, assessing the content of legislative and executive acts and overturning any acts by those bodies that contravene the constitution (Stone Sweet 2000: 37). Constitutionalism, then, contemplates limits on governmental behaviour that are determined by courts of law. A vision of courts as rights protectors can serve as a way of harmonising rights-oriented constitutionalism with traditional democratic theory (Hubner-Mendes 2013; Grimm 2009).

Given the important role of constitutional rights in realising individual rights, it is perhaps no surprise that judicial review is critical to the performance of the modern 'liberal' vision of democracy. Courts exercising judicial review play a vital role in protecting and preserving individual rights and liberties, particularly the rights of minorities against majority tyranny. This vision of rights-protecting judicial review was canonised in Justice Harlan Fiske Stone's famous footnote in *US v Carolene Products Co.* (1938), in which Stone suggested the Supreme Court might drop its usual presumption that congressional legislation is constitutional when laws are directed at 'discrete and insular minorities' in society. Yet the vision of individual rights-protecting judicial review has a pedigree that goes back even beyond the New Deal Supreme Court. Tocqueville wrote in the 1830s that providing courts the power to rule statues unconstitutional 'forms one of the most powerful barriers that have ever been devised against the tyranny of political assemblies' (Tocqueville [1838] 1966: 103). Even earlier, Alexander Hamilton stated in Federalist 78 that strong judicial power protects the people from both dictatorial power and 'the encroachments and oppressions of the representative body' (Hamilton *et al.* 1961). Judicial review in this rights-protecting sense may be considered counter-majoritarian, yet when majority rule produces decisions that harm minority groups or thoughts, advocates of this rights-protecting vision argue that judicial review becomes a legitimate method to ensure that liberty and equality, the cornerstones of the liberal democratic order, are protected.

In many ways, a vision of judges as rights protectors extends even beyond strict arguments over judicial review. Discussing rights more generally, Puchta, Maine, and other late nineteenth century jurists also spoke of the overriding interest of law to protect the individual liberties of all in society.[12] Many ideals within natural law similarly fit within the rights-protecting vision. The idea that there exists some form of natural justice – one that is separate from mere 'legal' forms of justice and that does not need formal acceptance from a political community – goes back at least to Aristotle. The rediscovery of natural law ideas in Europe by St Augustine and St Thomas Aquinas ultimately led to its introduction into American legal and constitutional thought through Hobbes and Locke. Notably, in a natural law framework the judgment of a democratically elected legislature need not be the touchstone for determining what is the correct answer to rights claims. Instead, the job of the judge is to discern whether any higher order fundamental values would supersede the ordinary laws passed by current governments.

Natural law principles formed the basis for an early justification in favour of judicial review powers. In *Calder v Bull* (1798), Justice Samuel Chase stated his

---

12. Puchta (1887: 5), for example, wrote that freedom of the individual 'is the foundation of Right' within law.

famous view that 'certain vital principles' fundamental to democratic government must stand as superior to any simple legislative act that seeks to infringe those principles.[13] Though traditional ideas of natural law are often derided in modern legal thought as illusory, unrealistic, or incompatible with changing social values, Stone Sweet (2000: 136) has noted a tendency even in contemporary times among modern Kelsenian positivists to describe the 'supraconstitutional' status of some rights, thus placing them – like natural law – above the normal legislative and judicial process.

Writers and jurists like Brennan and Waluchow describe an activist view of rights protection: that judges should – indeed have a duty – to go beyond majority preferences or morals and apply higher order fundamental values. Justice Chase's defense of natural law describes a similar judicial duty. John Hart Ely (1980) presents a more measured model of rights protecting judicial review. Ely's general theory advocates that judicial review is necessary in a democratic system because of the unique ability of judges to protect rights. But – importantly – he argues that judges must not introduce their own substantive value judgments into constitutional adjudication. Instead, they should take an active role only in (1) removing the defects from the democratic process and (2) safeguarding the participatory and representative rights of disfavoured groups, notably social or political minorities, against the sentiments of current majorities (Ely 1980: 135–79). In essence, Ely argues the process of democracy can introduce distortions that impede full realisation of democratic values and democratic rights. In these situations courts stand as the most democratically legitimate actor to ensure democratic rights are realised for all.

Dworkin's (1977) theory of principled constitutional decision-making similarly can be situated within a rights-protecting framework. Dworkin separates decisions based on policy from decisions based on principle. While the former are generally valid in the democratic political process (in fact, they occur all the time in the legislative arena), it is principled decisions that are necessary to ensure proper protection of rights within democratic society (1977: 84–85). Judges are the actors in a democracy best placed to evaluate and make decisions based on principle (and thus best placed to make rights-based decisions), largely because they are insulated from 'the demands of the political majority' (1977: 85; Black 1960). Victor Ferreres Comella (2009: 34) similarly suggests that the ultimate hope for constitutional review is for courts to act as the forum of principle to determine fundamental rights claims. In later work defending a morals-based reading of constitutions, Dworkin sought to differentiate 'majoritarian' views of democracy from his proffered moral understanding of constitutional democracy, which strongly protects the liberal democratic values of equality, liberty, and community, particularly (1996: 10).

---

13. This statement, though not binding precedent, helped to shape the larger argument regarding the place of fundamental rights and principles within democratic society. In *Calder*, the Court ultimately ruled the law under review did not violate the U.S. Constitution, and so did not consider the question *Marbury* ultimately decided.

Moral readings of constitutions would still need to comport with the traditions and principles of constitutional practice, lest morals-based review revert to decision-making based on personal judicial preferences.

Importantly, not all scholars find democratic benefits in the rights-protecting vision for judicial review just sketched out. Alexander Bickel (1971), a noted sceptic of strong court power, warns that judicial review under such guises as 'rights protection' or the 'forum of principle' can become a dangerous effort to use 'the possibilities of law as a method of ordering society' in the judge's own image. Michel Troper (2003: 115) similarly argues that such theories fail to 'demonstrate why a constitutional court would be more likely than a legislature to take such [fundamental democratic] values into account' in their decision-making. Judges, just as much as legislators, can create outcomes that fail to meet democratic principles, or fail to protect fundamental rights. Anna Harvey's (2013) research into the Rehnquist era Supreme Court concludes the judiciary has been a very poor protector of individual rights, and suggests rights protection would be stronger if the legislature served as the final arbiter.

What should the liberal rights protecting vision mean for judicial behaviour? To many, the vision is expressed in activist, open review of legislative and executive acts. In the rights-protecting mould, the judicial task can become an effort to change society from the top down, using powers of persuasion and moral right to even the playing field and impose 'just' solutions in society. Due to the focus on rights protection, the type of activism seen in the rights-protecting vision should best be seen in specific areas of the law – particularly in equality and in individual rights and liberties claims, which should be prioritised in the judicial docket. This, at least, is the prevailing view in the common law world. In the United States, the Supreme Court's jurisprudence in voting rights and desegregation efforts are emblematic of judicial review as an effort to right moral and political wrongs in society. In these areas, the Court took for itself the capacity to ensure the principle of 'one man, one vote' after Congress and state governments refused to ensure the fundamental principle of equality (*Baker v. Carr* (1962)), and assumed the responsibility to address the fundamental inequality of segregationist laws (*Brown v. Board of Education* (1954)). Later decisions took the Court in a notably activist direction, reshaping the racial composition of schools through student busing programs. The Canadian Supreme Court's prioritisation of civil rights, particularly women's rights, in the 1980s and beyond was also emblematic of an active rights-protecting turn (Epp 1998).

Similarly, the German Constitutional Court has emphasised the role of individual minority rights against majority overreach in several notable cases, including the controversial Bavarian crucifix case.[14] And in its noted *Solange* verdicts, the German court permitted European Court of Justice (ECJ) legal supremacy, but only 'so long as' fundamental rights of Germans are maintained.[15]

---

14. The Bavarian Crucifix Case, BVerfGE decision of 16 May 1995, 93, 1.
15. Re Wuensche Handelsgesellschaft, BVerfGE decision of 22 October 1986, 3 CMLR 225, 265.

The constitutional court, in effect, proclaimed the role of rights defender for German citizens even against larger EU principles. In their own EU accession cases, constitutional courts in Poland and the Czech Republic similarly reserved the right to ensure the protection of the individual constitutional rights of citizens, notwithstanding acceptance of EU law (Sadurski 2006). In a later 2011 decision, the Polish Tribunal again reserved the right to review EU rules when they might interfere with individual rights and liberties of Poles (Walencik and Domagalski 2011).

The Hungarian Constitutional Court during the 1990s used its ability to directly accept citizen constitutional complaints to fundamentally restructure the post-communist Hungarian political landscape. Rules ranging from reductions in pension payouts to laws limiting offensive speech were overturned, as was the death penalty, despite large public support for the practice. And in 1995 – eighteen years before the US Supreme Court took a similar case – the Hungarian Court ruled that same-sex couples must be treated equally to heterosexual couples in social and economic matters, fundamentally altering social relationships in the country and taking on public beliefs on morality and religion in the process (Schwartz 2000: 93). A similar outcome was seen in Slovenia, where the constitutional court in 2009 overturned laws that limited the ability of same sex couples to inherit their partner's property after death.[16]

Other behaviours should be present, as well, if the liberal rights-protecting vision holds true in judicial behaviour. Given the need to ensure individual rights, the liberal rights-protection theory of judicial review minimises the role of ideological, party-line decision-making in the exercise of judicial review. Instead, activism is based on the need to uphold fundamental rights. Epp (1998: 42), for example, writes that the development of the US Supreme Court's strong women's rights agenda was highly unlikely given the conservative makeup of the Court at that time. In fact, Stern and Wermiel's (2009) biography of Justice Brennan notes that Brennan, the main driver of the liberal women's rights agenda, held very traditional views of male and female roles in his own Supreme Court office: he flatly refused to consider hiring female law clerks, instead taking on women only as secretaries. At the same time, he authored legendary decisions making differential treatment for men and women the subject of 'heightened scrutiny' by the Court.

As a theoretical matter, the liberal vision for judicial review also downplays strategic aspects of judicial decision-making, and for good reason: if rights are rights to be enforced and protected regardless of circumstances, then there should be little room for the bargaining over outcomes that often arises in strategic models of decision-making (as described in Maltzman *et al.* 2000: 1–5). Similarly, the liberal rights-protection vision downplays the possibility that public opinion or public pressures drive judicial decision-making. In fact, many of the most important decisions rights-conscious judges announce will involve overriding majority preferences, and indirectly majority opinion. However, judges seeking

---

16. Blazic and Kern v Slovenia, U-I-425/06–10 of 2 July 2009.

impact could harness the power of interest groups and citizen engagement with the legal system to ensure their outcomes are implemented (Cichowski 2007: 259; Epp 1998). In protecting the democratic bargain, or working with interest groups, some would say the rights-protecting vision acts in accordance with majority-supported constitutional principles (e.g. Law 2009), though that point is conceptually distinct from being responsive to majority policy preferences through inducements, threats, or self-interest.

Vision 3: The legalist vision of judicial review

A final vision of democracy focuses on the need to ensure fair processes and to consistently apply legal obligations in democratic society. This vision for a limited democratic government ultimately involves the courts, through the exercise of judicial review, as protectors of the rule of law. The rule of law is a notoriously difficult concept to pin down. However, at a minimum, the rule of law entails a system in which laws are publicly known and are applied neutrally and equally within society (Carothers 1998). In a system where 'the Constitution governs the legislator as much as the private citizen', courts have a fundamental duty to ensure that democratic actors remain accountable and that the constitutional order is consistently applied (Tocqueville [1838] 1966: 101). To maintain the validity of judicial review, though, judges must subsume their personal views, or even the popular views of the day, and deliver internally coherent, durable, and consistent decisions in neutral, universal terms.

This final vision integrally involves the judiciary in what is often termed a 'legalist' vision of judicial review. Legalism has often been termed a 'simple' method of decision-making,[17] though as explained below legalist arguments for judicial review, and judicial decision-making broadly, contain a diverse set of theories and ideas for the proper role of judges in governmental life. At its core, the legalist conception of judicial review rests on the view that the primary job of the judge is to find and apply the 'correct' answer to constitutional issues, using doctrine and other neutral methods. In their legalist defense of judicial supremacy, Alexander and Schauer (1997: 1372) state the primary job of the constitutional judge is in fact to get 'the right answer', and apply it consistently. Yet reaching the right answer does not end the judicial task. Judges, trained in the law and neutral principles of reasoning, must then describe why their answer is correct. As unelected actors with the power of making law, this requirement of 'giving reasons' provides court opinions a necessary democratic legitimacy: courts are unelected actors, yet by providing reasons for their decisions, the people are given an open account of the deliberations and considerations that led to the case outcome (Shapiro 1992; Ferejohn and Pasquino 2002).[18]

---

17. e.g., George and Epstein (1992: 324).

18. And, as Sunstein and Posner (2006) note, when greater numbers of judges consolidate on one answer, there is greater certainty that answer is correct.

The traditional, perhaps stereotypical, vision of legalism as a solution to uncomfortable issues arising from judicial power has a long tradition in the legal world. Both common law and civil law traditions were arguably formed on the idea that courts of law should serve as impartial, reasoned forums for dispute resolution. The early nineteenth century German jurist Friederich Karl von Savigny believed it necessary for judicial decisions to be grounded in and governed by *law* precisely because judges, like others in society, could be subject to partisan or personal influences. Following the law then ensures impartiality in decision-making and subsequent legitimacy in outcomes (Beisner 2011: 228).

In Europe, the implications from the legalist vision mirror many of the traditional concerns arising from the 'government of judges': that, to prevent an anti-democratic takeover of policy making, judges must limit their own exercise of judicial power, including judicial review power. In a separation of powers framework, legislatures make laws and judges apply them, often mechanically. Adherents of this legalist vision of courts and law in society dominated European legal thinking during the latter part of the nineteenth century and well into the twentieth century – though with exceptions, including the Scandinavian legal realists, Hermann Kantorowicz and the free law scholars, and their forerunner Jhering (Rytter and Wind 2011; Stone Sweet 2000; Jhering 1915).[19] Remnants of this view can still be seen today: Bernard Schlink (1992) decries the deference paid by German law professors to constitutional court decisions, treating (and teaching) court outcomes 'as though they were codified law' rather than living documents.

Similarly, despite the early twentieth century rise of Llewellyn, Frank, and the American legal realists, the dominant story of constitutional judging in the United States was for many years built around the notion of judges deciding cases in a restrained fashion, working out solutions by reference to competing precedent and neutral processes, as Levi (1949: 5) described in his famous work (still assigned in many US law schools) on legal reasoning. In the modern world, the role of the judge in this legalist vision of judicial review can, in Chief Justice John Roberts' confirmation hearing analogy, be related to that of a baseball umpire, an official who calls balls and strikes, who applies the rulebook and makes the right call, but is not an active player in the game of politics or policy making. To engage in substantive rights analysis necessarily involves weighing competing policy choices, a process which is better left to the political branches of government. Instead, according to Henry Hart, Jr (1959: 99), judges in the legalist model are responsible for 'articulating and developing impersonal and durable principles' to guide society.

As intimated above, many traditional theories of law and jurisprudence fit well within a legalist framework. *Formalist* theories of decision-making view

---

19. Jhering (1915: 1–2), who described the law as 'not mere theory, but living force', also believed 'the life of the law' to be 'a struggle' between interests for power over its word – similar to Justice Oliver W. Holmes' (1881: 5) classic proto-realist statement that 'the life of the law has not been logic: it has been experience'.

law ideally as a 'rationally determinate' entity – i.e., that the law is capable of providing logical, structured and largely complete answers (Leiter 2010).[20] The judge's job is then to find the most appropriate law for the dispute in question and dispense a legal answer. Often, formalist answers are presented as the product of an inescapable logical deduction – the answer must be so, because the law says 'x' and logical deduction leads us to the answer 'y' (Schauer 1988; Dyevre and Jakab 2013). In a formalist framework, neutral application of these deductive legal decision-making practices will ultimately reach the best answer. Yet, to adherents it also can do more: by ensuring rational predictability in law, formalism potentially allows for greater freedoms to develop, and a better ability for citizens to clearly know what their freedoms are.

Formalism often is associated with eighteenth and nineteenth century legal thought, particularly in France post-Revolution. Even today, most French court opinions are still written in this logical, deductive format, and opinions emanating from the European Court of Justice (ECJ) often utilise a modified formalist style (Lasser 2004). Though largely out of favour today, Anna Harvey notes formalism shaped early debates on the role of judges in colonial America, as well. In 1776, Thomas Jefferson advised that the will of the democratic legislator must be supreme: any notion of justice or 'mercy', in Jefferson's words, should come from the lawmakers in the assembly; judges should act as 'a mere machine', dispensing the verdicts written in the legislative code (Harvey 2013).

Legal *positivism*, which, contra to a liberal rights-protecting vision, separates valid legal rules from moral claims of right, also can be placed within the legalist vision. Like the formalist theory of adjudication, positivism maintains that valid legal rules are those that emanate from a legitimate sovereign authority (such as a legislature).[21] Judges, then, must look to these sovereign authorities and rules when making decisions. A positivist theory of judging can be compatible with judicial review, though it sits uneasily with many aspects of it. Rather than questioning the existing rules, as many rights-protecting or majoritarian judges might be wont to do, judges in a positivist framework instead look to valid rules to resolve any ambiguity when making decisions (e.g., Hart 1961).[22] In practice, this means judges must adhere strictly to one type of rule – legal precedent and *stare decisis* – in decision-making and opinion writing (Epstein and George 1992). The decision for positivists exercising judicial review, then, is not to analyse dynamically or produce new principles for the state, but rather to merely 'describe the state through an analysis of its constituent principles and justifications' (Troper 2003: 99).

---

20. Some scholars have created different degrees of formalism in law (Kuhn 2011: 75).

21. Leiter (1999) describes formalism as a theory of *adjudication*, or decision-making, while positivism is a larger theory of *law*.

22. However, Hart's (1961) more contemporary iteration of positivism allows for judges to be guided by social acts – generally laws, administrative rules, and court opinions, but also social norms and customs – when creating outcomes.

However, not all arguments within the legalist vision of judicial review focus on the mechanical application of facts to law. In the present day, theories of textualism and originalism relate closely to legalist arguments. Originalism proposes that the democratic legitimacy we provide to courts of constitutional review arises because – and only because – judges rely on the original, and not contemporary or personal, understandings of the constitutional bargain (Scalia 1989a). Judges, then, must find the original meaning of the legal text and apply it to the current problem without adding substantive value judgments. Though in the context of opposing the borrowing of foreign law, Argentine scholar Carlos Rozenkrantz (2003) similarly argues that law is democratically legitimate only because it is created in a procedurally fair manner by the people's representatives. Judges, then, must focus on that text and tradition in their own interpretation.

Ideas of originalism and textualism are currently popular, though they also have a long pedigree. Savigny's idea of the *Volksgeist*, and the German historical legal school it inspired, allowed for problems of law to be worked out both analytically and historically, with the correct legal answer deriving from the history of the principle at stake in the case. By solving problems in this manner, judges would ensure objectivity while also removing any arbitrariness from personal judicial biases.

Savigny's *Volksgeist* was a rebellion against codification, positivism, and the stultified but 'mechanically precise administration of justice' spreading through continental Europe in the early to mid 1800s (Savigny [1831] 1975: 21). Yet, despite the promise of an animating spirit of the law guiding legal interpretation, to many the aim of the *Volksgeist* theory of law still was the creation of a 'scientific positivism', or a 'modern legal science, a system perfectly suited to resolving all problems that a mature society could present' (Dawson 1968: 455).[23] Duncan Kennedy later remarked in a similar vein that Savigny's theory still led continental legal thought towards a 'legal science' predicated on a complete and rational system of laws (Kennedy 2010: 812).

Legalist descriptions of judicial review also need not focus on the creation of a complete theory of jurisprudence. In a recent book discussing the value of courts in deliberative democracy, Hubner-Mendes (2013) argues that by engaging in argumentative, reasoned deliberation, the collegial court of constitutional review uses a comparatively stronger method to reach decisions than other democratic deliberative bodies. By using collegial methods and consistent and rational discourse, courts are able to enhance democratic performance by being able to reach the best, most justified answer to a given social problem. To Hubner-Mendes and others (including Charles Black), it is not the mechanics of the legal method, but rather the deliberative quality of judicial decision-making that enhances democracy.

---

23. Jhering's theory of law as 'an idea of force' rather than a set of abstract, scientific legal principles perhaps avoids these problems better than Savigny's *Volksgeist*, and thus avoids Dawson's critique.

What are the implications for judicial behaviour in the legalist vision for judicial review? In some ways it is difficult to generalise outcomes, though some concrete expectations can be discerned. At its core, there is a commonality within a legalist vision: the job of the judge exercising judicial review is most certainly *not* to impose personal policy values on case outcomes. Such impositions of personal policy generally lead to charges that judges are usurping the proper role of democratically elected policymakers, with deleterious consequences for judicial prestige and legitimacy. Instead, by developing and applying neutral legal principles judges can effectively separate the judicial decision-making process from their personal preferences on policy choices (Scalia 1989a: 864; Rozenkrantz 2003; Savigny [1831] 1975).

Another implication of the legalist vision is a necessary focus on the law as expressed in the legal code, past cases, and the constitution to reach these 'best' solutions. Thus, we should see discussion of legal principles, past cases, and citation to precedent. The outcomes (though not necessarily the rationales for outcomes) should be qualitatively different from the majoritarian vision, though, because they are based on vastly different premises. The legalist view of judicial review implicitly assumes case outcomes will not be informed by the personal policy views of judges. In fact, adherents of the legalist view find that policy discussions have no place in the legal rule making performed by courts (Scalia 1989b; Edwards and Livermore 2009; Ferejohn and Pasquino 2004). Rather, as Louis Favoreu (1990) noted, constitutional judging should be an arena in which politics has been reined in by the law. Thus, there should not be variation within the bench consistent with the majoritarian ideological or political incentives visions. At the risk of oversimplifying, judges following this vision of judicial review instead will rule 'by the book', examining the relevant statutes, constitutional texts, and past cases on point, and then, using established legal decision-making criteria (such as canons of interpretation or even balancing tests), reach the right and best legal outcome.

Summary

To what extent does constitutional review, as practiced in contemporary democracies, in fact fulfill these visions? This is a difficult question to answer because, as noted in Chapter One, any one ruling by a court often can be interpreted as consistent with multiple visions. Thus, to assess the democratic performance of judicial review we need to assess judicial behaviour across a large number of rulings and we need clear and discriminating expectations regarding which types of behaviour are consistent with which visions. Below I lay out the empirical implications of these visions for judicial behaviour. In subsequent chapters I test whether these implications are seen in the assembled data, keeping in mind that, in the end, none or several of the visions may have corroborating evidence.

The majoritarian vision of democracy offers several competing rationales for judicial review, and a number of competing, and partially overlapping, implications for judicial behaviour. Within Dahl's 'ruling regime' conception, judges should vote based on their own ideological preferences. To this degree, the model is similar to the so-called 'attitudinal model' popularised by Segal and Spaeth (2002), in which Supreme Court justices vote almost exclusively based on their attitudes or preferences over policy. Yet, to Dahl and others, this policy-based judicial review can be majority-enhancing due to the ideological agreement between judges and the parliament that should arise from the political court appointment processes and related judicial bench turnover. Without high turnover, we should expect to see disputes between the judiciary and the new ruling legislative regime. The related 'allied' court view of majoritarian judicial review, in which political majorities use favourable judicial review to overturn mutually disfavoured laws, presents several distinct empirical implications. One implication is that judges should exercise judicial review to strike down older laws, specifically laws passed by past governments. At the same time, judges should be much more deferential to the legislation enacted by a current, allied majority. Thus, decisions to overturn legislation enacted by parties or coalitions still in power should be much more rare. Chapters Four and Five address these questions.

The 'institutional incentives' vision of majoritarian judicial review should lead to direct and observable empirical implications for judicial behaviour. First, appointment and reappointment processes should lead to straightforward differences in voting behaviour. Career-oriented judges subject to reappointment could try to maintain a closer connection to the anticipated reappointing actor, and thus indirectly the majority will. Conversely, those not subject to reappointment should vote more closely with their appointing actors' interests. Thus, there should be clear differences in judicial decision-making based on the presence or absence of the reappointment incentive. Second, there could be additional motivations based on future, post-court career incentives, as well. I address these issues in detail in Chapter Six.

Finally, the 'public support' model anticipates ideological voting on the part of judges, yet acknowledges that judges must stay within the boundaries of public support to effectuate their rulings. This means that judges seeking legitimacy and compliance for their rulings should be able to read current public views on the court and either temper or expand their decision-making to stay within the constraints of public opinion. Greater public support for the court should lead to greater activism, while lower levels of public support should lead to greater deference to other branches. Public support could also work indirectly. Judges reviewing the constitutionality of legislation could choose greater activism when the enacting coalition either lacked or is lacking solid, durable majority support. These issues are discussed in detail in Chapter Five.

The need to ensure compliance should also lead to observable and distinct judicial behaviour. Judges, fearful of retribution and lacking true powers of enforcement, should defer to the views of more powerful political actors. Therefore, one possible implication from compliance-based review is more deferential review in cases involving political actors, with perhaps only rare instances of courts overturning existing legislation. With European constitutional courts receiving briefs from legislatures and governments, the amount of deference could depend on the briefs the court receives. I explain this in greater detail in Chapter Five.

The second vision, a liberal rights-protection vision for democracy and judicial review, also has distinct implications for judicial behaviour. Evidence of a rights-protecting judiciary could be seen in an expansion of the number of individual rights-based cases accepted for review, or otherwise an emphasis on individual rights protection in their caseload, as Epp (1998) shows in his comparative study of rights revolutions. However, Epp uses common law supreme courts to examine the development of rights protection. When examining the European constitutional courts, there is a jurisdictional difference that must be addressed. The US Supreme Court, the Canadian Supreme Court, and other decentralised common law courts have enormous discretion over their dockets; constitutional courts generally do not have control over their abstract review docket, and as a result must accept and review any case brought by recognised actors. The effect of this rule is to make more difficult the observation of rights-protection behaviour of the type noted by Epp and others. Nevertheless, rights-protecting judges should still exhibit activism in those cases of individual rights brought before them. In addition, judges in centralised systems who seek to emphasise rights protection could send signals favouring claims by rights-protecting actors. Chapter Four investigates whether greater activism is seen in certain constitutional issues.

Finally, the validity of the third vision, a legalistic vision of democracy and judicial review, could be established by the existence of several distinct judicial decision-making behaviours. In particular, we should *not* see systematic variation within the court consistent with political incentives or ideology. However, there are certain behaviours we should see: specifically, in formulating the best, most appropriate solutions to constitutional questions, we should see the use of neutral and impartial judicial decision-making practices. The use of precedent is one easily discernible way of observing the validity of legalist vision, as it both advances ostensibly neutral practices and potentially legitimates opinions. It is worth repeating that there should not be discernible ideological or strategic patterns to the use of precedent or a partisan slant to any of these ostensibly neutral practices. I investigate this vision, using new evidence from constitutional court decision-making practices, in Chapter Seven.

Table 2.1 below provides an outline of the visions described above, including the expected motivations of judges and empirical implications from these motivations.

Literature Review: Evidence of judicial behaviour in judicial review

The institution of judicial review makes the judicial branch an important veto point for policy. Given the importance of the judiciary in both the interpretation of constitutional texts and the making and breaking of policy, scholars have long studied the factors that influence judicial decision-making processes and outcomes. Despite the larger 'visions' established above, most current political science work has split the world of judicial decision-making into two different camps: the

Table 2.1: Visions of judicial review

Vision	Expected motivation	Empirical implications	Testing
1. Liberal rights-enhancing	Protect individual rights and civil rights	Larger number of rights-based cases accepted, overturned	Ch Four
2. Legalist	Find best, most correct legal answer	Development of legal principles; Absence of incentives- or ideology-based decision-making	Ch Seven
3. Majoritarian			
a. Ruling regime	Legitimise majority preferences	Policy-based decision-making Ratification of laws adopted by current majority	Ch Five
b. Allied review	Work with political majority to overturn older laws	Policy-based decision-making Overturn laws by previous majorities	Ch Five
c. Public support	Create rulings in line with public opinion	Retreat from active judicial review when public support low Greater activism when support is high	Ch Five
d. Incentive-based	Majority-enhancing decisions made based on incentives	Career-oriented voting Vote with policy interests of re-appointer	Ch Six
e. Compliance-based	Does not rule against powerful majority unless compliance met	Consider views of parliament Greater activism with outside monitor to help ensure compliance	Chs Four, Five

attitudinal model and the strategic interactions model. Most theories testing these models are based on the behaviour of the US Supreme Court, though comparative research involving countries outside the United States has increasingly been undertaken to examine the implications of these theories.

The classic attitudinal model finds judicial behaviour and judicial decisions to be driven by the ideology or policy preferences of judges. Similar to many aspects of the majoritarian vision for judicial review, the attitudinal model as formulated by Segal and Spaeth proposes that Supreme Court justices will vote in accordance with their attitudes towards the policies within the cases they decide. For example, Justices Thomas and Scalia favour conservative policy outcomes, and so their own votes will reflect these views. Yet, unlike many of the majoritarian vision sub-types, the attitudinal model predicts the justices will face few to no constraints on their decisions. This is largely due to the unique rules present on the Supreme Court: one, justices are appointed for life, which takes away a key avenue for political retribution against judicial rulings; two, the Court can largely set its own docket, and is thus free to select the cases (and the policies) it wishes to review; and three, it is the court of final review, and overturning or overriding Court opinions is exceedingly difficult under the US Constitution (Segal and Spaeth 2002). However, for the purposes of broader comparative theory-building, it is important to note that the first two rules above inspiring the attitudinal model are not present in most constitutional courts around the world.

Still, examinations of judicial behaviour in Germany, France, and Italy have generally corroborated the basic outlines of the attitudinal preference model (Hönnige 2009; Franck 2009; Pellegrina and Garoupa 2013). Similarly, judges on the Portuguese Constitutional Tribunal and the Spanish Constitutional Court similarly follow the basic policy preferences of their appointing political party (Amaral Garcia *et al.* 2009; Garoupa *et al.* 2013). Right-appointed judges on the Portuguese and Spanish Courts vote in favour of the constitutionality of rightist legislation at a much higher rate than left-appointed judges. Similarly, the decision of Spanish and Portuguese judges to engage in dissent mirrors the ideological left-right divide that exists on those courts (Hanretty 2012).

Unlike the legalist vision for judicial review, the attitudinal model largely rejects the value of case facts or legal decision-making rules like *stare decisis* and precedent in high court decision-making (Segal and Spaeth 1996). Instead, outcomes are almost solely predicated on the influence of judicial policy preferences, and the ability of judges to impose those preferences on the political world.

Most prominent attitudinal studies explicitly discount the importance of law or broader rights-protecting motives in empirical testing of high court decision-making, as well. Segal and Spaeth's (2002) classic account of attitudinal judicial decision-making concludes that law does not matter at all in high court outcomes. Many other political science studies focusing on judicial attitudes (both comparative and US-based) simply ignore the role of law, failing to operationalise items like legal merits or legal factors in their testing of decision-making by constitutional judges (e.g., Amaral Garcia *et al.* 2009; Garoupa *et al.* 2013). Carrubba *et al.* (2008) do consider legal merits in their study of the European

Court of Justice (ECJ), but as a control variable, using the ECJ's advocate general brief to determine the legal merits of each case. This final approach recognises the potential tension between law and politics – that a ruling that appears to reflect political considerations could also reflect the legal merits. The Carrubba *et al.* approach also recognises the tension that exists between judges' political goals and the strategic environment in which much of judicial decision-making takes place, and thus the importance of a second dominant theory in political science today – the strategic interactions theory.

The strategic interactions theory argues that judicial behaviour is determined by a combination of institutional factors, notably the actions and potential reactions of the legislature and the executive, as well as the beliefs of other judges and of the public at large. While not downplaying the desire of judges to impose policy preferences on case outcomes, the strategic view recognises that judges are limited or constrained in their ability to effectuate those decisions. Judicial behaviour, then, is influenced by policy preferences but mediated by intra-court relations, as well as the strategic interaction of courts in a separation of powers system of government based on mutual checks (Epstein and Knight 1998). Institutions mediate judicial preferences by structuring the choices available to judges, and by helping to shape judicial views about the likely consequences of their rulings (Maltzman *et al.* 2000: 14). This understanding of how other actors might react provides judges with useful information on how they should behave, and the types of rulings they should produce. Aspects of the strategic interactions theory fit well within the 'institutional incentives' and 'public support' iterations of the majoritarian vision for judicial review in democracy.

Though developed initially for the US separation-of-powers environment, strategic theories of judicial behaviour potentially have strong explanatory power in multiple environments. In established democracies, where courts already have established institutional legitimacy, judges can dominate court-legislative interactions if they are able to attract public support (Vanberg 2005). In other instances, judges may need to engage in conditional self-restraint, deferring to the legislative policy position or, more broadly, the policy position of important implementing actors (Carrubba *et al.* 2008). It is important to note that not all agree with the strategic nature of constitutional review, particularly in European constitutional courts. Taking up Jhering and Jellinek's earlier use of the terminology, Stone Sweet (2000: 75–76) argues that in a properly judicialised environment, it is legislative majorities that will need to 'autolimit' their own legislative product in order to ensure their policy will survive constitutional review. Implicitly, then, constitutional judges act as unchecked policy arbiters in this autolimitation environment.

In new democracies, as well, strategic behaviour potentially has even greater import for the use of judicial review. Without established court authority and independence, it should be even more important to acknowledge, react and respond to the interests of implementing actors in government – specifically, the legislature and executive (Epstein *et al.* 2001). Even in non-democratic environments, there are reasons to believe judges engage in strategic behaviour. Specifically, there is evidence judges on the Argentinian Supreme Court during the 1970s and 1980s would 'strategically defect' from the ruling regime once it became apparent the current regime was losing its grip on power (Helmke 2002).

Why we need comparative evidence

How high court judges make decisions and how they justify their outcomes are both vital questions for judicial politics and for larger theories on institutional design and broader democratic performance. Yet, most claims and most of the evidence regarding judicial behaviour and the relationship of courts to other governmental actors come from the United States. The United States is a valuable case for analysis, but in the 'global era of court power' it is increasingly difficult to draw larger conclusions on judicial behaviour from just one country. US-focused research has driven both theory and evidence on judicial decision-making, but it can be hard to translate these findings to other environments. Limitations include the institutional rules that govern the US courts, the federalist system in which the Supreme Court operates, and the different deliberative processes and practices in the Supreme Court.

The US court system has always operated under relatively unique institutional rules that are not often seen in other countries. At the national level, the Supreme Court – and the entire federal court system – operates under life tenure for judges, subject only to minimal constraints for illegal activities. The president has always appointed nominees, and the Senate has always confirmed nominees. Different rules govern both the appointment and retention of judges in many other countries. Notably, few constitutional judges elsewhere in the world have life tenure – most constitutional court judges have only limited tenures, with terms generally between six to twelve years (Ginsburg 2003).[24]

Additionally, few countries have emulated the US-style appointment process for their own national constitutional court appointments. Some, notably the Czech Republic, Slovenia, and Slovakia, use a variation of the 'collaborative' method of appointments used in the United States, in which two or more actors work together to appoint judges to the bench. Many other countries, including Spain, Italy, and France, have adopted a second type of appointment system, the 'divided' appointment system, in which different public bodies independently select a set number of judges. In Spain for example, four of the twelve judges on the court are appointed by the lower house, four by the upper house, two by the government, and two by the judicial council. A final method places appointment power exclusively in the hands of a single actor or body, generally the parliament. In Poland, the Sejm, the lower house of parliament, is the exclusive appointing body for the constitutional tribunal.

Numerous countries also include a supermajority vote requirement for proposed constitutional court nominees to be confirmed. For example, the four

---

24. Of the sixty-three countries listed in Ginsburg's (2003) analysis, only twenty courts were given life tenures.

constitutional judges nominated by Spain's lower house and upper house all must be confirmed by 60 per cent of MPs and Senators, respectively; judges on Hungary's court must be confirmed by a two-thirds supermajority of parliament, as do judges on the German Constitutional Court. These different constellations of power provide differing motivations for the judges. Notably, the final two methods open up the possibility of court capture by appointing bodies, with certain blocs of votes guaranteed for the president or for parliament. Additionally, supermajority requirements open the possibility of legislative deals being created, in which major parties agree to support each other's nominees (generally an equal number of nominees, as occurs in Spain, Hungary, and Germany). Such deals, and the institutional rules that enable them, are completely non-existent in the United States, where most research on institutional constraints and appointment rules has focused.

Apart from appointments, there are broader institutional frameworks that differentiate the US from most other countries. The United States is a federalist system, with a sovereign national government and states that also are sovereign within their own sphere. The US is also a presidential system organised through a system of checks and balances between the legislative, executive, and judicial branches. Most European democracies are structured in very different ways. With the possible exclusion of Switzerland, no European country can be considered presidential (Clark *et al.* 2013). Instead, European systems are either parliamentary, in which parliament determines the prime minister and government, or semi-presidential, in which government depends on support from a legislative majority and the head of state is popularly elected through a separate process. This difference is important: as Strom (2000) notes, parliamentary systems are not designed to operate in a strict checks and balances manner. Without the competing principals in the executive and the legislature, much of the separation of powers theory premised on the court interacting with two or more policy-driven actors (the legislature and the president) is inapplicable in parliamentary systems. This is not to say that the separation of powers theory itself is inapplicable to parliamentary systems, but it does mean that the strategies employed by the court should operate in distinct ways. Even in semi-presidential systems, presidents generally operate in ways distinct from those in pure presidential systems (Tavits 2009).

Finally, there are differences between the operation of the US Supreme Court and other major constitutional courts, particularly with regard to the parameters of judicial review. US courts operate in what is known as a decentralised system of judicial review, in which courts at any level in the legal system can review and potentially hold laws unconstitutional. Specialised constitutional courts, in Europe and elsewhere, operate in a centralised system of judicial review, in which only one court – the constitutional court – is able to review and potentially overturn legislation.[25] This means that constitutional courts have different relationships with the lower courts than the Supreme Court, or any high court

---

25. However, in Portugal all courts can exercise judicial review.

in a decentralised system has its own lower courts. The US Supreme Court has come to depend on the lower courts to settle most legal issues, including most constitutional issues; only the most important issues and most important splits in the law percolate upward to the Court.[26] The same cannot be said for constitutional courts. Citizens, lower courts, and institutional actors alike are given direct access to the court. Though most constitutional courts have adopted rules of procedure to dispense with or reject the many thousands of individual citizen petitions received every year, there are few opportunities for courts to avoid deciding claims brought by political and institutional actors using the abstract referral procedure.[27]

The US Supreme Court is also the supreme tribunal in the United States legal system, and so engages in non-constitutional statutory review in addition to its judicial review function, setting standards in evidence, contracts, and patents, among others issues. Constitutional courts, though, are courts of limited jurisdiction – they only consider matters relating to the constitution. In some countries this extends to related functions of overseeing election-based legal disputes or adjudicating the legality of political parties, but these extra functions are all based on their role as constitutional guardian. In this sense, constitutional courts have a more limited interaction with the lower courts, and a more limited oversight function. Legal parties generally cannot appeal their case up to the constitutional court; instead, when lower court cases bring up a matter of constitutional law, it is the lower court judge that is in charge of deciding whether to ask the constitutional court to settle the constitutional claim. Thus, constitutional courts interact with lower courts in a wholly different manner than high courts in decentralised judicial systems interact with their lower courts.

As described briefly above, constitutional courts also interact with political actors in a much different manner than the US Supreme Court. In centralised systems, parliamentary groups, opposition parties, presidents, and other assorted political actors have direct access to constitutional review, and can contest laws on theoretical or abstract (as opposed to concrete) grounds. Tocqueville (1838 [1966]: 102) wrote that American-style judicial review lets private interests take control of legislation, allowing the court to decide legal claims in which there are real individual harms, and protecting the judicial review function from 'the daily aggressions of the party spirit'. This, of course, is not the case in centralised review, where party-based litigation based on abstract, potential harms is routinely filed. Referring back to Table 1.1 in Chapter One, we see that nearly all countries allow opposition parties in parliament to file claims directly with the constitutional court. Thus, constitutional courts are at greater risk of being drawn into day-to-day politics, which is potentially troublesome for maintaining institutional legitimacy.

---

26. Of the more than 8,000 petitions filed each year, the Supreme Court decides around eighty to ninety per year (Epstein and Walker 2013).

27. Constitutional courts can dismiss abstract referrals if the legal claims fall outside of the court's jurisdiction, or outside of a specific actor's capacity to bring suit.

The limitations of the US case extend beyond institutional intricacies. Though the study of US judiciary, both federal and state, has seen a surge of new research over the past twenty years, most studies examine the twentieth and now twenty-first century courts. Yet there is little evidence from early years of the US court system. Epstein, Segal and Spaeth's (2001) empirical investigation of Chief Justice Morrison Waite's (1874 to 1888) records provides some evidence of late nineteenth century Supreme Court behaviour, notably the presence of a 'norm of consensus' during that time, but most pre-Roosevelt Court studies are anecdotal, due to the absence of accurate data for those early years. This means that existing judicial studies can tell us a little about the voting behaviour of judges and, perhaps more importantly, the pressures placed on judges during the early years of democracy, and of the court's life.

Outline of the book

Due to institutional rules and the general secrecy of Western European constitutional courts, it is often stated that scholars simply 'cannot systematically study' many aspects of European courts in the manner that we study the US court system (Stone Sweet 2000: 47). Given this sobering thought, what have we learned, and what could scholars still discover, about the exercise of judicial review in constitutional courts?

In Chapter Four, I examine the role of ideology, institutions, and rights protection in decision-making practices on several European constitutional courts. In most majoritarian justifications for judicial review, the ideological preferences of judges are assumed to be important factors (though not always the dominant factor) in judicial decision-making and outcomes. Recent studies have examined the role of ideological preferences on constitutional courts, though much of its scope is necessarily limited by the institutional rules and lack of information that characterise the operation of these courts. Does ideology factor into outcomes broadly, over all issues, actors, and across multiple courts? I also investigate whether certain types of actors help ensure compliance with rulings, thus better freeing the court to overturn legislation.

The role of legal issues also is largely unexplored outside of the United States: most existing work instead focuses on institutional limitations and potential ideological motivations. I address legal issues directly by examining the major legal issue for all cases included within my dataset. Thus, I am able to test the independent effects of legal issues. For example, do the courts, as is often claimed in the liberal rights protecting vision of judicial review, systematically favour civil rights claimants? Have these cases become an increasing part of the court's docket? I address this in Chapter Four, but also in other areas of the book.

In Chapter Five, I investigate in further detail the implications of the majoritarian vision of democracy and judicial review. Specifically, I examine how concepts like public support, governmental power, and government coalitions – variables that fit directly within the majoritarian framework – might influence the exercise of judicial review. In Chapter Six, I examine the role of institutional incentives and career motivations in judicial decision-making. Specifically, do judicial appointment and retention rules influence judicial decision-making? And, does variation in these rules affect the ability or desire of judges to vote their sincere preferences? Notable comparative studies on appointment processes have generally focused on the career judiciary in the lower level courts (Garoupa and Ginsburg 2010; Guarnieri and Pederzoli 2002), while investigation of retention practices generally has focused on dynamics in more unstable political environments (Helmke 2002; Serrano and Polga-Hecimovich 2013). I examine how judicial reappointments may influence decision-making, and also address other career-based theories of decision-making.

Apart from the potential effects from certain legal issues, there is a much broader, and deeper, lack of information surrounding the use of legal argumentation and decision-making methods in courts outside of the United States. To many in the legal field, the idea that *stare decisis* and precedent differentiate common law decision-making from civil law decision-making is almost second nature. Yet it is apparent that past cases shape and guide constitutional court arguments, and that precedent appears to play a major role in the decision-making and opinion-writing processes on these courts. In Chapter Seven, I examine the use of precedent on the Polish Constitutional Tribunal, developing a unique database of case citations to examine how judges on constitutional courts use legal argumentation within their opinions. Notably, this data can be used to test the validity of the legalist view of judicial review. Do judges use neutral legal methods of decision-making to reach the normatively best outcome free of political influences? Or is there an ideological or strategic component to legal argumentation?

In the end, there are still many more questions than answers when it comes to determining the factors that influence judicial decision-making and the exercise of judicial review in democracies. This study sets out to address these deficits and provide theory, data, and systematic evidence of constitutional court behaviour across countries.

Chapter Three

Background: Constitutional Courts in Eastern Europe

The march of democracy in the twentieth century, and now the twenty-first, generally has been accompanied by the development of strong rights for citizens, and strengthened courts to both guarantee those rights and ensure the proper functioning of democracy. From the rubble of World War II there arose a heightened realisation that the future progress of Europe necessitated the development of liberal democracies based on equality and individual rights, governed by the rule of law (*Rechtsstaat*) and monitored by strong judicial actors (Stone Sweet 2000). Similarly, the gradual progress of democracy in East Asia during the 1970s and 1980s was consolidated in part through the development of strong judicial review powers to protect the democratic bargain (Ginsburg 2003), a pattern that was repeated in Latin America, as well (Helmke and Rios-Figueroa 2011). When this global wave of democratisation reached Eastern Europe, major actors there similarly sought to consolidate the process of democratisation through the creation of strong constitutions with an increased role for courts. In Inga Markovits' (1996: 2272) words, leaders of the new governments sought to move from a legal system based on 'criminal law, ensuring citizens' compliance, to constitutional law, protecting their rights; from Party rule to the rule of law'.

The performance and endurance of modern liberal democracy, then, is of central importance to the new democracies of Central and Eastern Europe (Schwartz 2000). The importance of liberal democracy to the region has been paradoxically highlighted by current questions over the viability of democracy in Hungary, once the most promising of the new Central and Eastern European transitional democracies (e.g., Piana 2010). Hungarian Prime Minister Viktor Orban has consolidated government power around his Fidesz party after its strong showing in the 2010 election, changing the rules to allow closer party control over elections, the central bank, and ultimately the jurisdiction of the Hungarian Constitutional Court (Scheppele 2013). In a December 2014 speech, Orban noted that Hungarians have rejected liberal democratic principles and freedoms over past years, instead embracing 'illiberal democracy' through his party's rule (Keszthelyi 2014). Questions over the Hungarian government's crackdown on civil society organisations has led to criticism from the *New York Times*, Human Rights Watch, the Norwegian and German governments, and the European Commission, among others (HRW 2013). Questions over rising official corruption also prompted the US Department of State to cancel visas for several Hungarian government officials (Galyas 2014). Though democratisation seemed an inexorable path by the mid-2000s, the example of Hungary today shows the future of liberal democracy in Central and Eastern Europe is no longer a forgone conclusion. This chapter examines the development of courts and judicial power over the twentieth century – a path that converges with the development of liberal democracy, as well. I then turn to the development of constitutional courts in Eastern Europe, with particular emphasis on the four countries studied in this work: Poland, the Czech Republic, Latvia, and Slovenia.

The development of constitutional judicial review in Europe

Liberal democracy was not always the norm. Boix (2003), Acemoglu and Robinson (2005), Lipset and Rokkan (1967), and others describe the gradual path towards democracy taken in many European countries. In the United Kingdom, for example, it was not until the end of World War I that property requirements for voting were removed, finally clearing the path for nearly all adult citizens in the UK to obtain the right to vote.[1] The end of the Great War in continental Europe also saw the first halting moves towards the widespread adoption of judicial review. Denmark's Supreme Court, for example, claimed for the Danish courts the power of judicial review in 1921, while Romania also briefly adopted judicial review in the 1920s (Rytter and Wind 2011; Sadurski 2014). Austrian jurist and political philosopher Hans Kelsen saw a potential difficulty with the adoption of rights-based constitutions in continental Europe: how to ensure the continued protection of constitutional rights and constitutional order? The continental civil law systems were largely built on the notion of 'parliamentary supremacy' – the idea that popularly elected parliaments are the legitimate holders of the general will, and are best able to advance the interests of the whole community (Levine 1993: 18–35; Stone 1992). Kelsen recognised the civil law court system, in which ordinary judges applied the law but could not make or develop law, stood as an obstacle to the realisation of higher order constitutional rights. How could courts and judges enforce the constitution if parliamentary supremacy dictated that they had no power to overrule the will of the parliament?

Kelsen's solution was the constitutional court, a stand-alone body of judges created specifically to exercise judicial review. Kelsen believed that the constitutional interpretation done by these courts made them, by necessity, a law-making body. However, unlike the forward-looking, creative lawmaking role of parliament, the constitutional court only stood as a 'negative' lawmaking body, with the ability to strike down legislation for violating the constitution but not the ability to positively create new rights (Kelsen 1945: 269). Kelsen's court was implemented for a time in the newly independent states of Austria and Czechoslovakia in the 1920s and 1930s. Yet rising authoritarianism in Europe led first to the dissolution of democratic rule in those states before ultimately triggering the end of Austria and Czechoslovakia as independent states.[2]

---

1. The Representation of the People Act of 1918. Females under 30 who did not meet minimum property qualifications still did not receive the right to vote until 1928.

2. The 1938 Anschluss, whether considered unification or an annexation, did effectively eliminate the political independence of Austria. The 1939 German invasion into Czechoslovakia also eliminated Czechoslovak independence.

Austria's Constitutional Court was dissolved in 1934 with the new authoritarian constitution; its successor court was dissolved again in 1938 after the annexation of Austria by Germany.[3] The Czechoslovak Constitutional Court was effectively dissolved in 1931, when no judges were appointed to fill expiring terms. The court met again briefly in 1938 and 1939, but never resolved a case during that time (Sadurski 2014).

The end of World War II saw the re-establishment of democratic constitutional order in Western Europe, a democratic consolidation that was aided by economic redevelopment assistance from the United States government's Marshall Plan. The US influence in the constitutional drafting process helped prod West Germany and Italy, particularly, towards legal systems guided by rule of law (or *Rechtsstaat*) principles, with strong individual rights for citizens and strong courts to enforce those rights (Stone Sweet 2000). As Ginsburg (2003) notes, this choice – to provide rights and courts as venues to enforce those rights – provided the first nail in the coffin of parliamentary supremacy in Europe and elsewhere. Hans Kelsen's idea of the constitutional court to adjudicate constitutional law ultimately was included within the German, Italian, and Austrian constitutional systems, where it has flourished and expanded its influence over time.

Countries in Central and Eastern Europe, however, fell under Soviet influence post-World War II. These countries did not (or could not) accept the US economic aid or other post-war political and economic reconstruction assistance. By the late 1940s, communist coups throughout Central and Eastern Europe allowed the region to fall directly under the Soviet sphere of control, with dramatic results for the region's political future (Roberts 1996; Applebaum 2013). While Western Europe re-developed strong multi-party systems with open debate on policy choices and a real possibility that parties in power could be voted out of office, the communist-controlled governments of Eastern Europe implemented strong central governments, with little to no room for policy debate or even for the existence of opposition groups or parties.[4]

In Czechoslovakia, Poland, Hungary, and elsewhere, communist governments created constitutions with strong individual rights for citizens, though these rights often were meaningless in practice. Communist-inspired constitutions all allowed for the communist-controlled parliaments to override any constitutional provision, thus bringing individual constitutional rights dependent under the control of authoritarian government (Elster 1993). Constitutional freedoms like expression and speech rights were guaranteed only 'if consistent with the interests of the working people'.[5] The result, as Markovits (1982: 522) explains, was an explicit

---

3. Constitutional Court of Austria. Available from: https://www.vfgh.gv.at (Accessed: 8 April 2015).

4. There are examples of government sanctioned opposition parties. In the 1980s, Poland's leadership allowed for the formation of several parties other than the Polish United Workers Party (Communist Party) [PZPR], notably the United Peasant Party and the Democratic Party, though both parties were still to be led by the 'guiding political force' of the PZPR (Brzezinski 1992: 101).

5. Czechoslovakia Constitution, article 28.

attempt *not* to develop a constitutional order built on 'bourgeois *Rechtsstaat* ("rule of law") notions', but rather to create an orderly, controlled society through legalism and law.

Thus, legal development was at once overly complete yet abstract. Scheppele (2002: 241) writes that despite the presence of 'telephone justice', the main problem in the socialist legal systems was not too little law, but rather *too much*. Communist governments established complex and often contradictory sets of legal codes, full of traps for the unwary or even well intentioned citizen (Boros 2003: 201). Completing the circle, huge state security apparatuses regularly intruded on the lives of citizens, demonstrating along the way the power of the state to control the destinies – the future prospects, hopes, and dreams – of its citizens (Glaeser 2011).

Given the perceived power of the communist state over its citizens, the fall of these governments from power seemed unthinkable to many on both sides of the Iron Curtain. Yet, cracks had formed over time in the social and political structures that the communist regimes had created. In 1980, the Solidarity movement in Poland was born in the Gdansk Lenin Shipyards and quickly took hold, gaining popularity and strength throughout the country. By 1981, nearly 10 million people, one-third of all Polish workers, were members of the Solidarity Trade Union. The rapid rise of the organisation ultimately led to a government crackdown and the imposition of martial law in December 1981, yet the strength of Solidarity as a non-governmental opposition force remained throughout the 1980s. An election in June 1989 thought by many in the Communist *nomenklatura* to legitimate their power instead showed the political power of Solidarity and the bankruptcy of communist rule (Ash 1993). By September 1989, Solidarity was in charge of government.

A similar crack emerged in Hungary, where during the summer of 1989 the government removed an electrified fence separating Hungary from Austria. Waves of Hungarians and East Germans fled into Austria during the summer of 1989, despite a temporary re-imposition of the border in the early autumn of 1989 (Rothschild and Wingfield 2000). In East Germany, demonstrations that began in Leipzig in September 1989 gradually grew in size before spreading to East Berlin and other large East German cities, culminating in the resignation of Erich Honecker and the opening of the Berlin Wall. Czechoslovak, Bulgarian, and Romanian regimes soon toppled, as well. Thus, in an extraordinary series of months during the late summer and fall of 1989, all of the major communist regimes in Eastern Europe had vanished, overtaken by the sudden 'power of the powerless' (Havel 1992; Ash 1993).

The legacy of communism and the redevelopment of legal culture

The legacy of communism presented unique difficulties for the development of the rule of law and judicial authority in Central and Eastern Europe. Of most pressing immediate concern, these formerly communist countries had to navigate a seemingly 'impossible' simultaneous dual transition from command economy to market economy while also moving from authoritarian to liberal democratic government (Elster 1993: 267). Compounding these concerns, years of communist rule left many citizens with inherent distrust for the formal institutions of government, including an under-resourced and increasingly illegitimate court system. Many new court systems also had to contend with an under-developed civil society, as well as a poorly developed legal culture – both of which served as impediments to the establishment and consolidation of the rule of law (Febbrajo 2010; Moffet 1998). In most communist societies the state prohibited the formation of independent groups outside of party control, from unions to reading groups. In East Germany, Poland, Czechoslovakia, and elsewhere, '[t]he party state aimed to be civil society, as well' (Glaeser 2011: 143). With the legacy of state monopolisation of group formation, post-communist societies faced challenges in generating outside groups that could bring claims to the courts.

Novak (2003: 94) describes the communist era in Slovenia as a time of 'extreme politicization' of the courts, with judges serving as 'a tool in the hands of the governing communist autocrats, rather than [...] a shield used to safeguard individual freedom'. Boros (2003), Kuhn (2004), and others emphasise the deleterious influence the communist system had on the prestige and reputation of the judiciary. Few resources were given to the judiciary or the legal system as a whole, and low wages were provided to those in the judiciary. A complex web of often-conflicting regulations left most who were forced to live within the communist-authoritarian system distrustful of it (Scheppele 2002). At the same time, literal readings of the law prevalent in socialist jurisprudence allowed many judges to avoid facing the complexities of real world problems (Kuhn 2004: 553).

The loss of prestige in the judiciary at that time was apparent.[6] Far from holding positions of independence and status, judges during the communist era instead operated in a subservient role to the ruling class that demonstrated 'the political power of the state over the judges' (Wagnerova 2003: 168). Part of this lack of prestige can be seen in the salaries paid to communist-era judges and prosecutors. Judges in East Germany earned approximately DM 1,400 per month in 1980, less than the wage paid to plumbers and electricians (Markovits 1996: 2277). Judges in communist Czechoslovakia earned less than state prosecutors, but also less than bus drivers and mine workers (Wagnerova 2003: 170; Kuhn 2011: 53).[7]

The first step for many countries during the transition period was the lustration or de-communisation of the ordinary courts. Czech judges had to go through a lustration process, in which any individuals found to have collaborated with the secret police or to have been agents of communist officials were barred from continuing in office (Open Society 2001). The results were dramatic, with more than one-third of Czech judges on the bench in 1990 out of the judiciary by 1993 (Kuhn 2011: 165; Wagnerova 2003). The Czech lustration law thus placed

---

6. Though perhaps not in all societies. Iglicar (2003: 181) notes that the Slovenian (Yugoslavian) judiciary increased in respectability from the 1950s to the 1980s.

7. Wagnerova and Markovits both claim the high number of women in the judiciary contributed to the low salaries paid to judges.

government officials – specifically Ministry of Justice officials – in a strong position to control the future composition of the ordinary courts (Piana 2010).

Similarly, upon reunification in 1990 the German government initiated investigations into all East German prosecutors and judges, dismissing nearly 50 per cent of each group in the first year alone. By 1994, over 90 per cent of judges and prosecutors no longer worked in their former positions (Markovits 1996). In the new German capital, the Berlin's new Ministry of Justice fired all East Berlin prosecutors and judges, rehiring 15 per cent through a competitive application process (Borneman 1997: 60). Other countries, notably Poland, did not purge their judiciaries in the post-communist transition, though Poland did require judges to submit declarations on their cooperation with state security during the communist period (Open Society 2001). Still, Poland has gone through its own transformation within the judicial branch during the 1990s and 2000s, one in which career judges left the country's highest courts to be replaced by legal academics relatively untouched by the communist legacy (Kuhn 2011: 173).

In the post-communist transition, then, re-establishing trust and legitimacy in the judiciary was of paramount concern to those actors involved in orchestrating the turnaround (Piana 2010: 93).[8] To a large extent, the re-development of the Eastern European judiciaries occurred with the aid and support of outside actors, including the US Agency for International Development (USAID), the American Bar Association (ABA), both through its Rule of Law Initiative and the recruitment of top US law professors,[9] and the European Union (EU), most notably through the PHARE program.

On a structural level, the EU's main strategy to bring about legal reform was the larger program of *conditionality* – a policy in which candidate countries must adhere to democratic standards and conditions before gaining admission to the EU as a Member State (Mendelski 2012). One primary condition placed on all candidate countries was the development of the rule of law (Sadurski 2004: 374). Developing the rule of law, in turn, required developing judicial capacity and reforming the role of the judiciary within society. To increase judicial capacity, the EU's major assistance program, the PHARE program, directed major outlays of funds towards civil society, public administration, and legal reform. PHARE originally was established to provide support to Hungary and Poland, though the program gradually expanded to include nearly all of the formerly communist Eastern European transition states (Europa 2007).[10] PHARE's 'twinning' program allowed judges and legal officials in the newly democratic East to be paired with

---

8. Kuhn (2011: 164) notes, however, that some modernising economists during the early transitional phase attempted to limit the role of legal reforms as a point of emphasis in the transition, instead focusing on reducing the role of government regulation, and thus the centrality law, and presumably increasing market-based factors in the new governments.

9. Erwin Chemerinsky, Cass Sunstein, and Peter Maggs were some of the many law professors who contributed to constitutional development in these countries.

10. Countries benefiting from the PHARE program include: Bulgaria, Croatia, the Czech Republic, Estonia, Hungary, Latvia, Lithuania, Poland, Romania, Slovakia, and Slovenia.

experienced counterparts in more established Western European democracies. The program was designed to create meaningful relationships across countries, though its most important aspect arguably was the 'transfer of best practices' from West to East (Piana 2010: 36–37). This included collaborative re-writing of important aspects of civil and criminal codes in Eastern European states, as well as programs to develop new methods of legal interpretation.

The PHARE program also developed systems of training for judges, organising seminars and workshops to develop judicial knowledge among other items. Such reforms made practical the notion that, for legal change and modernisation to occur, '[structural] legal reforms must be accompanied by reforms in thinking' (Wagnerova 2003: 176). There also were more practical reforms in legal operation, notably the creation of usable websites to find out information on the courts, the adoption of e-filing and tracking systems for lawsuits, and the modernisation of equipment in judicial offices.

Similarly, the ABA judicial reform programs in many Central and Eastern European and other post-communist states created seminars for judges, prosecutors, and other attorneys. The ABA programs were in many ways born out of President George H.W. Bush's 1990 vision for a 'citizen democracy corps' of private sector individuals and organisations that would venture to Eastern Europe to develop needed skills and 'support democratic change' (Devroy 1990). Reform programs developed by the ABA's Rule of Law Initiative also helped to draft new judicial codes of ethics for judges and prosecutors. The Rule of Law Initiative also assisted local attorneys, judges, and legislators in the creation of new commercial codes and other substantive legislation.[11] Much of this work occurred through the Central and Eastern Europe Law Initiative (CEELI), established in 1993 by the ABA with the support of USAID (ABA 1993). By 1999, ABA and USAID had established the CEELI Institute in Prague to serve as a permanent judicial training centre for judges, attorneys, and law students throughout Eastern Europe and Eurasia.

Required monitoring of reforms by the European Commission was a major – perhaps the major – aspect of the EU's legal reform strategy for the Central and Eastern European candidate countries. The EU, and specifically the European Commission, worked with Hungary, Poland, and the Czech Republic to ensure their legal codes and judicial standards met the *aquis communitaire*. Yet, as Sadurski (2004) and others explain, in many candidate countries local political elites welcomed the introduction of these programs, which often aided local efforts to improve capacity and resources, and ultimately the legitimacy, of the new democratic governments.

Nowhere was the need for modernisation better seen than in the area of judicial decision-making, which had been described as stuck in a 'European legal culture that prevailed in the 19th century' (Hondius 2004: 527). This predominant legal culture was characterised both by excessive deference and passivity to authority

---

11. ABA Rule of Law Initiative. Available from: http://www.americanbar.org/advocacy/rule_of_law.html (Accessed: 13 February 2015).

and by rigidly formalist decision-making methods, notably lacking both the incorporation of outside authority and the use of case law and jurisprudence (Emmert 2003). Kuhn (2004) blames the overly formalist decision-making seen in the lower courts of Eastern Europe on the decline of the rule of law and the lowered status of the judiciary that took place during communist rule. Though the communist state and its governing authorities became an omnipresent force within society during its rule, judges and lawyers were largely excluded from participating in this power. The socialist legal system was 'composed exclusively of written law' – the development of case law was not permitted, and judicial interpretation was virtually non-existent in these socialist legal systems (Kuhn 2004: 542). Markovits (1996: 2274) similarly describes the overriding concern within the East German legal system was for 'uniformity of the law'. The result in many areas of the Eastern Bloc was the establishment of a highly mechanical jurisprudence that appeared ever more out of step with the judicial freedom developing elsewhere in Western Europe and North America (Kuhn 2011).

Thus, even after the end of communist rule, many judges steeped in that tradition still expressed slavish adherence to the literal application of the code, and the limited role of judges in substantive decision-making. Given changes in the Western legal landscape and the increased confluence between common law and civil law systems, such practices were increasingly out of step with modern judging. Equally important, it became apparent to many experts that these types of formalist practices were inadequate for the social and legal transformation taking place in Central and Eastern Europe throughout the 1990s and 2000s (Kuhn 2011; Trochev 2008; Hollander 2003; Morawski and Zirk-Sadowski 1997). Rather than formalism, dynamism in judicial decision-making could be necessary to resolve concrete legal cases, particularly when working within poorly drafted, out-of-date, or simply incomplete laws.[12]

Despite this often-stultified review in the ordinary courts, constitutional court judges have from an early time engaged in a different style. In fact, important battles developed in the Czech Republic, Poland, and elsewhere between constitutional courts and supreme courts over the methods of judicial decision-making and opinion writing, with constitutional court judges developing dynamic, purposive decision-making styles that often clashed with the more traditional methods used in the many ordinary courts (Trochev 2008; McCormack and Summers 1997). It is to these constitutional courts I now turn.

Courts in Poland, Slovenia, the Czech Republic, and Latvia

This study focuses on four countries: Poland, Slovenia, Latvia, and the Czech Republic. The four countries are united in being a part of the wave of

---

12. Rogers (2001) notes that, given the inability of the legislature to see into the future and create fully complete legislative codes at time t, the ability of courts to use their temporal advantage to solve unanticipated problems at time $t+1$ should be a primary rationale for politicians to maintain judicial independence and judicial power.

democratisation that followed the end of communist rule in Eastern and Central Europe. During the transition from authoritarian to democratic rule, these countries all chose to adopt constitutional courts to serve the role of protector and arbiter of their new constitutions. Subsequent chapters will use data from these courts to empirically test different visions and predictions of how judicial review operates in modern democracy. In this section I explore briefly the four courts selected for study. How were these courts established? What are their powers? How are they staffed? Below is a brief exploration of these questions.

Poland was the first of the Eastern Bloc countries to establish a separate constitutional court (Brzezinski 1998). Poland's Constitutional Tribunal was established in 1982 by the communist government of General Jaruzelski as an attempt to placate reformers following the 1981 crackdown on Poland's nascent democratic movement, though it did not start operation until 1985. Yet, at the outset there were important limits to the new court's power. First, the Tribunal only ruled with finality on executive decrees – rulings on legislation were only advisory. Second, and perhaps most notable, the court when it was established only had jurisdiction to consider laws and regulations enacted after 1982, which would exclude considerations of the legality of Jaruzelski's imposition of martial law in 1981 (Brzezinski 1992: 99). After the fall of the communist government in 1989, the Constitutional Tribunal was not only retained but also gained additional powers, though until the adoption of the 1997 constitution the Sejm still retained the power to override Tribunal decisions if they could garner a two-thirds supermajority.

Today, the justices of the Polish Constitutional Tribunal are selected by an absolute majority vote of the lower house of the Polish parliament, the Sejm. The current Tribunal has fifteen justices; all justices serve nine-year terms. The judges on the court have a variety of backgrounds: some are career judges, some are primarily academic law professors, and some come to the court with political backgrounds. In fact, several current members of the Tribunal have retained their academic positions while also serving on the court.[13] According to one former Tribunal justice, many of the judges initially appointed to the court in the 1990s were law professors because the MPs in charge of appointments wanted to avoid the charge of politicising the institution. Still, the role of party politics in appointments remains strong: nearly all judges to the Tribunal have been appointed with the support of the majority party or coalition in parliament (Garlicki 2002).

With its prominent role even before the democratic transition, the Tribunal has from an early time been asked to decide cases with major implications for social policy. In the early 1990s, the Tribunal overturned key parts of the new government's economic revitalisation plan, including a recently enacted reduction in pensions for many retirees. As described in Chapter Four, pensions and other social welfare matters have remained a large part of the court's docket in subsequent years, as well. The justices also weighed in on important civil rights

---

13. Confirmed through interviews with Tribunal staff. Several judges have maintained their academic positions in various law faculties around the country while serving their term on the court.

issues. In addition to its protection of assembly rights and rights to equality seen in the Equality Parade Case, Tribunal justices have also tackled sex discrimination in a series of cases that overturned laws allowing sex-based differences in mandatory retirement ages and pension accruals. Given the popularity of the Catholic Church, the court has hewed a fine line in religious freedom cases. In 1991, the Tribunal upheld a new law introducing religious education and religious symbols in public classrooms, with an allowance for students to opt out of religion courses. In a 2007 ruling, the court held that state funding of religious education at the university level, which appeared to benefit the Catholic Church, did not violate the constitution's requirement of state impartiality towards religious practice.

Overall, the Polish public views the Tribunal as both competent and impartial. The Polish polling firm CBOS has conducted two polls investigating in-depth the views of citizens towards the Tribunal. In 2007, 82 per cent of Poles believed the Tribunal was impartial (up eight points from 2004), and 88 per cent believed the Tribunal was effective in guarding the constitution (CBOS 2007). According to more recent polling, the Tribunal is regularly found to be among the most publicly popular institutions of government.

The new Slovenian Constitutional Court was established in 1991, shortly after Slovenia's declaration of independence from Yugoslavia. Like Poland, Yugoslavia adopted a constitutional court during its own communist era.[14] Slovenia's own government within the Yugoslav state also adopted a constitutional court, though like the Polish Tribunal it too was limited in its powers to review and annul legislation (Cerar 2002: 216; Mavcic 2009). Thus, the new independent Slovenian government did have some experience with a higher court potentially capable of checking the legislature and executive. Still, the new Slovenian Constitutional Court was given expanded powers to rule laws and regulations unconstitutional, and also was granted important formal independence powers (Nowak 2003). Of particular note, the Slovenian Constitutional Court is permitted to go beyond the bounds of the case presented and consider the constitutionality of laws not challenged by the initiator of the constitutional complaint (Sadurski 2014: 15).[15]

Judges on the Slovenian court are appointed by the parliament after being nominated by the Slovenian president. However, parliament has, from an early time, taken the dominant role within this appointment process – a process that also has been from an early time 'highly politicised' (Cerar 2002: 218). It has become common practice for the president to consult with parliament before making any nominations, and parliamentary majorities regularly 'impose [their] will' in the appointment process (Cerar 2002: 217). And, from an early time the judges on the Slovenian Constitutional Court earned a reputation for engaging in judicial activism and political decision-making (Cerar 2002: 216). In fact, this activism

---

14. In fact, it was adopted in 1963, much earlier than the Polish Constitutional Tribunal.

15. Slovenia Constitutional Court Act, article 30 ('In deciding on the constitutionality and legality of a regulation or general act ..., the Constitutional Court is not bound by the proposal of a request or petition.')

led to early calls on the part of some politicians to reign in the court by adopting a supermajority confirmation vote for nominees. Still, the Slovenian court has appeared to successfully weather these initial storms to take a prominent place in national government.

In fact, the Slovenian court has been at the forefront of changes in several important social policies. In the late 1990s, the court expansively defined the meaning of equality, finding that in some cases the state could actually take positive remedial action – in this case allowing women to draw pensions after accumulating fewer years of work – to remedy past disadvantages women have faced in the workplace. In a 2009 case, the court struck down a key part of the same sex partnership law that limited that ability of same sex partners to inherit property. In doing so, the court opened a path for full and equal rights for same sex couples.

Similar to the Slovenian court, the Czech Constitutional Court was the product of two earlier, short-lived Czechoslovak Constitutional Courts. The first Czechoslovak Constitutional Court was established in 1920 in the newly independent Czechoslovakia after the break-up of the Hapsburg Empire. The 1920 court was the first based on Hans Kelsen's idea of the constitutional court as a 'negative legislator' in a new separation-of-powers-based European democratic order. The seven-member court was appointed in 1921 to serve ten-year terms, though none were re-appointed after the expiry of their terms and the court sat vacant until 1938.[16]

The second Czechoslovak court was established after the end of the communist government, but only lasted eleven months due to the dissolution of the Czechoslovak Federation (in the so-called 'velvet divorce'). The Czech Constitutional Court was established at the end of 1992 and began work in July 1993. Like the US Supreme Court, the fifteen members of the Czech court are nominated by the president and confirmed by the Senate, the upper house of parliament. Each justice serves a ten-year term, with the possibility of re-appointment by the Czech president. The appointment scheme for Czech judges was tested in 2004 and 2005 by then-President Vaclav Klaus. Klaus effectively 'blocked the Court's ability to function by not appointing new judges' in 2004 (Sadurski 2014: 9; Trochev 2008). Without new justices, the court could not gain a quorum, and thus could not rule on the constitutionality of laws. When he did put forth nominations, the Senate rejected seven nominees before the court was able to re-gain full strength in December 2005.

The court has power to review the constitutionality of law and regulations, both national and local, as well as individual constitutional complaints, though it also can review the judgments of the ordinary courts to determine whether rights have been violated. This final jurisdictional power gives the Czech court a potentially greater influence than other constitutional courts over the output of the ordinary

---

16. The Czech Constitutional Court: History. Available from: http://www.usoud.cz/en/history (Accessed: 20 March 2015). See also The Constitutional Act of 1920, Article III [Czechoslovakia].

judiciary (Kuhn 2011: 194). Perhaps for this reason, the Czech Constitutional Court and the Czech Supreme Court were involved in several high profile battles over judicial interpretation and the respective powers of each court (Priban 2002: 380; Trochev 2008). As intimated above, the Czech Constitutional Court also had a sometimes-rocky relationship with former President Vaclav Klaus. Klaus on several occasions questioned the neutrality and impartiality of the court's judges, pointedly describing the Czech Constitutional Court's 2009 Lisbon treaty decision as 'not a neutral legal analysis but a biased political defence' by a 'political' court (CTK 2009). Klaus later attempted to alter the powers of the court after it ruled against a bill that would have shortened the terms of MPs in the lower house of parliament. However, when Klaus was impeached by the Senate for treason as he was leaving office in 2013, the court threw out the case, determining that as he was out of office by the time the case reached the court, impeachment could not proceed as a procedural matter.

The Latvian Constitutional Court was the final of the four courts to be adopted. It was approved by parliament in 1994, but did not begin hearing cases until the end of 1996. The court has seven members, selected on a separation-of-powers system of appointment: parliament, by absolute majority vote, appoints three judges; the cabinet appoints two more, and the judicial system appoints the final two judges. Despite its late start, the court has become an important policy maker in Latvian society, notably in taking on issues of pensions and other socio-economic rights, prisoner's rights, and, to an extent, the rights of the ethnic Russian minority in Latvia (Kruma 2009).

From an early time the Latvian Constitutional Court judges have been in the middle of high profile and high risk cases. In 1999 the court was asked by members of the former governing cabinet to rule on the constitutionality of parliament's dismissal of the telecommunications council, a council which the former cabinet members claimed was under the jurisdiction of the transportation minister, not the parliament. Latvia's new court ruled against the parliament and in favour of the former government, though did so knowing the possibility that the new government (led by the confectionary millionaire Andris Skele) and parliament would not respect the decision. Also in 1999, attempts were made by Skele and the Justice Ministry to dissolve the Constitutional Court by merging its functions into the Supreme Court. The president of the Constitutional Court, Aivars Endzins, later noted in a Latvian television interview that the court's rulings that year may have been tied to the effort to dissolve the court (BBC Monitoring 2006). The Constitutional Court has been the subject of other attempts to alter its role in government, including a 2006 bill aimed at giving the court the role – unwanted, according to the court president – of providing consultative opinions to the government (Sloga 2006).

Overall, these countries provide an ideal area to test comparative theories of judicial review. Notably, the countries selected for this cross-national and longitudinal study have several commonalities that can help to control the potential effects of outside factors. All the countries have a roughly comparable current history of democracy, as all moved from communist-authoritarian governments to democratic governments in the early 1990s. Within these countries there are certainly differences in democratic consolidation. Grzymala-Busse (2007) describes how differences in party system development led to the varied development of governmental oversight institutions and ultimately democratic consolidation in Poland, Slovenia, the Czech Republic, and Latvia. Yet all four currently meet the Przeworski *et al*. (2000) definition of a democracy. Similarly, all four countries also faced significant incentives from the European Union to democratise, to reform state agencies, and to adopt institutional protections, notably independent courts (Orenstein *et al*. 2008; Sadurski 2004). Thus, the types of outside pressures, particularly those from international organisations, placed on these countries have been roughly similar. Currently, all four are members of the European Union, and so must abide by the *acquis communitaire* – the body of common rights and obligations that unite all EU member states. Similarly, they must follow the principles contained with the EU treaties, as well as regulations and directives of the EU institutions.

At the same time, these countries differ on important institutional rules, which will allow for full testing of a range of theory regarding the practice of judicial review. As described in greater detail in Chapter Six, appointment and retention practices differ: in the Czech Republic, judges are nominated by the president and confirmed by the Senate. In Slovenia the president also nominates judges, though the president *de facto* consults with parliament to choose a safe nominee before nominating (Cerar 2002). In Poland, judges are appointed by a simple majority vote in parliament. Perhaps most important, they vary in retention practices. The Czech Republic provides judges the possibility of re-appointment by the parliament, while the remaining countries mandate fixed, non-renewable terms in office for constitutional court judges.

As described in greater detail in Chapter Five, all four countries have experienced democratic consolidation and institutionalisation, but also differ in party system institutionalisation and the types of government that have arisen after elections. Latvia has experienced some level of party continuity over time, but also the rise and fall of significant parties from one election to the next (Bloom 2011). Poland's party system has experienced less volatility than Latvia, but also has twice seen governing parties suffer significant declines in support from one election to the next. For example, Solidarity Electoral Action (AWS) was the government formateur in 1997 after receiving 44 per cent of seats in the Sejm, but received only 5.6 per cent of votes and no parliamentary seats in the 2001 election. Slovenia arguably has seen the most stable party system. The left-leaning Liberal Democracy of Slovenia (LDS) party dominated governing coalitions in the 1900s and early 2000s before losing power in 2004. Yet after the 2008–09 financial collapse, Slovenia's party system has been more unstable.

Overall, the differences in appointment practices, combined with the turnover in government, has created an environment in which it is possible to examine the potential influence of ideology and/or policy-based decision-making, which will be examined in greater detail in Chapter Four. The variations in the party system also have allowed for the creation of multiple governments, some with solid public support, others lacking true support. In Chapter Five, I use these differences to examine how the type and the breadth of citizen support for executive government might influence the operation of judicial review. While the commonalities in democratic consolidation should control for extraneous factors, these differences in institutional design and the particularities of democratic practice should result in different incentives for judicial decision-making.

The dataset

To examine the general visions of judicial review described in Chapters One and Two, I utilise a unique dataset of constitutional court cases from Poland, the Czech Republic, Latvia, and Slovenia. The information contained within this dataset is focused at the level of the legal issue presented in the case, with legal issues representing distinct national laws or regulations being challenged. That is, each observation in the dataset is either a law or regulation the court reviews. Most cases analysed in this study arise through 'abstract' review, a process through which specified actors challenge laws even in the absence of a concrete complaint. Yet in Latvia, any person who claims 'fundamental' constitutional rights are violated can file suit through the same abstract review procedure.[17] And in Slovenia, private individuals also can present claims under a similar type of suit that enables legal challenges with the same effect as the abstract review procedure. I include these cases here, as well. Following Carrubba, Gabel, and Hankla (2008), most analysis in this book centres on the legal issue, rather than the case, because in some instances the courts consider the constitutionality of multiple laws within one constitutional referral. Many of the instances where multiple laws are considered involve two closely related (yet distinct) laws,[18] or else the constitutionality of a law and its related regulation(s). Most such instances of multiple issues within one legal case occur in Poland. In total, 965 legal issues arising from over 800 cases in these four countries are included. For individual-level data analysis, the unit of analysis is the judge's decision for each legal issue. Below, I explain the information contained within this dataset.

To create the dataset, I first read the final decisions from all cases, searching for key case facts and variables in the process. Case outcomes are the primary consideration in this study; accordingly, most of the key variables are those that might help us discover how judges and court panels engage in decision-making and outcome-creation. Perhaps the key consideration for this project is the outcome of the case: does the court decide that the law or regulation under review is unconstitutional or constitutional? This decision is key because of the policy implications within that choice, and the primary importance, both practical and theoretical, of the decision to overturn in theories of judicial review. In overturning legislation, these courts rule with finality on the policy

---

17. Latvia Constitutional Court Law, section 17.

18. That is, the laws are separate entities, with one not being simply an amended version of the other law.

decisions within those cases. I consider any law that is overturned, in whole or in part, to be ruled 'unconstitutional'. Given the focus on the outcome of the case, many of the explanatory variables and control variables all are focused on helping to explain the larger case outcome. However, Chapter Six evaluates claims regarding judicial decision-making at the individual level, and certain individual-level variables will be used in testing. The key variables in this dataset, as well as their mean values, are listed below in Table 3.1, and are used throughout the book.

Table 3.1: Descriptive statistics for case-level and individual-level data

Variable	Mean	Description
Unconstitutional ruling	0.56	Whether the law or regulation under review is ruled unconstitutional
Duration	3.99	The number of years since the law or regulation that has been enacted
Opposite party review	0.56	Is the reviewing panel majority comprised of judges chosen by opposing parties?
Panel size	7.00	The number of judges deciding the issue
Dissent	0.41	The number of dissents filed
Oversight agency challenge	0.19	Did an oversight agency refer the issue to the court?
MP group challenge	0.12	Did a group of MPs refer the issue to the court?
Local government challenge	0.08	Did a town, city, mayor, or other local government official refer the issue to court?
President challenge	0.03	Did the president refer the issue to the court?
Number of parties	3.42	Number of groups filing briefs in the case
Minimum winning coalition	0.57	MWC enacting coalition
Surplus coalition	0.22	Surplus enacting coalition
Minority government	0.21	Minority government
Current government law	0.42	Is the party or coalition whose law is under review still in government?
Reappointment	0.38	Is the judge eligible for reappointment?
Public support for court		Public approval of constitutional tribunal, from CBOS
Vote proximity	0.47	Does the judge rule in accord with appointing party's interests?
Last two years in office	0.22	Is the judge in last two years in office?
Years in term	5.7	The number of years a judge has been in office
Age	59.6	The age of a judge when case is announced
Political background	0.36	Does the judge have background in politics?
Judicial background	0.41	Does the judge have previous legal experience?

Chapter Four

Beginnings: Majoritarianism and Rights Protection

Introduction

'Who will do the governing and to whose interests should government be responsive?' (Lijphart 1999: 1). This question, one central to broader issues of democratic quality and endurance, has often been answered by examining the performance of political institutions. Lijphart's own discussion focuses on electoral rules and parliamentary institutions as primary contributors to good democratic performance (see Lijphart 1984, 1999).

Yet, relatively few studies have broadened this focus to include the role of the judiciary. In many countries today the answer to the question, 'who will do the governing?', must include the courts, as the decisions of these courts have the power to bind other actors and shape subsequent outcomes (Stone 1992; Hönnige 2011). This is all the more true with the constitutional courts of Eastern Europe, which have been highly active in defining constitutional values and shaping policy – more active, many say, than their counterparts in Western Europe (Sadurski 2006; Robertson 2010). This can be seen in numerical terms: in 2005 alone, the Polish Constitutional Tribunal overruled twenty-two of thirty-five legislative acts challenged through abstract review. This activism also can be seen in specific policy areas. After the 2008–09 global financial collapse, the Latvian government, hit hard by the economic slowdown, passed a new austerity budget after financial bailouts by the EU and IMF. Yet a key aspect of the reform plan – pension cuts – was repeatedly overturned in a series of Latvian Constitutional Court decisions in 2009 and 2010. Early in its life, the Polish Tribunal similarly overturned key aspects of the new democratic government's economic plan. And when Equality Parade organisers sought to march in Warsaw, it was the Constitutional Tribunal that ultimately secured their right against the objections of the new Polish president and government.

Increasingly, broader questions of democratic functioning and performance involve examination of the courts, and the relationship of the courts to other actors in government and society. In this chapter I take an initial examination of the data on judicial outcomes and test some preliminary claims presented in the previous chapters. Specifically, I first examine the baseline claim from the majoritarian model of judicial review specified in Chapters One and Two. Do judges on constitutional courts decide cases in an ideological or policy-based manner? Do judicial outcomes differ based on the composition of each panel? This key, baseline condition within the majoritarian model potentially ties judicial review and judicial outcomes to democratic legitimacy (Peretti 1999; Dahl 1957).

Writing in 1957, political theorist Robert Dahl found policy-based based judicial review was a given, though turnover within the bench should allow the courts to represent, generally, the views of the political majority of the day. This thesis has spurred a diverse range of judicial scholars to continue with a policy-based view of high court judging, albeit not necessarily with the majority-promoting outcomes Dahl anticipated. The 'attitudinal' model of judicial review works on the assumption that high court judges decide cases based on their own policy preferences, which, given the political nature of appointment processes, happen to correlate well with the policy preferences of the politicians who appoint judges to the court (Segal and Spaeth 2002). Comparative scholars who examine the role of policy or politics in constitutional court judging often follow the assumptions of the attitudinal model. Christoph Hönnige's (2009) examination of the French Constitutional Counsel and the German Constitutional Court compares the party affiliation of the pivotal judge in each judicial panel with the likelihood of success by opposition parties. Garoupa, Gomez-Pomar, and Grembi's (2013) study of the Spanish Constitutional Court similarly examines the validity of policy-based voting by judges on that court. Given the adoption of attitudinal voting theories outside the United States, this chapter also can help confirm the validity, or possibly show the invalidity, of policy-based judicial decision-making in new environments.

Second, we can examine the validity of a liberal, rights-protecting vision of judicial review. Do courts use their powers of constitutional review to aggressively ensure the protection of civil rights or other social protections? To examine this question, I look both to the types of issues courts decide (and how they decide), as well as the actors bringing cases to these courts.

Ideology, court deference, and rights protection

A long line of existing theory, largely built from examination of the US courts, suggests judges are motivated by ideological goals and personal policy preferences (Pritchett 1948; Dahl 1957; Murphy 1966; Segal and Spaeth 2002). For many years, American political scientists viewed Supreme Court justices as almost pure political actors. Contemporary scholars have added important qualifications to this conclusion: notably, that the policy goals judges attempt to advance may be tempered by the competing demands from judicial doctrine, jurisprudence, and inter-branch relations (Eskridge 1991; Epstein and Knight 1998; Maltzman *et al.* 2000; Hansford and Spriggs 2006). For many years a different idea held sway outside the United States, one in which democratic politics occurred solely within the executive and the legislative branches of government; the judiciary's function was *law*, independent of politics. The idea that judging carried a political aspect was seen as anathema to the proper judicial role of describing the law. Alec Stone Sweet (2007: 73) explains how many prominent French constitutional scholars, including Louis Favoreau, separated 'things political' from 'things legal', treating investigations of policy-making in the constitutional courts as 'an accusation' that courts were illegitimate. In the 1990s, professor Bernhard Schlink (1992: 735) noted a fundamental unwillingness of German legal scholars to engage with constitutional court decisions as outcomes that carried implications for social policy – or as outcomes that could possibly be incorrect. Instead, they were treated purely as code-like legal pronouncements.

Today, the idea that European courts, too, may respond to policy motivations and institutional rules is perhaps not as contested (Dyevre 2010; Hönnige 2011). In fact, in recent years scholars have found a clear policy-based dimension to aspects of German, Italian, Spanish, and French Constitutional Court voting (Pellegrina and Garoupa 2013; Hanretty 2012; Hönnige 2009; Franck 2009). However, difficulties remain within the study of European constitutional courts. Perhaps the most important limitation is the inability to fully observe the responses of many European constitutional judges. Much of our current comparative research has been focused on Western European courts, but institutional rules within many of those countries limit or outright prevent researchers from observing the effects of policy preferences and institutional rules. France, for example, prohibits judges on its *Conseil Constitutionnel* from filing dissents, and further prohibits the name of the opinion author to be known (Stone 1992). In the Italian Constitutional Court deliberations and voting are secret and dissents are not allowed, which largely precludes observing the voting behaviour of individual judges (Volcansek 2000; Pellegrina and Garoupa 2013). As a result, it is difficult for researchers of these courts to observe ideological decision-making, or see the strategic effects of institutional rules.

Other institutional rules, such as supermajority appointment requirements, attempt to remove the direct role of politics from constitutional court confirmations. Germany, Hungary, Spain, and Italy are some of the many countries that mandate these supermajority voting rules. The intent of these rules was to encourage compromise and remove the role of party politics in appointments. The effect, however, has been to incentivise the major political parties to create deals in which major parties of the right and left will vote in favour of the other's slate of nominees in return for reciprocal support for their own slate of nominees (Hönnige 2009; Scheppele 2005; Stone Sweet 2000). In Germany, the leftist SPD and the centre-right CDU/CSU have long engaged in such bargains. The result has been an equal number of SPD and CDU/CSU judges on the court at nearly all times, which has made observation of ideological outcomes particularly difficult (Vanberg 2005).[1]

The rules described above greatly limit the amount of observable data, and, as noted in Chapter Two, have led some to conclude that scholars simply 'cannot study systematically' many aspects of European court behaviour in the same way that US courts can be studied (Stone Sweet 2000: 48). Yet, this pessimistic conclusion has not stopped researchers from making use of the observational data that is available in individual countries. Pellegrina and Garoupa (2013), for

---

1. Though the observation of ideological outcomes is difficult, this should not lead to an absence of political decision-making among individual judges on the court. Additionally, Hönnige (2009) notes that the court has occasionally had left or right majorities within the panels due to imbalances in terms of office. At such times, ideological voting is apparent.

example, determine the ideology of Italian constitutional court judge rapporteurs influence the success rate of the prime minister when the court hears Italian regional government/central government constitutional cases. Hönnige's (2009) examination of abstract review cases initiated by abstract political parties in the French and German courts is able to make use of cases decided during the few periods of imbalance between SPD and CDU appointees to find a similar link between judicial ideology and opposition party success in Germany.

These findings are important because the basic majoritarian vision for judicial review anticipates ideological voting among judges on courts of constitutional review. For Dahl (1957) and others, the recruitment and selection processes for these courts drives ideological voting among judges. In systems where democratically elected political actors are responsible for appointments to the court, we should see judges who are appointed reflect the interests of those appointers. Provided a close connection between voter choices and government composition, these judges should also reflect the basic preferences of the median voter. Conversely, a rights-protecting (as well as legalist) vision of judicial review in democratic government largely subsumes the desire of judges to decide cases based on ideological preference in favour of other paramount interests (i.e., the need to protect individual rights).[2] Given this backdrop, do we see evidence supporting any of these visions in their basic form?

The newer democracies in Eastern Europe are ideal environments in which to test a policy-motivated vision for how judicial review operates, as well as theories in which judges serve as rights protectors in democratic society. In the four countries selected here, selection processes should allow for ideological or policy preferences to play a significant role in judicial decision-making. Partisan political actors have extensive abilities to nominate and/or appoint favoured actors to the court, with anecdotal evidence already suggesting a strong partisan role in judicial selection. In Poland, judges are selected through a simple majority vote of the members of parliament. The same process exists for selection of the Latvian parliamentary blocs.[3] This process almost invariably allows the preferences of the popularly elected parliament to be translated into judicial selections. For example, Poland's parliamentary majorities have almost always been successful in appointing their preferred nominees to the court. Former Polish Justice Lech Garlicki (2002: 268) notes only two instances from the first twenty-nine Polish court appointments in which nominees from non-majority parties were proposed and confirmed in the Sejm. Even the Latvian Constitutional Court president has described as political the process by which nominees are selected to his court (Diena 2006; BBC Monitoring 2006). These appointment processes create a direct link between majority preferences and judges on the court, a link that

---

2. There is, of course, the possibility, even likelihood, that judges may respond to multiple incentives – i.e., the desire to protect rights and to vote ideologically. I explore this possibility later in the chapter.

3. It is important to keep in mind that the Latvian Supreme Court appoints two judges to the Constitutional Court.

politicians certainly recognise: according to a close watcher of Polish politics, one of incoming prime minister Jaroslaw Kaczynski's main goals in 2005 and 2006 was to 'gain control of the constitutional court' (Millard 2010: 148). As head of the PiS party, Kaczynski himself noted a need to appoint his own more conservative justices, as it was 'evident in their verdicts' that certain 'individuals in the Constitutional Tribunal ... are associated with the SLD [Democratic Left Alliance]' (Safjan 2006).

Slovenia uses an appointment process similar to that in the United States, where the president nominates and the parliament approves nominees – though in practice the president consults heavily with the parliament before even making nominations (Cerar 2002; Mavcic 2009). With this ability of parliamentary majorities to appoint preferred actors, there should be a significant correlation between parliamentary preferences and the preferences of the judges they select. Thus, the Czech Republic represents the only true deviation from the parliament-dominated model of judicial appointments. The appointment process for constitutional court judges in the Czech Republic largely mirrors the process in the United States, where the president is responsible for nominating judges who are then confirmed by the Czech Senate. The president, then, holds the balance of appointment power, with a check on this power retained by the upper house of the legislature (Priban 2002).[4] Overall, the direct and discernible role of political actors makes the constitutional courts within the four countries studied here particularly suitable for examining the role of ideology in constitutional court outcomes. Further, the existence of these favourable rules should not necessarily change the *presence* of certain factors (such as ideology and strategic interactions), merely the ability to *observe* them.[5]

In addition to the expected role ideology should play in appointments, the very nature of many constitutional court cases brings up important policy implications. This is particularly true for 'abstract' review challenges – constitutional referrals made by authorised governmental and non-governmental actors after a law has been adopted and potentially before it has been enforced – i.e., without a concrete injury.

---

4. However, until 2012 the Czech president was elected through a vote of the Czech lower house and upper house, with victorious candidates needing to secure majorities in both houses of parliament. The Czech president is now elected by popular vote of the people to serve a five-year term.

5. There is one possible exception to this statement, though, that must be addressed: the rules allowing public voting records. If we imagine that judges, regardless of locale, care about their job, the decisions they make, and the effects these decisions have on larger society, then the public availability of this voting information should not lead to any comparative differences between environments with public and transparent voting and environments where judicial voting is private (e.g. Italy). However, similar to the problems of observation in legislative roll call voting (see Carrubba *et al.* 2006), the presence of observable voting in courts could lead some judges to alter their voting behaviour. Because their votes can be observed, it is possible that some judges could face incentives to alter their voting behaviour to please either the party in power or their own appointing party. This should be particularly true for those judges near the end of their term and facing reappointment. This is an issue I will examine in Chapter Six. Only the Czech Republic allows re-appointments to the constitutional court.

Table 4.1: Constitutional courts of Poland, Slovenia, Latvia, and the Czech Republic

Country	Size of court	Appointment	Terms in office
Poland	15 judges	Majority vote of parliament	9 years, fixed terms
Slovenia	9 judges	Majority vote in parliament, on proposal by president	9 years, fixed terms
Latvia	7 judges	Majority vote in parliament: three judges nominated by parliament; two judges nominated by the cabinet; two nominated by Supreme Court	10 years, fixed terms
Czech Republic	15 judges	Majority vote in senate, on proposal by president	10 years, reappointment possible

For example, as seen in Table 1.1 in the first chapter, rules of standing in nearly all constitutional courts allow opposition political parties in parliament the right to challenge legislation and executive rules at the constitutional court. Many national rules allow for other political actors – notably, the president, but also unions, political parties, religious groups, and institutions of government oversight – to challenge legislation in the constitutional court, as well. These abstract challenges place the court directly as a conflict-resolver between two opposing partisan political camps – a situation that is all the more true when these courts hear challenges to legislation presented by opposition political parties, in many cases after they have lost an earlier fight over legislation in parliament. The Latvian court's ruling – early in its life – on the competencies of the cabinet and the parliament (described in Chapter Three) is but one example of the political nature of many abstract cases.

Given this ideological, policy-driven environment, I propose as a first testable hypothesis (Hypothesis 1) that when there is a marked difference between the policy preferences of the court and the preferences of the legislature or government that enacted the act under constitutional review, we should expect, all things equal, that the court will vote to overturn that legislation. However, when the court and the legislature are similarly situated on the left-right continuum, we should expect greater agreement between the policy preferences of the enacting legislature or government and the court, and thus a greater likelihood that constitutional challenges to the act will be rejected. It is important to note that the court may be less deferential to the position of the legislature with certain issue areas the court finds particularly important – such as legislation that affects the judiciary, or civil rights. At the same time, the court may be more deferential in other areas – including tax law, or defense and national security law – often considered outside of the court's main area of influence. Nevertheless policy divergence between the court and the parliament should lead to greater activism by the courts in the review of legislation, while policy congruence between the court and the parliament should lead to greater acceptance of legislative policy. By testing this first hypothesis, we will be able to ascertain whether the basic building block of the majoritarian vision – ideological voting – holds true.

Rights protection

In contrast to the majoritarian vision, which focuses on the degree of connection between public preferences and court outcomes, a competing justification for judicial review focuses on the ability of courts to protect and expand civil rights and liberties. In US constitutional law, this view is expressed in Justice Harlan Fiske Stone's famous dictum that the Supreme Court would review more stringently laws that classified, or infringed the rights of, 'discrete and insular minorities' within society – those groups that, due to their minority status, could not avail themselves of the normal democratic process.[6] Along these same lines, noted Supreme Court scholars Erwin Chermerinsky (2010) and John Hart Ely (1980) have argued that the most important role of the high court is to protect the rights of minorities from majority overreach. Similarly, as noted in Chapter Two, Dworkin's (1977; 1996) principles-based and morals-based theories of constitutional rights propose a strong role for courts in protecting and advancing individual rights. This understanding of judicial review views courts as unique actors in democratic society, capable of limiting the majoritarian impulses that impede minority rights and prevent full realisation of democratic values.

Anecdotal examples of the judiciary's rights-protecting mission are often noted. *Brown v Board of Education* (1954), which overturned nearly a century of formal segregation in areas within the United States, is often cited as the consummate example of courts strongly protecting the rights of oppressed minority groups against the dominant political majority. Outside of the United States, Epp (1998: 194) describes the Canadian Supreme Court's protection of women's rights as a model of the modern global 'rights revolution'. Similarly, the South African Constitutional Court's *Grootboom* decision interpreting the right to housing contained in South Africa's constitution stands as a strong, yet practical, protection of expansive social and economic rights post-apartheid (Sunstein 2002).[7]

Eastern European constitutional courts have similarly been seen as particularly cognisant of rights protection within society (Schwartz 2000). In fact, British legal scholar David Robertson (2010: 87) finds pronounced differences between Eastern and Western Europe 'when we come to look at the rights-protecting role of constitutional courts' (2010: 87). Robertson's analysis focuses on the prominent guarantees of social and civil rights within the Eastern European constitutions,

---

6. Whether the Supreme Court, or any high court, has actually fulfilled this pledge is often questioned. After Stone's writing in the *Carolene Products* case, the Supreme Court mentioned the need to protect 'discrete and insular minorities' only once more – Justice Blackmun noted the need to protect such groups when striking down laws excluding all non-citizens from welfare programs.

7. Government of the Republic of South Africa v Grootboom, 2000 11 BCLR 1169 (CC).

though others have noted similarly broad rights outside of Eastern Europe (Stone Sweet 2000; Law and Versteeg 2012). In fact, individual rights have been at the forefront of several important, and widely publicised, constitutional cases. Hungary's Constitutional Court liberalised gay rights in 1995, mandating parliament pass legislation granting homosexuals equal rights in legal partnerships. Slovenia's Constitutional Court similarly has been active in civil rights matters. In 2009, the Slovenian court ruled unconstitutional a law that limited inheritance within same sex partnerships, clearing a broader path for increased rights for same sex couples.[8] And in an earlier 1999 case, the court ruled that the need to ensure functional equality in society permitted the legislature to create laws designed to compensate for historical disadvantages women have faced in the workplace and at home.[9]

Similarly, the Polish Constitutional Tribunal determined in 1997 that differences in mandatory retirement ages for women and men violated the constitutional right to equality, and, with a slightly different rationale, in 2007 also struck down legislation granting women shorter periods of accrued work before being able to collect pensions.[10] The court's interest in equality goes back to its early years: in 1987, the Tribunal ruled the principle of social equality prohibited the communist government from requiring numerically equal numbers of male and female students be admitted to medical schools, given that many more women than men apply to medical school.[11] This interest in equality extends beyond sex discrimination. In the Equality Parade case noted in Chapters One and Two, the Polish Constitutional Tribunal wrote strongly about the importance of 'protecting minority groups' to the larger democratic legitimacy of the state, with the justice Miroslaw Wyrzykowski concluding strongly that 'the moral views of the holders of political power are not synonymous with "public morals"' for all of society.[12]

Yet, examining the field broadly, the picture of rights protection is anything but clear. To find opposing evidence, we need look no further than the United States, the birthplace of modern judicial review. Reviewing constitutional outcomes, Gerald Rosenberg (2008) pessimistically determined the idea of court-inspired rights protection and social policy change to be a 'hollow hope': judges, to the extent they are interested in protecting rights, will not be effective in seeing these protections implemented unless and until they have assistance from other political actors. Chemerinsky (2014: 3) similarly concluded that the Supreme Court over its history 'has frequently failed' to protect many individual rights. Despite the guarantee of equal protection in the US Constitution's Fourteenth Amendment, the Supreme Court allowed the mass internment of Japanese-American citizens during World War II, and wrote, in denying the claim brought by the purportedly

---

8. Blazic and Kern v Slovenia, U-I-425/06–10, 2 July 2009.
9. Decision U-I-298/96, 11 November 1999.
10. Case P 10/07, 23 October 2007.
11. Case P 2/87, 3 March 1987.
12. Case K 21/05, 18 January 2006 (English translation).

'feebleminded' Carrie Buck that her forced sterilisation by the state of Virginia violated basic liberties: 'Three generations of imbeciles is enough'.[13] Anna Harvey's (2013) analysis of Court decisions also concludes that protections for social and economic rights in the United States would, in fact, be *stronger* if the institution of judicial review did not exist. Rather than protecting rights, the Supreme Court often holds back rights advancement. These arguments mirror the rationales that guided the French in establishing and maintaining the prohibition on judicial review throughout the nineteenth and much of the twentieth century: judges were seen to be traditionalist, anti-democratic actors who would hold back, not advance, the rights of citizens – a view only reinforced by the behaviour of the US Supreme Court in the early 1900s (Lambert 1921).

It is commonly accepted that, if judges take into account the need to strongly protect civil rights and liberties claims, this should be expressed in the outcomes courts produce. Specifically, we should see courts overturning legislation infringing civil rights and liberties at a higher rate than other constitutional claims, including tax, pension, federalism and local-national government disputes. However, when examining European constitutional courts we must take into account the different jurisdictional rules that govern the acceptance of cases. Unlike the US Supreme Court, which largely sets its own docket, or the Indian Supreme Court, which selects only a small number of cases for its 'public docket' (Epp 1998), constitutional courts must generally accept all cases that arise through their abstract docket. Thus, any over-time increase in civil rights cases seen in European constitutional court dockets could be largely spurious, a product more of outside groups deciding to bring claims than of any emphasis by judges. Instead, to examine this question we can look to outcomes of court cases: given the presence of a diverse set of issues to resolve on the court docket, do courts protect individual civil rights and liberties at higher rates than other constitutional claims? If the rights protecting vision is correct, we can hypothesise (Hypothesis 2) that civil rights and liberties claims will be protected at higher rates than other types of claims (i.e., federalism, tax, separation of powers cases).

Testing the predictions

To examine these questions, I created a unique dataset of constitutional court cases (described in Chapter Three), which includes all cases in which these four courts reach a final decision on the constitutionality or unconstitutionality of a law or regulation.[14] The theories presented above are focused on the ability and the likelihood of judicial panels overturning legislation or national regulations. Thus, the dependent variable I use for testing is a dichotomous measure indicating

---

13. Buck v Bell 274 US 200 (1927).

14. Reviews of local regulations are excluded from the analysis, largely due to the difficulty in determining key institutional and ideological values critical for the analysis. At the same time, reviews of local laws are overturned at an extraordinarily high rate. In Slovenia, 88 of 90 local regulations were overturned during this time period.

whether the constitutional court ruled a law or regulation unconstitutional. A ruling of unconstitutionality is coded as a 1 and a ruling affirming the constitutionality of the rule in question is coded as 0. This dependent variable was chosen because rulings of unconstitutionality represent the most fundamental challenge courts provide to the legislature and the executive. To rule an act unconstitutional places the court in direct conflict with political actors, and unconstitutional rulings generally require the legislature to take an affirmative action in response. Past work on court-legislative relations has often focused on the court's final result as the primary outcome of interest, including Vanberg (2001, 2005) and Staton's (2006) examination of public support and compliance for court decisions, and Hönnige's (2009) examination of opposition party referrals. Stone Sweet's (2000) theoretical examination of court-legislative interactions also takes as its main starting point the decision of the constitutional court to rule legislative acts unconstitutional.

My first hypothesis proposes that judges will decide issues in accordance with the ideological interests of their appointing party. Making this determination requires information on the government that passed the legislation under review and the ideology of the party that appointed each judge. I first identify the government responsible for the legislation under review. I code each piece of legislation as the product of either a leftist or a rightist coalition, as determined by the Comparative Manifesto Project (CMP) (Volkens *et al.* 2011). Similar to Hönnige (2009) and Pellegrina and Garoupa (2013), cases are then grouped according to whether the court majority was appointed by parties of the left or the right. The variable *Opposite Party Review* then captures whether the median judge is ideologically from the party whose bill is under review. Appointing party ideology is, admittedly, a blunt instrument to measure ideological effects. Yet, it is a proxy that consistently has been found to have 'significant explanatory value even after correction for other variables' that might influence outcomes (Epstein *et al.* 2013: 57).[15]

A second hypothesis proposes courts could be more likely to give close judicial scrutiny to specific issues, while remaining deferential to other types of issues. Justifications for judicial review based on the judiciary's ability to protect individual rights necessarily involves a strong judicial role predict that courts will be more likely to use judicial review to protect the individual civil rights of citizens. Laws involving certain issues, then, may receive closer judicial

---

15. I use left-right scores from the Comparative Manifesto Project (CMP) to determine the left-right ideology of the appointing parliamentary coalition, with the final score for each judge being either (1) the left-right score of the party proposing the nominee (if known) or, if the nominating party is not known, (2) the sum of the left-right scores for each government coalition partner multiplied by each party's respective parliamentary seat shares (Volkens *et al.* 2011). I use Tavits and Letki's (2009) CMP key variables for Eastern European parties to determine left-right ideology. For the Czech Republic I use the ideology of the president. I use several sources to determine Vaclav Havel's party affiliation, including the European Elections Database (EED), which lists Havel as a left-leaning politician, and the POLCON database (Henisz 2010), which affiliates Havel with the Civic Forum (OF). OF was a left-leaning party in the early 1990s, using Tavits and Letki's (2009) Comparative Manifesto Project scores for Eastern European parties.

scrutiny than others. I note each case in which the court is asked to decide matters involving speech, religion, and equality (based on differences in treatment based on gender, ethnicity, nationality, or sexual orientation) as falling within the 'civil rights' issue category. Yet, as seen in the earlier South African example, court protection of citizen rights could branch into other areas of constitutional law. Schwartz (2000), Garlicki (2002: 277), and Robertson (2010) note the interest of the Eastern European courts in ensuring adequate property rights and socio-economic rights. Thus, issues other than typical civil rights could also indicate court concern with protecting individual citizen rights.

At the same time, there could be issues in which these courts will be more likely to defer to the legislature or government. Notable areas include national defense, international relations, and tax, as Stephenson (2004) describes in his theory of the development of judicial power. Vanberg (2005) previously studied the role of issue areas, though he split issues into a 'simple' and 'complex' issue dichotomy. My operationalisation is different, in that I have created fifteen different issue areas in which cases may be grouped.[16] These fifteen issue types, which include civil rights, national security, pensions, social welfare, inter-branch relations, property, and tax, provide for greater coverage than an issue type dichotomy, as well as a greater opportunity for analysis of court decision-making. By grouping cases into specific issue areas, we can more precisely investigate the factors that contribute to judicial review and judicial decision-making.

In statistical testing, researchers must also be aware of and account for omitted variable bias. Omitted variable bias is a problem if the omitted variable is likely correlated with the dependent variable (*Judicial Overturn*) and causally prior to an independent variable of interest. Past work has, in fact, identified other conditions in which laws may be under greater risk for overturn. First, high courts may be more likely to overrule older laws, either because they are out of touch with now-current views, or because they conflict with newer legislative pronouncements. This conflict of laws may be even more likely in countries transitioning from a communist to a democratic system of governance. For example, in Poland and other Eastern European countries communist-era laws remained valid law for years after the democratic transition – particularly core portions of the civil code. To account for this possibility, I have included a variable (*Duration*) measuring the number of years the challenged rule has been law.

Additionally, the number of parties subsequently involved in litigation may also indicate a case of particular salience to outside groups and interests (Vanberg 2005). A larger number of litigants could indicate a more contentious issue, or a more publicly visible issue; both could lead to more court activism. The variable *Number of Parties Filing* provides a count of the number of parties filing briefs – including both private organisations and government agencies – and can be viewed as a proxy for case importance to specific interests and the general public.

---

16. The issues are: civil rights; criminal; economics; European Union; interbranch relations; judicial independence; labour; local government; lustration; national security; pensions; property; general social welfare; tax; and miscellaneous.

Table 4.2: Monitoring and oversight agencies included in this study

Country	Actor
Poland	Commissioner for Citizens' Rights (Ombudsman); Supreme Audit Office
Latvia	Ombudsman; State Audit Bureau
Slovenia	National Court of Audit; Ombudsman
Czech Republic	Public Protector of Rights (Ombudsman)

There are, of course, many other actors with the ability to file abstract constitutional challenges with their respective constitutional courts. Specifically, all countries in this study allow groups of members of parliament (MPs) to present a constitutional challenge after a law has been enacted. In practice, the MP groups presenting constitutional challenges are invariably minority or opposition political groups, as it is opposition groups that are, nearly without exception, the losers in parliamentary voting (Stone Sweet 2000).

Second, all four countries permit institutions of monitoring and oversight to refer legal challenges to their respective constitutional courts. Oversight institutions are government actors tasked with ensuring individual rights and overseeing the proper functioning of government. National auditing agencies have the authority to ensure proper public spending and to 'limit discretionary access to state resources' by political parties and government alike (Grzymala-Busse 2006: 273). Ombudsman offices generally focus on issues of the individual citizen rights, and are often empowered to act on citizen-driven complaints over the performance or functioning of government acts. It was the Polish Ombudsman that initiated the successful 2006 gay rights Equality March case mentioned in the introductory chapter, though it also has initiated many other cases, including cases regarding press freedom and the 2006 case overturning changes to the Polish National Broadcasting Council.[17] Officials in the Ombudsman's office have noted the 'close' relationship between the Polish Ombudsman and the Constitutional Tribunal, with both offices having a 'fundamental similarity' in the protection of individual rights (Pelc 2001). Therefore, these challenges could carry implications for rights-protection, as well. Table 4.2 shows the oversight agencies included in this study.

Outcomes of empirical testing

The key variables in this dataset are listed below in Table 4.3, and are used in both this chapter and Chapter Five.

Figure 4.1 provides an overview of the number of cases decided by each court, and how often courts in these four countries rule national laws or regulations unconstitutional. One preliminary observation from this data is how high the

---

17. Poland Constitutional Tribunal, Case K 21/05, 18 January 2006; Case K 4/06, 23 March 2006.

rate of overturn is across countries. Three of the four courts overturned over 50 per cent of the laws and regulations challenged within the cases. Just based on outcomes, then, it appears these courts all engage in a great deal of activism, at least if we consider activism to be the number or proportion of laws overturned by courts. This initial observation raises questions regarding the alleged deference that courts – particularly new courts – are believed to show towards the elected branches. Nor is this high rate of activism necessarily limited to the time period studied. Separate data not included in this study shows that Poland's Constitutional Tribunal also overturned more than 50 per cent of all abstract review claims from 1993 to 2002, as well.

Table 4.3: Descriptive statistics for case-level data

Variable	Mean	Maximum	Minimum	Std. Deviation
Unconstitutional ruling	0.57	1	0	0.49
Years law	3.99	47	0	5.44
Opposite party review	0.56	1	0	0.5
Panel size	7.00	15	3	3.76
Oversight agency challenge	0.19	1	0	0.39
MP group challenge	0.12	1	0	0.39
President challenge	0.03	1	0	0.18
Number of parties	3.42	18	1	1.45

Figure 4.1: Case outcomes, by country

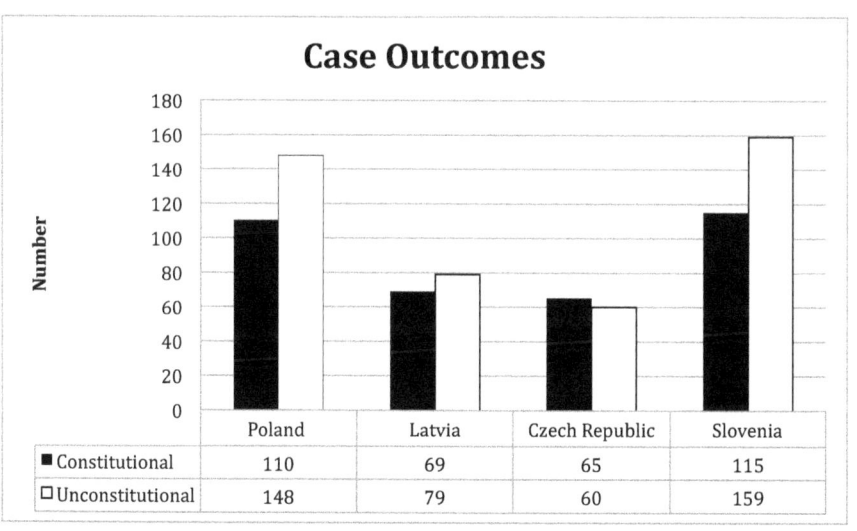

Case Outcomes				
	Poland	Latvia	Czech Republic	Slovenia
Constitutional	110	69	65	115
Unconstitutional	148	79	60	159

One notable exception to this trend is the Czech Republic, where we do not see the expected agreement between judicial appointments and case outcomes. In fact, legislation reviewed by judicial panels dominated by opposing judges has lower rates of overturn than review of legislation by judges aligned to the party whose bill is under review. I examine reasons why this may be so in Chapter Six.

Table 4.4 provides an overview of the outcomes of court cases given the ideological alignment of the judicial panel deciding the case. All four countries show distinct variation in case outcomes based on the alignment of the panel deciding the case. In Table 4.4, I differentiate outcomes based on whether the law or regulation under review was ruled unconstitutional, and whether the median judge on the panel was appointed from an ideologically opposing party ('opposition') or by the same party or coalition whose law is under review ('aligned'). In Poland, Latvia, and Slovenia, laws reviewed by panels of judges who were appointed by right (left) parties are much more likely to overturn left (right) legislation and regulations – all are at 64 per cent overturned or higher, compared to a roughly even chance otherwise. Again, the Czech Republic represents the only deviation from this pattern.

Finally, Table 4.5 provides additional information on outcomes grouped by common institutional actors that initiate challenges through the abstract review process. Notably, other than the small number of referrals from presidents, oversight institutions (Ombudsmen and national audit agencies) are the only major institutional actors whose referrals are successful in a majority of cases. Poland's Ombudsman is the initiator in the majority of those referrals.

Table 4.4: Type of review and overturning legislation

Type of review	Poland	Latvia	Czech Republic	Slovenia
Opposition	69% (93 of 135)	64% (9 of 14)	42% (36 of 86)	72% (53 of 74)
Aligned	48% (45 of 93)	53% (69 of 129)	56% (18 of 32)	52% (97 of 185)

Table 4.5: Constitutional outcomes from various institutional actors

	Unconstitutional	Constitutional	Total	% overturned
MP Group referrals	48	53	101	47.5
President referrals	13	8	21	61.9
Union referrals	14	34	48	29.2
Oversight agency referrals	98	43	141	69.5
Local government referrals	16	41	57	28.1

Table 4.6 presents results from logit regression models.[18] Right away, it is apparent that ideology is important to court outcomes. The variable Opposite Party Review captures whether the median judge on the panel is ideologically different from the party whose bill is under review. The results are clear: right-leaning judicial panels are much more likely to overturn leftist legislation, and vice-versa, a finding that is corroborated in the simple dichotomy of results by ideology seen in Table 4.4. The results reported in Table 4.6 are taken from logistic regression models, which make interpretation of the coefficients difficult. One way to better understand results from logistic regression is through predicted probabilities of outcomes (not shown in the Table). In the data assembled, the probability a law will be overturned rises from a baseline of 56 per cent, with all variables set at their mean value, to 65 per cent in cases when the median judge was appointed by an opposing political party. Even when controlling for the numbers of years a law has been in effect, the number of parties involved in the case, as well as the independent results of other major institutional players, there is still a significantly greater likelihood of a constitutional challenge being successful when the judicial panel deciding the case is comprised of a majority of members appointed by an opposing political party.[19] The effect is actually stronger for oversight agencies: courts are much more activist when oversight agencies bring claims before constitutional courts. In fact, the predicted probability of overturn rises from 56 per cent to 69 per cent in cases an oversight agency refers a law to the court for constitutional review, keeping all other variables at their mean levels.

Previous studies have shown that courts can overcome potential compliance issues by relying on either the public or organised interests to act as a type of monitor ensuring the legislature acts on their rulings (Staton 2010; Vanberg 2005; Spriggs 1997, 1996). In their dual job of referring constitutional complaints to the courts and also monitoring the work of the government, these monitoring and oversight actors have the ability to help courts overcome concerns of override and noncompliance. Could referrals from these oversight institutions similarly embolden the courts to overturn legislation? The sheer numbers of referred cases overturned suggests that these courts do find significant value in these referrals. A more detailed way of answering the compliance question is to see whether constitutional referrals from oversight agencies lead to the overturn of more legislation by current governing parties, as it is current governments that should present the most significant compliance problems. The numbers suggest this is not the case. I created a new model that accounted for whether the legislation under review was enacted by the current government, then interacted that variable with the oversight agencies. The coefficient for the interaction term in model 3 is not significant, though, and a look at the raw numbers shows that courts are just as likely to overturn laws enacted by a current government as an older government

---

18. Results do not include country-level clustering. Adjusted standard errors for country-level clustering do not meaningfully change the results of the logit models.

19. Results shown with the variable *Duration* as a continuous variable. A squared transformation of *Duration* does not significantly change the results.

Table 4.6: Influences on the decision to overturn legislation, logit estimates

Variable	Model 1	Model 2	Model 3
Intercept	−0.54*	−1.07*	−1.17*
	(0.24)	(0.60)	(0.58)
Opposite party review	0.54*	0.57*	0.55*
	(0.17)	(0.18)	(0.18)
Oversight agency	0.73*	0.68*	0.81*
	(0.24)	(0.26)	(0.30)
MP group challenge	−0.13	−0.16	−0.17
	(0.23)	(0.27)	(0.27)
Number of parties filing		0.00	0.01
		(0.06)	(0.07)
Duration		0.01	0.02
		(0.02)	(0.02)
Issue: Civil rights		0.30	0.38
		(048)	(0.49)
Issue: Judicial independence		1.48*	1.50*
		(0.59)	(0.59)
Issue: Pensions		0.61	0.75
		(0.64)	(0.66)
Issue: Property		0.23	0.31
		(0.50)	(0.50)
Issue: Tax		−0.11	−0.04
		(0.49)	(0.50)
Issue: Labour		−0.79	−0.73
		(0.50)	(0.50)
Oversight agency * Current government			0.38
			(0.49)
Poland	0.34	0.53	0.56
	(0.25)	(0.28)	(0.29)
Slovenia	0.72*	1.17*	0.96*
	(0.25)	(0.30)	(0.28)
Latvia	0.66*	0.81*	0.86*
	(0.28)	(0.32)	(0.33)
AIC	1025.80	1001.30	946.38
Log L	−484.89	−404.65	−369.19
N	760	748	714

*indicates significance at p < 0.05. Standard errors in parentheses. The Czech Republic is the excluded reference group.

when oversight agencies present cases to the court. Thus, the evidence ultimately seems inconclusive: current government laws are overturned at high rates when referred to the court by oversight agencies, but not at a rate suggesting these courts find particular value in the monitoring capacity of these actors.

Additionally, many of the claims brought by national Ombudsmen relate to individual rights violations. Again, though, civil rights issues are actually slightly more likely to be overturned when brought by other actors, suggesting these agencies do not play a decisive role in the court's civil rights protection decisions. In other areas, such as property (nine out of twelve cases), pension (three out of four cases), and social welfare issues (ten out of thirteen cases), the courts do agree with these constitutional challenges at high rates.

Table 4.6's models also include additional testing for the type of issue the court hears.[20] Previously, Vanberg (2005) found the German Constitutional Court was more likely to overturn laws when they pertain to publicly known and readily understood issues. The effect of many issues areas does not reach statistical significance, and for that reason several issues are excluded from the Table, though these courts generally overturn laws that threaten judicial independence. Notably, laws implicating classic individual civil rights are not more likely to be overturned than other laws, suggesting the absence of a classic rights-protecting vision of judicial review. Yet in other ways there is some evidence that courts attempt to protect individual rights. Laws affecting individual property and housing rights, and laws affecting social welfare are often overturned. At the same time, these courts are more lenient in their review of budget and tax laws, with both sets of issues generally receiving deferential review. The types of issues the court hears, and their importance to individual rights, are discussed further in the section below.

Rights protecting courts?

The results above suggest that ideological preferences play a role in judicial activism, yet so does the presence of an oversight institution as a litigant. Equally interesting, though, are the types of issues that are most successful at the court, and how different litigants affect these success rates. Few of the fifteen issue areas are significantly associated with court actions to overturn legislation (*see* Table 4.6). At the same time, there are suggestive trends from these results. Perhaps most notable, these constitutional courts take a dim view of laws that attempt to regulate or limit the judiciary. Given the need to consolidate court power, the high rate of activism with regard to judicial independence should not be surprising. More important for individual rights protection, the results show a strong interest in protecting several so-called second generation rights – social and economic rights to property, housing, pensions, and social welfare.[21]

---

20. All issue types are included in the regression equations, though some results are not reported in the table results.

21. Most pension laws referred for constitutional court analysis involve limitations on pension rights or reductions in payouts.

Poland, Latvia, and Slovenia all provide for specific constitutional rights to social security, education, and housing – Latvia's constitution even provides for paid holidays and vacations.

Figure 4.2 breaks down the success rate of constitutional referrals by certain key issue types. The success of constitutional referrals for property rights violations is particularly interesting. Thirty-eight of sixty-four property rights referrals were successful. At first glance, this trend could reflect the importance courts in these new democracies place on promoting property rights and projecting a credible commitment to economic development and economic rights, as North and Weingast (1989) and others have proposed. Yet many of the issues these courts are asked to decide involve laws removing rent controls, the availability of cooperative housing, and ease of transfer of property. These types of issues deal less with the protection of the economic rights of property holders than on the availability of and access to housing and property by the mass public. The strong protection given to these rights appears to reflect a desire on the part of these courts to support broad-based, citizen-focused issues of fairness and access that often lack organised interests in the political world. In this sense, then, courts do seem to operate in a way that protects under-represented interests in society.

With regard to housing cooperatives, the Polish Constitutional Tribunal has issued several rulings striking down laws that attempted to limit the rights of tenants.[22] The Czech Constitutional Court similarly upheld a challenge against the constitutionality of rent controlled dwellings, though it also chastised the parliament for failing to draft rules that would provide for more housing equality (Czech Radio 1 2006). And in a 2000 case limiting the ability of bailiffs and property owners to evict families from homes, the Polish Tribunal held that the constitution provides to all – including the less well off – a basic protection against the loss of dignity in losing a dwelling and a 'minimum level of subsistence guaranteeing the individual a possibility of self-reliant functioning in society'.[23] At the same time, it is important to keep perspective: not all court activism in property claims can be viewed as protecting the rights of under-represented interests. In a 1997 Slovenian case, the court struck down a parliamentary attempt to limit the re-privatisation of land acquired by the state back to large landowners by imposing a cap of 100 hectares per transfer.[24] The Polish Tribunal also has ruled in a series of cases that statutory limits on rent increases by landlords violate the rights of property owners.[25]

Apart from property claims, these courts have often been strong protectors of mass-based socio-economic rights, and from an early time. The Polish Constitutional Tribunal struck down key portions of the Balczerowicz Plan of economic austerity and reform, including limits on old-age pension payments (Schwartz 2000: 64). Though it is not a focus of this study, the neighbouring

---

22. Case K 23/98, 25 February 1999; Case K 5/01, 29 May 2001; Case K 32/03, 20 March 2004.

23. Case K 11/00, 4 April 2001.

24. Case U-I-121/97, 23 May 1997.

25. Case P 11/98, 12 January 2000; Case K 48/01, 2 October 2002; Case K 4/05, 19 April 2005.

Figure 4.2: Judicial outcomes by issue area

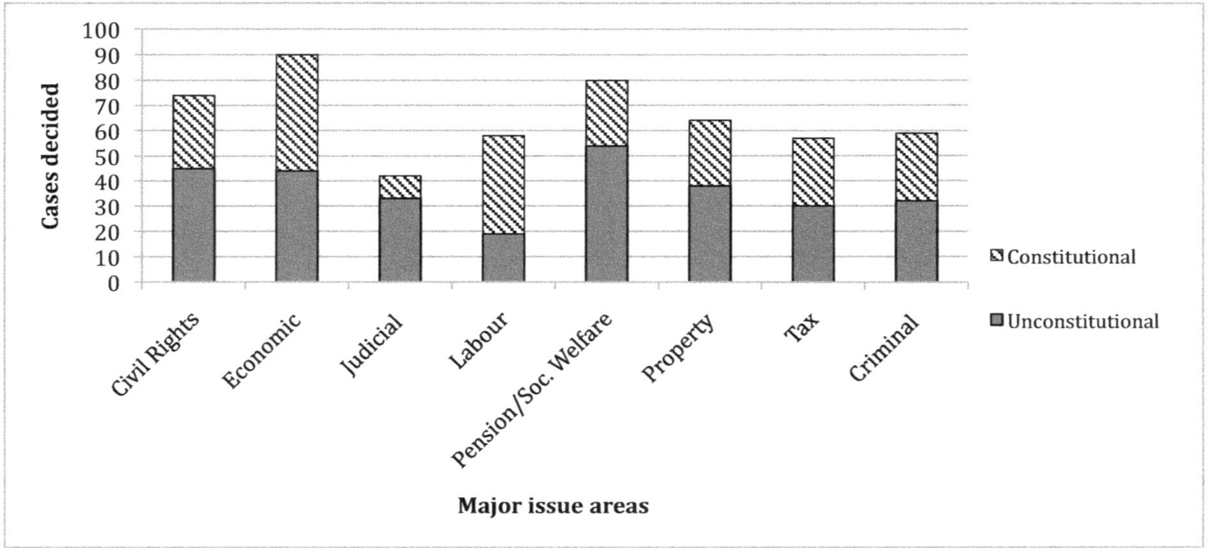

Hungarian Constitutional Court also earned a great deal of public popularity by striking down key portions of the Bokros Package, which implemented pension reforms, wage reductions, and other fiscal and economic austerity measures (Cook 2013: 201). The Hungarian government was forced to reinstate some of those benefit cuts after these constitutional court rulings (Tokes 1997: 144).

These Eastern European constitutional courts have been similarly active in less well-known cases, too. In a 2003 case, the Latvian Constitutional Court ruled in favour of prisoners who had to forgo state disability benefits while in prison (where, depending on one's perspective, they receive other state-imposed 'benefits' like housing, meals, and necessary services).[26] As noted in the introduction to this chapter, the Latvian court has similarly limited some of the most painful pension cuts implemented after the 2008–09 financial collapse, including striking down the 10 to 70 per cent pension reductions for several classes of current and former employees, despite briefs from the Latvian parliament (the Saeima) indicating such cuts were needed to meet commitments to the IMF and the European Commission.[27] In an interview after those rulings were announced, the president of the Bank of Latvia seemed to acknowledge the court's rationale that across the board cuts would have led to an unpalatable situation in which 'some [citizens] may not be able to make ends meet' (Paiders 2010).

Yet in other areas of individual rights, these constitutional courts are more deferential. In tax and (non-property or pension) economic issues, and in criminal procedure, these courts have upheld more laws than average. They also have been deferential in several high profile efforts to deal with the communist past, notably through lustration policies. Lustration is a vetting process in which people who seek to participate in the current regime must attest to any involvement in the past regime, with penalties attached for either (a) participation in or (b) lying about non-participation in the old communist regime. In general, constitutional courts have left governments free to adopt lustration policies, despite claims that these programs violate important individual rights. In 1998, The Polish Constitutional Tribunal ruled the terms of the Lustration Act did not violate constitutional rules against self-incrimination.[28] The Czech Constitutional Court affirmed two separate lustration acts, the first in 1992 and a more comprehensive law sustained in 2001, over a decade after the democratic transition and despite the objections of the petitioners that the return to totalitarian rule at that stage was almost non-existent and thus no longer constitutional in light of the rights limitations the laws place on certain members of society.[29]

Still, the courts have been assertive when lustration laws have crossed the line from vetting to score settling. After the Polish Law and Justice (PiS) party came to power in 2005, one of the first acts by the new government was the creation of a

---

26. Case 2003-22-01, 26 March 2004.

27. Judgment 2009-76-01, 31 March 2010, and Judgment 2009–43, 21 December 2009.

28. Case K 39/97, 8 October 1997.

29. Pl. US 9/01, 5 December 2001.

comprehensive new lustration bill that, among other items, expanded significantly the number and type of jobs subject to vetting, and changed the process and criteria for evaluation. Reviewing this legislation in a more comprehensive 2007 case, the court struck down significant portions of the law, finding that in a democratic state governed by the rule of law, the government cannot use the law to obtain 'revenge' or enact political retribution.[30]

Conclusion

What factors contribute to court outcomes – particularly the decision to overturn legislation and executive acts? As a basic point, the evidence here indicates that ideological considerations matter greatly to the decision to overturn government acts. This finding corroborates Pellegrina and Garoupa (2013) and Hönnige's (2009) results relating to the role of party preferences in Italian regional-central government cases, and French and German parliamentary opposition referrals, respectively. At the same time, the results here suggest a much broader effect: across multiple countries, and all legal issues and all parties, constitutional court judges express clear preferences in favour of their appointing party. Overall, the preliminary results in this chapter provide further evidence that ideology matters in high courts outside of the United States. If judges vote ideologically, then constitutional review could reflect the majoritarian vision for judicial review in democracy, to the extent that the court's majority ideology represents majority societal preferences. Thus, this chapter represents an important first step – though certainly not the final step – in examining the validity of a majoritarian vision of judicial review. However, deeper questions remain. Does the constitutional court represent or validate majority societal preferences, and if so, how? These questions will be examined in subsequent chapters.

At the same time, there is some evidence in these cases supporting the existence of liberal rights-protecting judicial review. Though we see little support for the claim that these courts take a more deferential view towards traditional individual civil rights claims, there is some hope that courts can and do exercise this vision in other areas of constitutional law: notably, property, housing, and social welfare claims. This may, in fact, represent a new form of individual civil right: rather than prioritise speech, assembly, equality, or religion claims, these courts may find a greater interest in securing and protecting the rights of all citizens to live free of hunger and deprivation. The evidence from this preliminary examination of constitutional court outcomes suggests these judges do, on aggregate, advance at least some of these goals in the modern era.

Finally, in their discussion of the development of constitutional courts in newer democracies, Epstein et al. (2001: 156) conclude that, for courts to be successful, they must limit themselves to 'reinforc[ing] those features of the constitutional system about which there is already substantial agreement. As for those issues

---

30. Case K 2/07, 11 May 2007 (English translation).

about which there is greater disagreement, new constitutional courts will [be wise to] leave those for another day'. The analysis above shows that courts need not always limit themselves to re-enforcing already-established policy. Instead, courts in many instances are assertive in striking down parliamentary legislation and governmental regulations and imposing their preferences in the policy realm. With this critical preliminary question satisfied, in the next chapters I examine aspects of the majoritarian vision in greater detail: is there evidence that judges respond to current majorities, or work with current majority governments to remove old policies? Does executive coalition size lead to differences in court outcomes? Are courts more active when public opinion is on their side? I address these more specific questions in the next chapter.

Chapter Five

The Public Will? Testing a Majoritarian Vision of Judicial Review

Introduction

The results in Chapter Four present clear evidence that politics and policy matter in constitutional court decision-making. The likelihood that laws passed by conservative majorities will be struck down is significantly higher when left-appointed judges review that law, and vice-versa. This is an important starting point, albeit one that confirms a host of past findings. Still, these results bring up an uncomfortable question for proponents of liberal democracy: are courts, unelected and largely unaccountable actors in democratic government, impediments to the realisation of the majority will?

With the ability to override the actions of elected actors, the power of judicial review to overturn legislative and executive acts is, as Justice Oliver Wendell Holmes, Jr wrote, the 'gravest and most delicate' action that courts in democracies undertake (*Blodgett v Holden* (1927)). This counter-majoritarian difficulty – the democratic concern that arises when unelected judges review and potentially overturn the policies of elected actors – raises serious normative questions about the desirability of judicial review in democracies where, nominally, the people rule (Waldron 2006; Bickel 1962). Given the prevalence of judicial review in democratic governance, scholars and jurists have developed many theories to explain and justify its use.

As described in Chapter Two, one common vision to justify the practice of judicial review – the legalist argument – states that judges are best placed to answer complex constitutional questions due to their ability to decide cases neutrally and apolitically (Scalia 1989a; Ferejohn and Pasquino 2004). A second vision for judicial review, the 'rights-protecting' vision discussed in Chapter Four, argues courts are best able to protect and defend the rights of citizens – particularly individual and minority rights – against overbearing majorities (Ely 1980). Finally, a third vision directly confronts the counter-majoritarian critique of judicial review. Rather than serving as an anti-democratic constraint, some scholars argue instead that court review can help to increase the correspondence between government actions and the preferences of the majority, whether by legitimating government policy (Dahl 1957), removing problematic legislation (Whittington 2005, 2007; Rogers 2001; Graber 1993), or moving policy away from entrenched interests and towards the majority view (Klarman 1997). Under this third view, judicial review can be majoritarian, or majority-enhancing, in practice.

In fact, a large literature has developed to answer the counter-majoritarian critique and advance a different view of courts as popularly accountable, majoritarian actors.[1] These scholars find that, in practice, courts generally 'promote [...] the interests of the dominant governing regime', thereby advancing the interests of the majority will (Hall 2012: 878). Even with independence protections, numerous scholars have found judges still have strong incentives to create outcomes that are acceptable to the elected majority. Anna Harvey (2013), for example, finds the Supreme Court in the Rehnquist era (1986 to 2004) can be divided into two periods. The first is a relatively moderate era that mirrors the solid Democratic majorities in the US House of Representatives. The second begins after the 1994 Republican landslide and coincides with a dramatically more conservative Supreme Court. For Harvey, Court deference to majority views kept the justices along a moderate path that reflected majority legislative preferences in the first period; the second period of conservative activism also reflects majority preferences – a changed set of preferences seeking more conservative outcomes and lesser protection of rights.

Despite empirical backing, these theories have potential limitations for scholars of judicial behaviour. Most of the above arguments concerning the desirability of judicial review in democratic government are conceived of and framed with reference to the US political system. Yet, as many comparativists know, the US political system operates under distinct institutional rules not present in many other countries. For one, the presidential system of politics creates separation of powers concerns not present in many other environments. In addition, the American electoral system is generally able to produce decisive single-party majorities – single member district (SMD) rules have allowed either the Republicans or the Democrats to rule as a majority party in the House of Representatives since the post-Civil War era. This is not the case in most European parliamentary democracies, where permissive electoral rules can influence the creation of multiple viable political parties and coalition governments. Thus, it remains an open question whether theories designed to explain judicial decision-making in the United States work on a comparative scale.

The different institutional rules in place outside the United States can create different incentives for compromise and constraint. As Powell (2000) describes in his classic work on democratic regimes, parliamentary systems can increase the likelihood of government representing the median voter, but it also can blur the voter-policymaker connection and ultimately alter the manner in which the voters approach elections. Thus, the type of government, as well as the type and number of parties in government, can increase or decrease the perception that the government represents the 'will of the people'. Could these institutional rules produce comparatively different influences on judicial decision-making?

---

1. Anna Harvey (2013) discusses aspects of this view, while Matthew Hall (2012) provides an overview and critique.

In the next section I address in further detail implications from the majoritarian vision of judicial review, in which judges use the power of judicial review to increase the correspondence between government policy and the preferences of the majority. Using the same data from the previous chapter, I investigate how the judiciary responds to democratic actors and democratic preferences. Specifically, I consider whether common factors – government coalitions, parliamentary preferences, public support, and governing status – influence court-legislative relations and the exercise of judicial review by constitutional courts. In doing so, I test whether different versions of a majoritarian vision of judicial review can help to explain judicial activism comparatively.

The Courts and the elected branches: testing specifics of the majoritarian vision

Modern democracies are built on popular sovereignty and equality among citizens, yet courts – perhaps the most unrepresentative of public actors – often serve as the final arbiter of policy disputes.[2] Many – perhaps even an increasing lot in the modern political science landscape – have begun to question anew why we should provide to unelected courts this power to override majority preferences. Cass Sunstein (1999) and Mark Tushnet (1999) have both argued, to varying degrees, that constitutional law in a democracy should be determined by the people themselves in the ballot box, not by judges. Jeremy Waldron (2006) has forcefully argued against the institution of judicial review as 'illegitimate' in a democracy. Similarly, Anna Harvey (2013: 293–295) concludes societies would be better to drop the unaccountable, undemocratic institution of judicial review and adopt the majoritarian model of parliamentary supremacy seen in the United Kingdom, New Zealand, and the Netherlands.

Yet, as noted earlier, an important strand of judicial research also has examined whether courts really do serve as anti-majoritarian institutions, or whether they possibly can serve majority preferences. There are many reasons to believe they might be able to serve such a role. Despite the protestations of mechanical jurisprudence adherents, judges are human beings and thus could be shaped by social forces, perhaps even the same social forces that influence the views of other citizens regarding appropriate policies in society. As human beings, judges also have beliefs over good and bad policies, and good and bad social outcomes. We may see these views sneak into outcomes. Though they are unelected actors, judges also may consider public preferences when creating outcomes just like other policy makers. Or perhaps courts can be active in the policy process by helping to move policy back towards moderate, majority-backed outcomes. These ideas are explored below.

---

2. Possibly excluding US state court judges chosen through elections.

Current governing majorities and court decision-making

In 1957, Robert Dahl wrote 'The Supreme Court as a National Policy-Maker', in which he noted that, despite the fact the US Supreme Court was an unelected actor in government, the Court's outcomes rarely were out of step with the policy preferences of the current ruling elite. As Dahl explains, high court judges are generally selected by politicians – actors who, in a democracy, have themselves been selected by popular majorities. If we expect, reasonably, that these political actors will select judges who share their policy and jurisprudential views, Dahl concluded there should be little reason to find judges challenging the will of the current majority. Instead, given their similar views high courts should instead affirm the policy of majoritarian elected actors. In doing so the courts then perform a valuable *legitimising* role, affirming the constitutionality of current policy and enhancing its intrinsic value to the public.

Could this 'ruling regime' theory of judicial review find support outside of the United States as a universal theory of judicial behaviour? Though not a focus of Dahl's story, rules in European constitutional courts could, in fact, create greater opportunities for confluence between majority preferences and judicial outcomes, and thus a comparatively better environment for confirmation of the theory. Recall from Chapter Two that US Supreme Court turnover was much more frequent when Dahl's initial testing was done, and it was this turnover that led to the connection between current elected majorities and court outcomes. Judges on constitutional courts rarely are given life tenure; instead, national rules create fixed terms in office that guarantee turnover on the court at regular intervals. These fixed terms and the accompanying increased turnover in judicial office they bring could allow for the replacement mechanism so crucial to Dahl's theory. In fact, as noted in the second chapter, research on the Portuguese Constitutional Court from the 1980s through the 2000s found that judges appointed by parties of the left did consistently vote to affirm leftist policies when those parties were in power, providing limited – but not total – support for such a theory outside the United States (Amaral Garcia *et al.* 2009).

Empirically, we should see distinct judicial behaviour if this theory is correct: specifically, courts should overturn fewer laws that have been enacted by current parties in power as compared to laws enacted by other coalitions. Under Dahl's view, this occurs largely due to the ideological congruence between the court and its appointers. Thus, as an initial hypothesis:

Hypothesis 1a: Court decisions will affirm the constitutionality of legislation produced by current governing majorities.

As noted in Chapter Two, confirming Dahl's theory of legitimising majoritarian review has been problematic at times. Funston's (1975: 807) examination of Supreme Court decision-making largely verified the Court's legitimising role in US politics, concluding that, in most cases, the Court does reflect the values of the dominant political coalition. Yet recent scholars have failed to find confirmation of this majority-enhancing decision-making pattern. Mishler and Sheehan's (1993) examination of the Court over a longer time period (1956 to 1989) found the Court's decisions increasingly out of touch with majority preferences. Though examining different questions, both Hall (2012) and Owens (2010) similarly concluded that current legislative and executive policy preferences are not strong influences on US Supreme Court voting, in doing so calling into question the ability of the Court to represent or legitimate the majority will. Instead, the Supreme Court often has been highly activist, but has done so by overturning policies in periods when it should be, under Dahl's theory, a passive actor.

How can such seemingly incongruent activism be explained? Whittington (2005, 2007) proposes a novel solution, one that allows for courts to be activist in the policy arena and still fit within a majoritarian vision of judicial review. Rather than merely legitimising current policy, high court judges who are 'allied' with current majorities can also aid in overturning older policies established by previous majorities or other opposition actors.[3] This allied theory of judicial review, too, has distinct empirical implications. If the 'allied' theory of activism is correct, we should expect to see ideological allies on the court use friendly judicial review to overturn legislation by opposing coalitions, and particularly legislation by older coalitions out of power.

Hypothesis 1b: Allied judicial review will lead to the overturn of legislation enacted by previous governing coalitions at higher rates than current governing majorities.

Parliamentary preferences and judicial activism

Courts are free to overturn any laws they wish, but past work indicates that strategic interactions within the political system should also influence the decision-making of high courts. Specifically, courts should try to limit the range of their opinions in order to stay within a strategic zone of compliance where other institutional actors (the executive, the legislature) will be more likely to adhere to court rulings (Epstein and Knight 1998).

The need to account for the preferences of elected actors could be of particular importance in newer democracies. In 1998, then-Polish Constitutional Tribunal Justice Lech Garlicki noted that one of the most pressing concerns for courts in new democracies, like Poland and the other three countries examined in this study, was 'ensuring compliance' with their decisions. According to Justice Garlicki, when courts strike down laws they must be aware that 'parliament can just as often ignore the court decrees and do nothing to ensure their implementation' (Moffett 1998). Speaking in 2008 on a likely court case to resolve a simmering dispute over the foreign affairs powers of the president and prime minister, one Polish law professor noted in the newspaper *Rzeczpospolita* that 'even if the Constitutional Tribunal agreed to decide this case, it is not certain that both sides will acknowledge its interpretation' of the constitution (Gielewska and Olczyk 2008). In such situations, courts might have an interest in creating rulings that actually will be implemented by other actors.

---

3. Whittington refers to this as the 'overcoming obstructions' or 'allied' account of judicial activism.

In many cases, the incentives for the judiciary to self-limit its responses are all too real – particularly in new or unconsolidated democratic regimes. The Chief Justice of Sri Lanka's Supreme Court was impeached in 2013 after defying the ruling party in several high-profile economic and anti-corruption cases (Economist 2013). Four Honduran Supreme Court justices met the same fate in 2012 for failing to rule with the government in a key police corruption law, despite an apparent lack of authority for the Honduran congress to even initiate impeachment proceedings against judges (Arce 2012). And in Hungary, long considered a democratic success story, the Fidesz government has in recent years openly defied the authority of the constitutional court to limit it through judicial review (Scheppele 2013; Petros 2012). Though these stories invoke democratic backsliding and the problems of democratic consolidation, judges in consolidated democracies also experience pressures to rule in line with majority behaviour. Clark (2011), Rosenberg (2008), and Pfander (2007) all detail how court curbing – proposals by the legislature to restrict or remove judicial power – can be used to constrain judicial actions in the United States.

These influences on decision-making, in which judges self-limit to avoid reprisal from political majorities, work directly into conceptions of majoritarian judicial review. Dahl's basic view of majoritarian review views judges and elected actors working together, symbiotically. But perhaps the true relationship between legislature and the courts is more of a superior-subordinate nature, in which courts feel constrained to respond to the policy wishes of the current governing majority. In the US legal system this type of dialogue between court and the legislature or government must work indirectly, as it is relatively rare for a court to directly receive the views of the legislature – due in large part to standing and justiciability requirements for plaintiffs filing lawsuits. With the general requirement that parties to a legal case receive a direct harm, it is difficult for Congress as a body to gain access to the court, though individual members may file *amicus curae* (friend of the court) briefs. Yet in European constitutional courts the parliament often submits a brief detailing its views on the merits of a constitutional challenge to a statute. When, for example, the Latvian Constitutional Court considered the pension reduction cases discussed in Chapter Four, they received a detailed brief from the Saeima (parliament) describing the 20 per cent budget drop that occurred from 2008 to mid-2009, as well as the requirement to cut state spending as a condition of the IMF and European Commission bailouts. Thus, judges on these courts often know important information regarding the goals of legislation as well as expected legislative responses.

Constitutional courts should be particularly responsive to parliamentary briefs requesting an overturn of the law under review. When parliament asks that a law be overturned, it is asking the court to take an action that the court can either fulfill or not fulfill. However, parliament is also implying a potential future action: if the court does not take action to overturn the policy, parliament subsequently will, in all likelihood, move policy from the current status quo to its own desired location. Given this scenario, it is better for the court to agree with parliament than to risk having their opinion negated by parliament in the not-too-distant future.

Hypothesis 2: Courts will respond to legislative briefs seeking to overturn laws or regulations by ruling the acts in question unconstitutional.

Government coalitions and court activism

Majoritarian judicial review can arise most simply when judges and the elected actors who appoint them share views on policy. Yet, again, existing theory is made with reference to the US political system, which operates distinctly 'majoritarian' electoral institutions, to use Lijphart (1999) and Powell's (2000) canonical typologies. Majoritarian electoral institutions operate with high levels of accountability to voters, but may feature lower levels of ideological congruence between voters and policymakers (Powell 2000).[4] Proportional representation (PR) parliamentary systems are thought to increase the connection between government policy and the preferences of the majority, but voting rules often lead to the absence of a majority party, and thus the formation of coalition governments – some of which may be close, some of which relatively far from the median citizen (Golder and Stramski 2010). Further, coalition governments also introduce important variation in the number of parties, and the number of the people's representatives participating in the executive branch of government – a difference generally not seen in majoritarian electoral systems (Lijphart 1999: 90). In this section I examine this more complicated coalition environment, where majority-enhancing judicial review could take different paths.

It has long been the case that voting rules used in parliamentary systems can lead to the absence of a decisive majority party. In this environment, parliamentary coalition formation provides a way for political parties to acquire power in government, and to realise desired policy outcomes in the process. Through coalitions, parties can solve potential commitment problems that would otherwise inhibit the passage of legislation. Yet political party coalitions differ in their size and their extensiveness. Generally speaking, minimal winning coalitions (MWCs) are coalitions that contain no more parties than are necessary to achieve a legislative majority (Riker 1962). Poland's October 2007 parliamentary election, for example, led to the formation of a minimum winning coalition comprising two parties – the dominant Civic Platform (PO), which won 45 percent of seats, and the smaller Polish Peasant's Party (PSL), which carried 6.7 per cent. Combined, the two parties carried just enough seats necessary to comprise a numerical majority in parliament. Traditional coalition theory holds that MWCs should be the most desired type of government, as the parties involved can split the benefits of office (like passing favoured policies, or appointing ministers) as tightly as possible. MWCs often are formed by ideologically compatible parties, which also cuts down on friction in the creation of government policies.

---

4. However, Golder and Stramski (2010) argue that PR systems do not have a consistent advantage in obtaining higher congruence between voters and policy makers.

Though some theorists state that minimal winning coalitions should be the only rational type – or at least the default type – of coalitional grouping for office-seeking parties, it has long been true that both minority and oversized coalitions are a regular occurrence in the political world (Lijphart 1999; Strom 1990). Oversized (also known as surplus) coalitions refer to any government that has more parties than are strictly necessary to obtain a majority. For example, if in the 2007 election PO and PSL chose to add a third party to the coalition, despite being able to form a majority without that third party, the resulting coalition would be oversized.

Given these different types of coalitional groupings, there should be certain environments that present distinct challenges for judicial activism. Assuming a court otherwise inclined to challenge legislative policy, the presence of a homogenous, cohesive, and stable governing majority can provide a difficult environment for courts to realise favoured policy.[5] Stable, homogenous governments are quite durable: single-party governments are the most long-lasting form of government, while MWCs have historically been the second most durable form (Schofield 1993). With its durability and stability, we might expect MWC governments currently in power to present courts with formidable override or non-compliance challenges. And, without unnecessary parties within the coalition, MWCs also should be close to the median voter and the policy desires of the majority of voters. Thus, outside of any non-compliance concerns, legislation produced by MWCs should present publicly desired policy that courts might be reticent to overturn.

Legislation created by minority governments, perhaps oddly, could present similar incentives for judicial restraint. Minority governments lack the support of a numerical majority in parliament, which means that executive and legislative coalitions are not necessarily identical (Strom 1990). However, minority governments are usually centrally located in the political space, giving them the ability to command a voting majority by 'lean[ing] slightly' left or right (Tsebelis 1995: 98). Thus, through bargaining and compromise minority governments can pass legislation while also maintaining close proximity to the median citizen (Powell 2000: 216). An illustration can be found in Latvia's short-lived 2004 three party minority government, comprising one conservative-right party and two centrist parties.[6] With a centrist prime minister, the coalition was able to exist through the participation of the rightist party (The People's Party – TP) and the sometime support of parties on the left representing Russian speakers (Bloom 2008). This need to maintain balance to remain in government is why Stone Sweet (2000) finds minority governments should produce better legislation – that is, legislation closer to the needs of the public and thus less likely to be challenged by other actors in the courts.

---

5. In their general theory of government oversight, Huber and Shipan (2002) note that homogenous governing majorities, like single-party majority governments, should present a less hospitable environment to challenge the legislature.

6. ZZS, the prime minister's party, received a left-right score of 5.3 on a ten point scale, almost perfectly in the middle.

However, there are also distinct legislative environments that could heighten judicial activism and increase the ability of courts to challenge policy – with or without agreement from the legislature. *Polarised* political environments represent one such circumstance. Polarised systems are generally defined by the large distance between parties on a left-right scale. In such deeply divided and fractured political bodies, any resulting legislation is more likely to be unpalatable to a large segment of parliament, and society. Political systems with high party *fractionalisation* represent another environment that could heighten judicial activism. Systems with high fractionalisation generally feature large numbers of viable parties, and often lack a strong formateur party capable of maintaining a coalition or enforcing political bargains (Crombez 1996). Logrolls formed by multiple coalition parties could more easily be broken, as well, as actors may readily defect from the coalition after obtaining their own favoured policy.

What do these environments have in common? Volden and Carrubba (2004) find *oversized* (or *surplus*) *governmental coalitions* are often formed within the two environments described above. Specifically, in polarised political environments and political systems with many parties, there exist incentives for legislative coalitions to include more parties and more legislators than are strictly necessary to govern. The end result of the oversized coalition – a fractious, overloaded group of parties with often-competing goals – makes the legislative output of these coalitions susceptible to constitutional challenges and court activism. With more parties than necessary, and with the looser ties that bind many of these parties, there exist incentives for parties to defect from the coalition once their piece of legislation has been enacted, ending the coalition in the process (Volden and Carrubba 2004). However, until defection occurs, there also is an incentive to produce legislation advancing the often-particularised interests of the coalition members.

The historical example of Italy shows the potential pitfalls of the oversized coalition. Post-World War II, the Christian Democratic Party (DC) dominated the Italian government, participating in every cabinet from 1945 to 1994. Yet the DC rarely held a numerical majority in parliament, and thus created coalitions – often surplus coalitions – with several smaller parties.[7] However, as Clark *et al.* (2011) note, the creation of oversized governments in Italy led to policy differences within government, which led to the collapse of government, which then led to the creation of a new 'crisis' government coalition that, too, was not built for the long-term and would ultimately collapse. In a twelve-year period from 1980 to 1991, Italy had twelve separate governments formed, eleven of which were surplus coalitions with four to five parties in the government. The concern with larger coalitions can perhaps best be seen in policy and spending, for many years a concern in Italy: larger numbers of parties within coalition governments leads to a larger public sector, as parties seek to distinguish themselves in government and deliver their own distinct policies to constituents (Martin and Vanberg 2013; Bawn and

---

7. In 1951, the DC gained a majority of seats, yet still created a government with its smaller partner, the PRI. Italian parliamentary coalitions can be found at parlgov.org.

Rosenbluth 2006). More bills to satisfy more interests could lead to improvident or unnecessary legislation being passed as a way to complete the logroll.

The more recent example of Poland during the mid 2000s also provides a good glimpse into the unsteady world of the oversized coalition. After a series of scandals, including the 'Rywingate' cash for legislation scandal, the governing SLD party lost considerable public support, but ultimately stayed in government in May 2004 after cobbling together a new surplus coalition with the UP, a newly formed splinter party called the SPDL, and the PSL, a former coalition partner. This new coalition only formed after several unsuccessful parliamentary confidence votes for the new SLD prime minister, Marek Belka, and only after the SPDL won assurances from Belka that the new government would enact a host of new social policy and anti-corruption laws (Scally 2004a). Yet even with guarantees over new policies, Marek Borowski, the new SPDL leader, warned that 'his party's support for the government might be temporary' – as little as three months before reconsidering his continued support (Scally 2004b). The PSL, too warned that it had a 'price' that must be paid for its participation in government: new laws to eliminate recently-enacted policies designed to make the agricultural sector more competitive and EU-friendly (Scally 2004c). Ultimately, Prime Minister Belka quit the SLD party less than one year later to join a new political party, triggering further crisis in government.

Perhaps more important, then, judicial review of oversized coalition legislation provides opportunities for courts to move policy towards the median – that is, to move policy towards a publicly supported, majority-backed outcome. Klarman's (1997) theory of majoritarian judicial review is realised when courts strike down unrepresentative, special interest legislation. The SPDL and PSL legislation guarantees above illustrate some of the bargains necessary when weakened parties engage in coalition bargaining. In fact, a main contributor to the formation of oversized coalitions is the presence of small formateur parties not located in the ideological centre (Crombez 1996), a situation that, combined with the addition of multiple parties, can shift policy away from the median. Greater distance between the ideological location of government policy and the median voter should lead to greater policy dissatisfaction on the part of voters, and consequent opportunities for courts to strike down these laws.

In sum, oversized government coalitions are more likely to require larger legislative logrolls, which also makes them more likely to enact legislation that is unwise, unnecessary, or distant from the median voter or legislator. Thus, I propose as a third hypothesis:

Hypothesis 3: constitutional courts will be more likely to overturn legislation produced by oversized coalitions than legislation from minimum winning coalition governments and minority governments.

Public approval

Finally, courts seemingly have no outward need to obtain public approval. As unelected actors beholden to the law, rather than the electorate, and with generally strong formal independence protections that insulate them from direct public pressures, judges should have little need to court public opinion.[8] How, then, to explain why judges still seem attuned to public opinion?

It may appear at first glance that institutional safeguards such as life tenure, which shield judges from the effects of public censure, give judges little reason to seek out the public's support for their decisions. But, most courts lack the power to enforce their opinions. Nor can they assume compliance from the legislature in amending and updating unconstitutional laws (Carrubba *et al.* 2008). Rather, the amount of authority that court decisions carry rests on 'sustained public confidence in its moral sanction' (*Baker v Carr* (1962)). This moral authority to give authoritative rulings binding on all in society is the court's only real power to help facilitate the enforcement of its rulings. Public confidence, then, can help encourage compliance with court rulings and protect courts from attack by other institutions of government. Given this scenario, it would seem logical for courts, both in the United States and around the world, to seek out public support and decide cases in line with public opinion.

In fact, several formal models of court-legislative interactions focus on the role of the public as a potential source of power (Carrubba 2009; Vanberg 2005; Stephenson 2004). Vanberg's theory states that when the public holds the court in sufficient esteem, they may punish public officials who refuse to comply with or implement court rulings. However, the public must also be sufficiently aware of and interested in the conflict to perform its monitoring duty. As a result, the court is more likely to be active in highly visible issue areas where the public is able to monitor the response of government. Vanberg's empirical testing bears out these claims, yet he treats public support, or legitimacy, for the courts as a given in Germany, the environment in which he tests his theory. Consequently, testing does not include whether the court is more or less responsive as a result of changes in the public's view of the court or the government. Staton (2010, 2006) endogenises public support in his model of court-legislative interactions, proposing that courts can selectively promote certain case outcomes, and by doing so generate media attention that the court can use to ensure compliance with their decisions. His analysis of the Mexican Supreme Court largely confirms the theory, though he also holds public support, or legitimacy, for the Supreme Court as a constant in empirical testing.

Clark (2011), however, directly examines public support for the US Supreme Court, using responses from the General Social Survey (GSS) question asking how much 'confidence' respondents have in the Supreme Court as a general proxy for the court's public legitimacy. Clark's findings demonstrate that higher levels of public support may influence the court's confidence to overrule the legislature, while lower levels of public confidence should reign in court activism.

As noted in Chapter Two, these past works all fit within a vision of democracy and judicial review that focuses on the ability of the public to aid or influence

---

8. Bolivia's Supreme Court is an exception, as it is as of 2010 an elected body, as are many US state courts.

the exercise of judicial review. Given that parliament and the government have a potential electoral check from voters, courts could view public support as a potential source of power to help them avoid sanction and attack from other political actors (Staton 2010, 2006). Or, courts could respond to decreases in public support by limiting their activism when public support falls. As a final testable hypothesis, I propose:

Hypothesis 4: Judges will be more active in overturning legislation when the public expresses greater support for the court, and more deferential when the public support is lower.

Testing the predictions

To examine these theories, I use the same database used in Chapter Four, though with different variables. To test these hypotheses, I use over 600 final decisions from the Polish, Slovenian, Czech, and Latvian Constitutional Courts from 2003 to 2010. As explained in detail below, the public opinion hypothesis is examined using only data from Poland. I include all decisions in which these courts provide final review and interpretation of the compatibility of national laws and regulations with their respective national constitutions.[9]

As in Chapter Four, the dependent variable is a dichotomous measure indicating whether the law or regulation under court review was overturned or not. Hypothesis 1a examines whether courts will be less likely to overturn legislation produced by current governing majorities. To operationalise this concept, I created a dichotomous variable, *Current Government Law*, that takes the value of 1 if the party or coalition whose bill is being reviewed is still in government. This is a straightforward exercise in most cases. However, due to the possibility of frequently changing coalitions, and the ability of some parties to stay in multiple coalitions over time, I employ the following rule to determine if a coalition is still in power: if either (a) the prime minister's party or (b) 25 per cent of the coalition (by seats) changes, then the coalition is no longer in power. Latvia, which is characterised by frequently changing coalitions, is the only country in which this rule was applied.

To test the effect of Whittington's 'allied' review theory (hypothesis 1b), I use the *Opposite Party Review* variable from Chapter Four, which captures whether the median judge is ideologically different from the party whose bill is under review. In all four countries, parliament often submits a legal brief on the merits of the claim when the constitutionality of a law is challenged (e.g., Brzezinski 1998). Through these briefs we may be able to observe a direct effect of elected majorities on court decision-making. My second hypothesis proposes that there should be a bias towards agreement with parliament's brief when the parliament asks the

---

9. Local laws are excluded for theoretical reasons. For example, if a group of MPs files suit to challenge the constitutionality of a local regulation passed by the Warsaw City Council, or the municipal council in Maribor, Slovenia, the constitutional court's subsequent ruling will not involve the current majority in parliament, or any parliamentary coalition at all.

court to overturn the law under review. Accordingly, I have created a variable, called *Parliament Overturn Threat*, that identifies cases in which the parliament has submitted a brief in favour of overturning the law in question.

To test hypothesis 3, I use a dichotomous variable indicating whether the law under review was passed by an oversized (or surplus) majority coalition. In general, government coalitions can be grouped into three different types: oversized, minority, and minimum winning coalitions (MWCs). As explained above, it is in the case of oversized coalitions that I expect courts to be most active and most able to see their own opinions gain compliance. Conversely, legislation adopted by MWCs and minority governments should present more difficult scenarios for courts seeking to overturn legislation. Coalition types were obtained from the ParlGov website (Döring and Manow 2015).

Whether due to a lack of data or a lack of differentiation within the data, direct testing of the role of public support on court outcomes is often missing from analyses of public support and judicial decision-making. For hypothesis 4, I will use public opinion data to measure the level of confidence citizens have in courts. This data is limited to Poland, so this analysis will be included within a separate test using only Polish data. Opinion data on the Constitutional Tribunal and other government institutions is collected by CBOS, a Polish public opinion research firm (captured in the variable *Public Support*). Since 2003, CBOS has surveyed the Polish citizenry regarding their support for the Polish Constitutional Tribunal. These surveys have been conducted on a regular basis: in most years, citizens are surveyed in February, July, and October. In all, there are twenty-one surveys capturing public support for the Tribunal from 2003 to 2010. The number of respondents queried is between 1,000 to 1,500 people. In all cases, CBOS asks Polish residents their opinion – 'good', 'bad', or 'hard to say' – of the Tribunal. The structure of this question more closely resembles a respondent's specific, as opposed to diffuse, support for an institution (Gibson and Caldeira 2009). Thus, it is likely that this opinion data best represents the public's approval with the short-term outputs of the Tribunal, though it could be argued, as Clark (2011) does with GSS data, that the general nature of the responses captured deeply-held or over-time opinions of the Tribunal.

As in Chapter Four, I add several control variables. First, I include a variable (*Duration*) measuring the number of years the challenged rule has been law. I also include the same variable used in Chapter Four that accounts for the types of issues the court hears, which places each case into one of fifteen separate issue categories. Finally, I add *country controls* to account for any country-specific variation in outcomes.

Results

Table 5.1 reports information on one of the main variables used in this study: the type of government from which challenged legislation has arisen. Overall, most cases arose from minimum winning coalitions, with roughly equal numbers of challenges arising from minority and surplus coalitions. All four countries have

Table 5.1: Legislation overturned, by government type

	Minority	Minimum winning	Surplus
Constitutional	85	176	57
Unconstitutional	71	264	112
Total cases	156	440	169
Per cent overturned	45.5	60.0	66.3

Table 5.2: Legislation under review, by country and government coalition type

	Minority	Minimum winning	Surplus
Poland	57	64	78
Czech Republic	60	83	3
Latvia	32	62	45
Slovenia	7	231	43

legislation from minimum winning, surplus, and minority governments, though the Czech Republic has relatively few cases arising from surplus coalitions, and Slovenia has relatively few cases arising from minority governments (*see* Table 5.2). As an initial observation, surplus legislation is overturned at high rates, with minority government legislation – perhaps surprisingly – overturned at the lowest rate. Still, these are only simple percentages: could other factors be at work in the activism of constitutional courts?

Table 5.3 provides the results from a series of regression models testing different aspects of a majoritarian vision of judicial review. Models were estimated using a logit function, with the dependent variable the dichotomous outcome of whether a law was ruled unconstitutional or not. I include country variables in all models to control for country-level factors. Due to the absence of a large number of parliamentary briefs filed in both the Czech Republic and Slovenia, the number of cases analysed in model 3 is smaller than other models. In addition, due to some imprecision in dates within the case opinions, it was not possible to accurately determine the enacting coalition for all laws under review. Laws in which I could not determine the date of enactment were excluded from the analysis. This results in a slightly lower number of cases than in Chapter Four.

The first consideration is whether judges engage in legitimising judicial review, with the expectation that legislation adopted by parties currently in power will be significantly less likely to be overturned. There is no evidence this practice occurs. In model 2, we see there is no strong likelihood that parties or coalitions currently in power receive any legitimation, on aggregate, by the constitutional courts. In fact, when looking at the raw numbers, legislation by current governing parties is overruled at a higher rate than legislation by older coalitions.[10] The predicted probability of overturning legislation actually increases from 55 to 60 per cent when reviewing legislation by current governing parties, holding all other variables at their means. Instead, the ideologically-based *opposite party review* – which occurs when a majority of the judges deciding the case were appointed by parties different ideologically from the party whose bill is under review – is still the main driver of court outcomes, as it was in Chapter Four. And in model 3 there is limited support for the opposite conclusion: that legislation enacted by parties currently in power is more likely to be overturned, as opposed to affirmed. Though this result is limited to the subset of cases in which parliament submits a brief on their desired outcome for the case, it also shows the limited impact of parliamentary preferences.

Overall, when examining this cross-national over-time data there is little support for Dahl's legitimation hypothesis: legislation adopted by current governments is, on balance, more likely to be overturned than legislation adopted by past governments. Why might there be such little support for the legitimation hypothesis? One reason could be the types of cases these courts decide. Given that abstract review cases present the court with more overtly political issues – policy clashes that often are disputes between sets of political actors – the high rate of overturn could show an active judiciary confident of its ability to rule with finality.

High rates of overturn could also show the power of friendly or 'allied' judicial review. Does friendly judicial review lead to lower rates of overturn for parties currently in power, and higher rates of overturn for legislation from previous coalitions? To test this theory, I interact (a) whether the party whose bill is under review is in or out of government with (b) whether the judicial panel reviewing that legislation is comprised of ideological allies or opponents. Examining both models 2 and 3, we see the interaction term is not a significant predictor of overturn.

Another, simpler test of allied review is to examine whether legislation from parties or coalitions out of power is overturned at higher rates when the court is comprised of appointees from ideologically opposing parties. Table 5.4 shows that constitutional courts are most active when faced with a challenge to a law enacted by a government still in power that is ideologically different from the panel majority. Legislation from parties out of power is overturned at a lower rate. Thus, it appears part of the allied thesis is validated: judicial review can be used to remove legislation mutually disfavourable to the court and their allies in the parliament. However, there is no temporal aspect to this process – and courts still overturn a large percentage of laws adopted by supposed 'allies'.

Model 1 in Table 5.3 examines whether the type of government influences judicial activism of legislation. Overall, the data strongly supports the idea that legislation adopted by oversized coalition governments is more likely to be overturned than legislation adopted by other governing types. In fact, the predicted probability of overturning legislation rises from 55 to 65 per cent when courts review legislation from an oversized coalition. These findings are robust to several

---

10. Legislation by current governing coalitions is overturned in 214 of 347 cases, while older legislation is overturned in 259 of 473 cases.

Table 5.3: Testing the majoritarian visions, logit models

Variable	Model 1	Model 2	Model 3
Intercept	−0.68* (0.25)	−1.10 (0.58)	−0.21 (0.79)
Oversized coalition	0.48* (0.21)		
Opposite party review	0.43* (0.19)	0.53* (0.24)	1.04* (0.35)
Current government law	0.29 (0.17)	0.32 (0.22)	0.64* (0.31)
Current govt. law * Opp. party review		0.10 (0.34)	−0.22 (0.50)
Parliament overturn threat			1.82* (0.44)
Duration		0.02 (0.02)	0.06* (0.03)
Number of briefs		0.00 (0.00)	0.02 (0.07)
Issue: Civil rights		0.32 (0.49)	0.27 (076)
Issue: Judicial independence		1.41* (0.59)	2.37 (1.24)
Issue: Pensions		0.80 (0.65)	1.21 (0.96)
Issue: Property		0.27 (0.49)	0.85 (0.83)
Issue: Labour		−0.87 (0.49	−1.22 (0.77)
Poland	0.45 (0.27)	0.91* (0.26)	−1.10* (0.31)
Slovenia	0.67* (0.26)	1.07* (0.27)	n/a n/a
Latvia	0.68* (0.30)	0.95* (0.33)	−0.45 (0.37)
AIC	858.34	953.11	506.84
Log L	−401.17	−380.55	−157.42
N	630	715	409

*indicates significance at $p < 0.05$. Standard errors in parentheses. Not all issue areas reported in the Table. The Czech Republic is the excluded reference group.

Table 5.4: Rates of overturn by ideology and governing status

	Party/Coalition out of power		Party/Coalition currently in power	
	Opposite party review	Same party review	Opposite party review	Same party review
Unconstitutional?	97	126	91	96
Constitutional?	66	124	50	70
% Overturned	60	50	65	58

different formulations of the model. Though not included in Table 5.3, additional testing shows surplus coalitions remain significantly more likely to be overturned when MWCs are included in the model and minority governments are the excluded reference group, and vice-versa, and also when controlling for whether the reviewed legislation was produced by a party that is currently in government.

The increased likelihood of court activism when reviewing oversized majority legislation is critical to understanding when and why judges overrule legislation. With surplus coalitions often forming when the party system has wide ideological differences, and thus may be unable to come to a median compromise, and also in highly fragmented systems in which it is generally hard to maintain bargains, it should not be surprising that the legislative output produced by such coalitions would be amenable to overturn. Due to these particular conditions, legislation produced by these unwieldy governments often is distant from the median voter or legislator (Mitchell and Nyblade 2008). Courts appear to recognise this, and overturn legislation from such governments at a higher rate.[11]

Could this increased activism with surplus coalition legislation be a product of courts challenging current governments perceived to be weak institutional actors? One way to test this claim is to examine whether rates of overturn are higher for surplus coalitions *currently in power* when the court decision is announced. A logit model testing this claim (not shown) does not support such a conclusion.

Finally, the variable *Parliament Overturn Threat* captures the effect of parliamentary preferences, as expressed in the case brief submitted to the court. Again, due to the absence of a large number of parliamentary briefs filed in both the Czech Republic and Slovenia, the number of cases analysed in model 2 is smaller than in other models. The results in model 2 show that parliamentary preferences also matter critically to court outcomes: when parliament submits a brief to express its desire to have a law or act overturned, the probability of that act being overturned increases significantly. Thus, it appears that the information given by parliament of potential override may be a critical constraint on court outcomes. When parliament expresses its desire to have a law overturned, a subsequent

---

11. Table 5.1 above provides additional visual confirmation that courts are much more likely to overturn legislation produced by surplus coalitions.

Table 5.5: Public approval and judicial activism

Variable	Model 1	Model 2
Intercept	−5.38*	−2.96*
	(1.51)	(1.65)
Public support for the court	0.10*	0.06*
	(0.03)	(0.03)
Current government law	1.11*	1.38*
	(0.36)	(0.39)
Opposite party review	1.15*	1.10*
	(0.31)	(0.32)
Duration	0.12*	0.10*
	(0.03)	(0.03)
Number of parties		−0.26
		(0.29)
MP group challenge		0.19
		(0.42)
N	227	227
AIC	281.13	285.79
Log L	−120.56	−110.90

*indicates significance at $p < 0.05$. Standard errors in parentheses.

constitutional ruling will likely be mooted by subsequent parliamentary action. Courts seem to respond by complying with the wishes of parliament. However, even with the independent effect of parliamentary preferences, the role of ideology (seen through opposite party review) remains a strong predictor of outcomes.[12]

In sum, ideological differences between the court majority and the party whose law is under review leads to significant increases in unconstitutional rulings. Yet the increase in judicial activism when reviewing legislation produced by surplus coalitions suggests that judges may seek to move policy back towards centrist positions.

Finally, does public support have any connection to court outcomes? This potentially critical aspect of the majoritarian vision of judicial review is examined next. Clark (2011, 2009) previously observed that rates of overturn on the Supreme Court vary over time according to levels of public support for the institution, with examination based on the number of cases the Court overturned on an annual level. The models in Table 5.5 test whether we can see a similar influence of public support on court outcomes at different points in time, taking advantage of the multiple survey responses per year in Poland. The information on public support

---

12. The results in model 2 show conditional coefficients for these two variables, due to the presence of the interaction term. Coefficients and significance levels do not substantively change when the interaction term is removed.

is roughly contemporaneous to the time in which the court is making its decision, which should allow us to see whether public support matters to court outcomes.

In Table 5.5, we see a significant correlation between higher levels of public support for the Polish Constitutional Tribunal and higher probabilities that the court overturns legislation. Model 1 shows the basic independent variables and controls listed above, while model 2 expands this to include several additional variables included in Chapter Four. Judges appear to respond to current public perceptions of the court's behaviour, as we see a greater likelihood of overturning legislation in cases when public opinion for the court is high, even when controlling for other possible factors.

Figure 5.1 shows predicted probabilities that legislation will be overturned based on different levels of court approval. During the time period studied, approval for the court ranged from a low of 36 per cent to a high of 56 per cent. At the lowest point of public approval, judges are much more reticent to overturn legislation, with a less than 45 per cent predicted probability of striking down legislation. Given that the Polish court overturned slightly more than 50 per cent of abstract referrals during this time, low rates of public approval appear to put a brake on court activism. At the other end, when public approval for the constitutional court is high, the judges are much more assertive and active in the policy arena. In fact, there is a predicted 85 per cent probability of overturning legislation when the court's own public approval is at 56 per cent, holding all other variables at their means.

Figure 5.1: Predicted probabilities of activism, based on level of public support

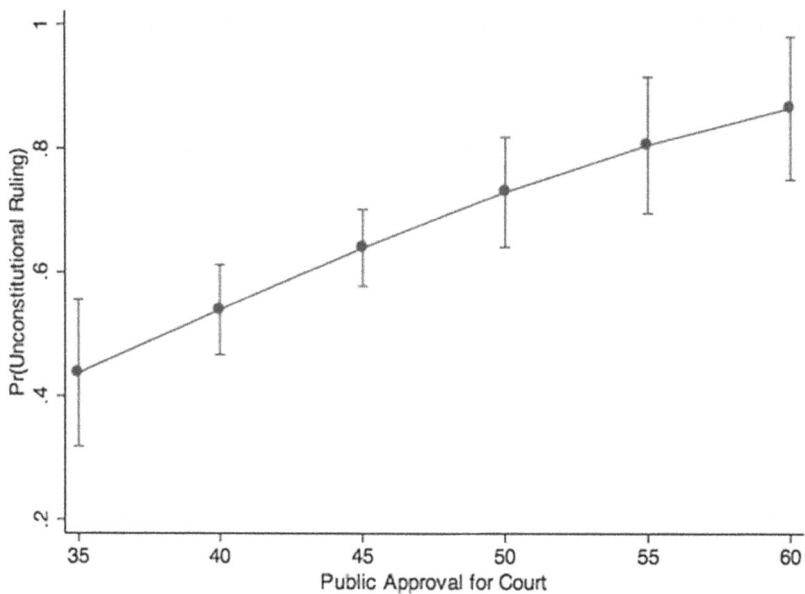

Conclusion

The power of judicial review in democratic societies places courts in a normatively difficult position, and scholars have long attempted to justify the ability of courts to review and potentially overturn the actions of democratically elected actors. To some, judicial review can be justified because of the neutral, apolitical manner in which judges decide cases, or by the ability of courts to act as rights protectors in society. And while several prominent scholars have begun to question the real democratic value of judicial review, other theories question just how counter-majoritarian courts truly are. This chapter has presented analysis of several theories of majoritarian judicial review.

First, I examined the classic theory of majoritarian review, in which the judiciary is able to legitimate current policies of the governing majority, largely due to the political connection between the government and the court. In both simple comparisons of rates of overturn and in more sophisticated logit regression models, there appears to be little evidence in support of the legitimation hypothesis. Current laws are, in fact, more likely to be overturned than older laws. The role of politics or ideology is at play, though it generally does not serve to legitimate current policies. Another theory, one of allied judicial review in which courts ally with friendly majoritarian actors, does have some measure of support: legislation passed by parties out of power is more likely to be overturned when reviewed by judges appointed by ideological opposites. However, current legislation, by both allies and opponents, is more likely to be overturned than legislation by parties or coalitions no longer in power, which cuts against part of the allied review theory. Even with these ambiguous findings we can still say that courts appear to show some amount of cooperation, though they are not completely faithful allies.

Examining court-legislative interactions, again both with simple and more sophisticated techniques, we see that courts are much more likely to overturn legislation produced by oversized coalitions, and more reticent to overturn legislation produced by minority and minimum winning coalition governments. Thus, there is some indication that courts can act, in a majoritarian manner, to rein in legislation that often is far from the median voter or part of a special interest logroll. Given the low rates of overturn for minority government legislation, these findings also corroborate Stone Sweet's (2000: 54) prediction that minority governments will produce 'less audacious legislation' that is less likely to be the subject of constitutional controversy. Finally, higher levels of public support are associated with a more activist court. At the same time, when public support for the court is lower we see a more cautious court emerge, and legislation is more likely to be upheld.

This chapter tests majoritarian theories, but the findings also have larger implications for the study of judicial politics. Clark's (2011) findings regarding court activism and restraint are corroborated here in the case of Poland, providing important confirmation of public approval outside of the United States. The chapter's findings also provide the first cross-national, over-time evidence of strategic behaviour by constitutional court judges with regard to executive government types. Despite some theoretical predictions of court behaviour when faced with differing legislative coalitions, up to now there has been little to no evidence showing that courts do respond to different government coalition groupings. The results here thus provide an important addition to the expanding literature on court-legislative interactions and court-executive interactions (e.g., Harvey 2013; Epstein *et al.* 2001).

The majoritarian vision for judicial review attempts to reformulate the way we consider judicial power and judicial interactions in a separation of powers system. Instead of viewing judicial review as a potential threat to democratic legitimacy, court actions reviewing – and potentially overturning – legislative majorities can in fact bring necessary balance in the policy arena. Yet this conclusion also is potentially problematic from a normative perspective of judging. Given the attention paid to judicial independence and principled decision-making, we might expect judges to consider principles higher than just the currently popular view. Could other factors – legal, strategic, or career-based – also play into the judicial decision-making? I consider these issues in the next two chapters.

Chapter Six

Institutional Incentives and the Choices Judges Make: Career-Oriented Judging

Introduction

The judiciary is often differentiated from other branches of government. While the executive and legislative branches are often defined by political dealing and partisan avarice, courts are generally viewed by the public as neutral, impartial decision-makers (Caldeira and Gibson 2009). Much of this perceived difference comes from the impression that judges are independent of politics or public pressures. In both the English common law tradition and the continental European tradition, judges are not elected actors.[1] Instead of a popular vote, judges in the English tradition are nominated by public officials to serve the interests of justice and the rule of law. And in the continental European legal tradition, a strict separation of powers, in which legislatures make laws, executives implement laws, and courts adjudicate discrete conflicts over laws, was designed to ensure that judges would maintain an independence from the political world.[2]

Much has changed from this traditional picture. With the global spread of judicial review, courts are ever more involved in the creation of policy. This increase in judicial power is not without problems for the judicial branch. Though Ferejohn and Pasquino (2004: 1672) note that European constitutional courts have been successful in avoiding the 'politicisation of judging', as judges around the world are increasingly brought into the policy-making world, they begin to look (to some, at least) like politicians in robes. As noted in Chapter Three, Czech President Vaclav Klaus certainly tried to feed this perception at times, pointedly describing the Czech Constitutional Court's 2009 Lisbon treaty decision as 'not a neutral legal analysis' but rather a biased opinion by a 'political' court (CTK 2009). The evidence in Chapter Four suggests some element of policy-based decision-making at the broad level, while Chapter Five also provides evidence that public support, and the court's own perception of its power vis-à-vis other actors, could influence outcomes. And as constitutional judges become more involved in delineating the bounds of social policy, the pressures and potential influences on judicial decision-making are ever more relevant. In this chapter, I examine whether a career-oriented model of judging can help to explain judicial

---

1. In the United States, federal court judges are appointed, though many US states have adopted judicial elections.

2. In the continental legal system, lower court judges often are appointed into the system through a process that includes a rigorous set of exams.

decision-making. Specifically, I investigate whether individual characteristics and career-based incentives, like reappointment concerns, influence the decisions judges make.

This chapter thus engages a final, and critical, argument within the 'majoritarian' vision for judicial review: to examine whether career incentives can influence judicial decision-making practices by creating opportunities for judges to ensure they remain in judicial office, or to find some other post-judicial career. If constitutional judges are now more involved in the policy-making process while on the bench, they also can be – and often are – involved in policy-making after their judicial career is over. In 2012, Czech Constitutional Court judge Eliska Wagnerova was elected to the Senate as an independent with the support of the Green Party just months after leaving the Constitutional Court.[3] Long-time Hungarian Constitutional Court president Laszlo Solyom became president of Hungary in 2005 after leaving the court. Eva Zarembova worked as an assistant for ten years in the Czech Constitutional Court after her own term as justice ended in 2003. For these and many other judges, it is apparent that the end of their term on the bench is not the end of their public careers.

Judicial independence and judicial decisions

To discuss meaningfully the importance of career motivations in the judiciary, we must begin with the value and importance of judicial independence. It is difficult to overstate the importance of independence to the judiciary: perhaps *the* critical concern for judges is the degree of decision-making independence they receive from other actors. In Chapter Four, we saw that judges in these four countries closely guard their independence: thirty-three of forty-one laws potentially intruding into the independence of the judiciary were ruled unconstitutional. At the same time, judicial independence is not a panacea – and, like other actors in a separation of powers system, we probably do not want the judiciary to be too independent from other parts of the government. Hilbink's (2008) description of the very independent and hierarchical Chilean judiciary before and during the Pinochet era shows the potential problems that unsympathetic and unaccountable judges can have for democratic rights protections.

Though most people support the general notion of judicial independence, it is a notoriously difficult idea to describe precisely, largely because what we want from judicial independence often helps inform what we think it is (Burbank and Friedman 2002). One common definition, which I utilise for reference throughout in this chapter, is *the ability of judges to make decisions free of undue outside political pressures.* Functionally, this means that judges are given discretionary space to decide cases in a manner that reflects their true beliefs and 'sincere judicial preferences' on law and policy (Rios-Figueroa and Staton 2010: 9;

---

3. The year before, Czech Constitutional Court president Pavel Rychetsky had to shoot down rumours he would run for Czech president.

Epstein *et al.* 2001b).[4] Sincere preferences could include a judge's view on the legally correct outcome, their view on the correct policy, or a merger of the two, where views on legal doctrine anchor views on the correct policy. In the political science literature, it is often assumed that greater independence at the high court level will allow for greater expression of ideological values in voting.

In continental Europe, concerns over independence stretch back to the 1500s, when many courts were subject to annual 'visitations' by political leaders, who could review and hold accountable individual judges for decisions they made (Dawson 1968: 243). Well into the eighteenth century, the limited tenure of many German judges – subject either to renewable contracts or to insecure appointments by the local ruler – continued to provide pressure to decide in accord with the wishes of the ruling powers. Yet at the other end of the spectrum, the relative freedom (and inheritable life terms) given to the pre-revolutionary French judiciary fed great corruption that ultimately led to complete reformation of the French judicial system.

Common law judges in England also generally served at the pleasure of the monarchy. Judicial independence in England was strengthened after the Glorious Revolution of 1688, which saw the newly-powerful parliament grant the English common law courts independence from the monarch (North and Weingast 1989). Judicial independence was similarly a concern for those drafting the US Constitution. To Alexander Hamilton, writing in *The Federalist* as Publius, life tenure for judges was necessary to avoid the 'the despotism of the prince' and the 'oppressions of the representative body' alike. The judiciary, the weakest of the three branches of government, required strong institutional protections to promote the 'independent spirit in the judges which must be essential to the faithful performance' of their role (Hamilton *et al.* 1961).

Despite Hamilton's vision of principled independence from the political world, scholars have often found potential pressures on judges lurking even in ostensibly neutral processes. The possibility of appointment to higher office may serve as a prime influence on judicial decision-making. Examining US federal court voting, Epstein, Landes, and Posner (2013) found lower court judges 'auditioning' for appointment to higher judicial office imposed higher criminal penalties, a conclusion others have found in the decisions of elected US state court judges in the years before their re-election dates (Huber and Gordon 2004, 2007). More generally, studies examining state supreme courts in the United States have found that elected judges often vote strategically to maximise their chances of re-election, moving away from publicly unpopular views and towards decisions popular with voters (Hall 1987, 1992), or towards their reappointing agents' interests (Shepherd 2009). For many years Japanese judges decided politically charged cases in favour of the ruling LDP party in

---

4.   Peretti (2002), relying on US federal courts for examples, states this definition is not a hard standard to meet. I contend this is a hard bar to clear in many US states, and in many countries around the world.

order to gain career advancement (Ramseyer and Rasmussen 2001). Thus, the evidence so far suggests there is more to court – and particularly high court – decision-making than the purely legal merits of a case. In particular, career-based concerns, such as the need to stay in office or gain a promotion, could lead to the creation of judicial outcomes favoured by elected actors.

However, despite the growing examination of how institutional rules influence US federal and state court decision-making practices, relatively few researchers have directly examined the effects of appointment and retention practices outside of the United States (but see Epstein *et al.* 2002), despite their obvious importance to European constitutional courts. Kischel's (2013) description of the byzantine system of appointments to the German Constitutional Court illustrates the myriad differences between US and European appointment process. On a larger scale, there are reasons to question whether US-based theories can help us answer questions comparatively. The vast majority of US states now utilise some form of judicial election for seats on the high court – rules that are almost unheard of outside of the United States.[5] The Supreme Court, for its part, has always operated under life tenure and with a presidential appointment and Senate confirmation process. Yet, most constitutional courts elsewhere in the world provide only limited terms in office – generally six to twelve years (Ginsburg 2003). These differences in formal rules could give rise to different incentives in judicial decision-making.

Much of current comparative theory on the role of high court retention dynamics is inspired by Helmke's (2002, 2005) work on the Argentinian Supreme Court. Helmke found that judges who lack independence or secure tenure will try to 'strategically defect' from the current ruling regime when those rulers show signs of losing power in order to win favour with incoming actors. During the period studied (1976 to 1995), Argentinian judges increased their anti-government rulings in the two years leading up to a change in political power. Perhaps sensing a shift in the political winds, Argentinian judges altered their decision-making to favour the expected interests of the new governing power. This decision-making pattern is seen even though Argentinian judges are formally granted life terms in office: thus, it was the informal ability of new regimes to remove or retain judges that drove judicial behaviour. Similarly, in Ecuador, where no judge has successfully served a full term in office, the primary determinant of judicial removal has been the ideological distance between judges and the new legislative coalition (Besabe-Serrano and Polga-Hecimovich 2013). Like the regimes in 1970s and 1980s Argentina, new Ecuadorean parliaments seek to remove most sitting judges after coming to power.

However, Helmke's defection theory also leaves out an important, and growing, segment of the world: legal and political systems in which judges actually have gained some real measure of *de facto* independence. In Central and Eastern Europe, for example, societies have moved over the past two decades from communist-authoritarian rule to nascent democracy, and, in many cases, to more stable democratic regimes. In these countries, do institutional rules provide

---

5. The Bolivian High Courts being one notable exception to this statement.

for similar 'strategic' incentives to rule with current elected majorities? Is there evidence of other career-based voting? Few answers exist in the comparative literature when the discussion moves to more stable democratic environments.

Poland, Slovenia, and the Czech Republic

Poland, Slovenia, and the Czech Republic all provide this more stable democratic environment with which to test career-based theories of judging. To determine this, I rely on the 2014 World Justice Project's (WJP) comprehensive Rule of Law Index, which creates a score system on justice, rights, corruption, and government accountability for 102 countries. Of note, Latvia is not among the countries studied, and so I exclude it from analysis in this chapter. All three of the remaining countries score high on this index, though. Poland and the Czech Republic both have scores close to the United States and France, while Slovenia's score is slightly lower, but does place it just above Italy. With scores roughly double to that of Argentina, all three also place high on the Linzer and Staton (2012) judicial independence index (*see* Table 6.1).[6] Thus, phenomena seen in these three countries should be from a qualitatively different environment than that seen in Argentina or Ecuador. At the same time, they also differ in important regards – perhaps most notably in the ability of constitutional judges to be reappointed. The Czech Republic allows for reappointment of judges by the Czech president, while Slovenia and Poland mandate fixed terms in office.

Despite their greater stability, concerns over judicial independence still have, at various times, become important political issues in most of the new Eastern European democracies, including the countries studied here. All notably faced difficulty ensuring adequate salaries were paid to their respective judiciaries during the 1990s, though this situation had brightened considerably by the end of the decade (Open Society 2001). Apart from this general concern over payments and equipment during the transition, several larger independence issues arose, as well. In the Czech Republic, President Vaclav Klaus' unsuccessful attempt to remove Czech Supreme Court president Iva Brozova in 2004 stood as a black mark for rule of law development. The constitutional court ultimately ruled against Klaus in his effort to remove her from office, and also overturned a subsequent effort by the Justice Ministry to appoint a new Supreme Court judge without Brozova's consent (CTK 2006). Both rulings raised the ire of the president. Just a few years later, President Klaus and party leaders in parliament called for limiting the powers of the constitutional court after the court overturned a law that would have shortened the terms in office for the lower house Chamber of Deputies (CTK 2009a). When the court ratified the constitutionality of the EU Lisbon Treaty, Klaus, an opponent of the treaty, called the court a 'biased political' body (CTK 2009b). President Klaus' efforts to influence the powers, composition, and even outcomes of the courts are important, as Czech Constitutional Court justices face reappointment by the president. Similarly, Poland also saw verbal threats and other questionable

---

6. In the Linzer and Staton index, scores closer to 1 indicate higher levels of independence.

Table 6.1: Constitutional courts of Poland, Slovenia, and the Czech Republic

Country	Size	Appointment process	Terms in office	WJP ROL Index	Linzer-Staton Index
Poland	15 judges	Majority vote in parliament, proposal by 50 MPs	9 years, fixed terms (no reappointment)	0.67	0.86
Slovenia	9 judges	Majority vote in parliament, proposal by president	9 years, fixed terms (no reappointment)	0.65	0.93
Czech Republic	15 judges	Majority vote in senate, proposal by president	10 years, reappointment possible	0.67	0.74

tactics directed against the Constitutional Tribunal and other judicial officials by the PiS government in 2006 and 2007 after a series of government setbacks in the Tribunal (Kurski 2007). In particular, PiS head Jaroslaw Kaczynski accused the Tribunal in 2006 of deciding cases in a manner that 'undermines the state and state institutions' – a strong statement that drew an even stronger public rebuke from the Tribunal president in *Gazeta Wyborcza* (Safjan 2006). The PiS party itself also was accused of trying to 'search for dirt' in the backgrounds of tribunal justices, including combing through the old communist informer files (Kurski 2008).

Despite these (largely unsuccessful) efforts to rein in or intimidate the courts, in aggregate judicial independence protections generally are seen as strong in these countries. In these more stable environments, where judges do not fear for their livelihoods after a change in government, does a career preservation theory of judging still apply? I examine this question below. As I explain below, there are good reasons to expect single term and reappointment systems to produce different decision-making dynamics.

Single-term appointment dynamics

Why might fixed terms in office or the possibility of reappointment matter at all to judicial outcomes? At least since the writings of Alexander Hamilton in Federalist 78, life appointments for judges – subject to certain limits (e.g., good behaviour) – have been presented as a key component of judicial independence. With life appointments, judges are free from both public sanction and pressure from political actors when making decisions.

Yet, due to the history and legal culture in European countries, as well as the recognition of their important policy-making functions, limited judicial terms are the norm on constitutional courts (Stone Sweet 2000). Though life tenure may be thought of as the most desirable rule to encourage judicial independence, fixed terms with no possibility of reappointment have also been thought to be independence enhancing (Epstein *et al.* 2002). If we use, as I do in this chapter, a definition of judicial independence that focuses on the ability of judges to decide cases free of outside pressures, then fixed terms with no possibility of reappointment could be an ideal way to ensure the independence of European constitutional court judges while in office.

The primary reason involves the lack of an incentive to deviate from their sincere preferences on law or policy. At first glance, judges with fixed, single terms in office should have no need to make decisions to please current or future political actors to stay in office. Regardless of the decisions they make, these judges serve a set term in office and then leave. Fixed terms in office without the possibility of reappointment thus enhance functional judicial independence by removing incentives for judges to behave and make decisions in ways that maximise their ability to stay on the bench. In fact, similar arguments have been made regarding term limits for legislators in parliament. According to proponents of term limits, fixed terms in office should give incentives for legislators to focus more on legislative issues and less on their own re-election goals. However, it also is important to acknowledge that maximising the ability of judges to decide cases free of outside pressure does not necessarily mean we will see judges deciding cases without bias or policy motivation. Voting based on policy is, in fact, a distinct possibility given strong independence from other actors.

With the assumption that greater independence should lead to more 'sincere' voting,[7] and the assumption that at the high court level we should see greater ideological voting, if given the freedom to do so,[8] one testable hypothesis (Hypothesis 1) is that judges serving single, fixed terms will show greater ideological consistency with the party that appointed them than judges with a reappointment incentive. Fixed terms can then be majority enhancing, though mostly to the parties or actors in government at the time of appointment. As a result, there could be potential conflicts over time as new governments, or new judges, enter the court.

The simple scenario above assumes a more or less uniform effect from single, fixed terms in office. However, there is a more complex view, one that acknowledges potential pressures can still be placed on judges who serve fixed terms. Post-court career opportunities provide one such pressure. In practice, constitutional court judges are appointed with the explicit support and backing of political parties. With fixed terms in office, appointing parties may be able to exert pressure on judges by offering inducements for post-court career prospects. As noted in the introduction, such concerns are not just theoretic. At least nine former Italian Constitutional Court judges have gone on to hold office in either the parliament or the cabinet after leaving the court. To Italian court scholar Mary

---

7.   As is found in Rios-Figueroa and Staton (2011) and Epstein *et al.* (2002) definitions of judicial independence.

8.   See Epstein *et al.* (2013); Epstein *et al.* (2002).

Volcansek (2000: 24), this pattern carries at least the implication that decisions while on the bench could be made with an eye towards future perquisites off the bench. However, partisan voting patterns on the Italian court are hidden by its consensus voting procedure – dissenting or separate opinions are not allowed.

Outside of Italy, additional examples abound of constitutional judges continuing their careers after leaving the bench. As noted earlier, former Hungarian Constitutional Court chief judge Laszlo Solyom remained active in the public sphere after leaving the court, and later became president of Hungary. Former Slovenian Constitutional Court judges Joze Tratnik and Zvonko Fiser were appointed to head the Slovenian state prosecutor's office after their terms in office were complete, and former leftist politician and constitutional court judge Ciril Ribicic was appointed by the centre-left Social Democrats to a much-desired position as Slovenia's representative to the Council of Europe's Venice Commission shortly after leaving office – a post that the subsequent conservative government tried to annul (Demokracija 2012).[9] Marek Safjan was appointed to be Poland's representative on the European Court of Justice (ECJ) after leaving the Polish Constitutional Tribunal. In short, the possibility of a future position in government – for example, in the Ministry of Justice or the ECJ – is very real and could influence current decision-making.

Despite the potential for concern, there is no consensus that (a) all post-court careers require ideological litmus tests and (b) post-court career incentives create real problems. First, many judges appointed to the constitutional courts come from either the ordinary court system or academic positions, where career advancement depends less on political influence (Vanberg 2005). For example, former Polish justices Miroslaw Wyrzykowski and Marian Grzybowski returned to prominent academic positions after leaving the Tribunal in 2010. The likelihood of a return to academia or the bench should lead to less credible career pressures on judges, which should also increase independence of decision-making. Second, for many the appointment to a high court represents the culmination of a long legal career – whether in academia, politics, or the ordinary court system. Many judges may simply retire at the end of their tenure on the court, thus reducing – if not eliminating – the potential for threats to their career. Finally, not all post-court careers necessitate ideological adherence. Appointments to the ECJ, for example, may not be based primarily on ideology, but rather on judicial merit, or knowledge of EU law or, as Carrubba and Gabel (2014) show, on having the political and strategic acumen necessary to navigate a difficult institutional and legal environment.

The arguments downplaying the practical existence of career incentives may be true in some cases, though not all. While a position on the constitutional court is, for some, the culmination of their legal career, the examples above show that for many judges it is not the end of their involvement in public affairs. Thus, the

---

9. Ribicic was formerly head of the ZKS–SDP (League of Communists of Slovenia–Party of Democratic Reform), a successor party to the old Communist party (Glaurdic 2012: 83).

potential pressure from an appointing actor remains valid for many judges. Yet, for research purposes it is difficult, theoretically and practically, to parse out (a) judges agreeing with elected actors simply because of similar views on law and policy from (b) those judges who agree with elected actors because they seek future favours from them.

Younger judges are one group of judges for whom this career incentive should exist. Volcansek notes the youth of many (though certainly not all) Italian judges with post-court political lives. It would make intuitive sense for younger judges to be more swayed by the prospect of future careers. For example, a hypothetical judge appointed to the Polish Constitutional Court at the age of 45 would be only 54 years old at the end of his or her term, and potentially desirous of a similarly prestigious position. Younger judges, then, could produce more ideologically consistent decision-making with their appointing party, as those younger judges have greater need for a post-court career. To be clear: the age of a judge cannot explain all decision-making, and there is no direct theoretical correlation between age and ideological attachment. Nevertheless, age can serve as a suitable proxy for the possibility of future career prospects for judges. Thus, a second testable hypothesis (Hypothesis 2) is that judges serving fixed terms will be more likely to respond to potential future career incentives by ruling more consistently with the interests of their appointing party. However, this effect should be seen at younger age intervals – that is, as judges grow older on the bench, there should be fewer career-based incentives to rule with their appointers.

Reappointment dynamics

Would the possibility of reappointment change the dynamics presented above? There are good reasons to believe the answer is yes. When compared against single term appointments, judges who are subject to reappointment are presented with direct political incentives to deviate from voting their sincere preferences. Renewable terms could maximise the likelihood of judicial responsiveness towards reappointing agents, much like what is seen with the elected US state courts, and should provide a lesser motivation to rule in line with their appointers.

The incentive for reappointment means that judges face career-based incentives to gain favour with reappointing parties or agents that could comprise future governments. Though judges are often appointed with the support of one party, the terms of office for constitutional court judges are long enough to present a distinct possibility that the appointing party will no longer be in office when that judge is eligible for reappointment. This situation presents its own unique decision-making dynamic for judges. In a strategic and career-oriented view of judging, we may expect that judges seeking reappointment could behave similarly to Helmke's preservation-minded Argentinian judges, turning variously more leftist or rightist depending on the preferences reappointer. In the United States, there is some evidence that lower court judges on the 'short list' for a Supreme Court appointment do attempt to become more ideologically rigid in an effort to gain favour with the nominating president (Black and Owens 2015; Epstein *et al.* 2013).

In the case of the Czech Republic, sitting judges could respond to uncertainty regarding the future appointer by either avoiding ideological voting patterns, or by turning towards the interests of their reappointing actor at the end of their term. The Czech president reappoints justices to the court; accordingly, it is the interests of the president that justices should seek out. However, during the period studied in this chapter, a new Czech president was appointed by the parliament in March 2003, only a few months before the end of nine judicial appointments. As a result, the new Czech president may not have served as a direct constraint on voting for all judges facing reappointment. At the same time, the anticipated interests of the full parliament, which at that time chose the president, could be a factor in judicial voting. Both houses of parliament, the lower house Chamber of Deputies and the upper house Senate, voted together to select the Czech president. After June 2002 Chamber elections, the leftist CSSD party won a plurality of seats, and formed the government with centrist and centre-right parties. However, Klaus' rightist ODS party came in second in seats in the 2002 Chamber election, and was the top vote- and seat-getting party in the Czech Senate election in October 2002. As a result, the parties of the left and right held nearly equal voting strength when seats in both houses were added together. And, from the 1998 and 2000 Czech lower and upper house elections, parties of the right even held a slight numerical advantage over parties on the left on an aggregate level.[10] For judges at the end of their terms, the uncertainty regarding the identity of the next president could lead to less ideologically rigid voting, and perhaps even a move towards more conservative voting in their final years on the bench.

Therefore, in the Czech Republic, which allows for the reappointment of judges, as a third hypothesis we should see less ideological consistency in voting, and perhaps greater end-of-term changes in judicial decision-making towards the interests of the anticipated reappointing body. From a theoretical point, whether the judge is actually reappointed is not a relevant consideration, as the focus is on the incentives faced by the individual judges, not the ultimate outcomes.

Individual characteristics

Finally, ideological or party line voting on the bench may be influenced by past experiences and backgrounds. We might expect judges with political backgrounds to have greater preference alignment with their appointing party, and to better express this alignment in their decisions. For example, Polish justice Marek Kotlinowski moved directly from serving as deputy Sejm speaker for the LPR party (when LPR was in a coalition government with PiS) to serving on the Constitutional Tribunal. On the other hand, there is some indication that appointees with past careers in the judiciary could be less likely to be influenced by ideological or other pressures. Judges with previous judicial careers could very easily move back into the regular

---

10. Based on left-right scores from parlgov.org, there were 159 members from parties of the right and 116 members from parties of the left after the 1998 Chamber and 2000 Senate elections.

court system or into the academic world. For example, Bohdan Zdziennicki, a former administrative judge, moved into an academic position after leaving the Polish Tribunal. And Eva Zarembova, a long-time Czech judge, stayed in the judiciary, becoming an assistant at the constitutional court for another ten years after her term on the court was complete.

Past studies have investigated the role of judicial backgrounds, though results have varied. In Portugal, for example, career judges appointed by the judiciary to the constitutional court have exhibited slightly different voting behaviour to the judges appointed by the parliament, though these behaviours are not statistically different (Amaral Garcia et al. 2009). Early research by Tate (1981), however, found that past judicial, prosecutorial, and political experiences are associated with differences in voting among US Supreme Court justices. Clearer patterns of behaviour exist among actors in another traditionally non-majoritarian institution: central banks. Examining central bank officials, Adolph (2013) concludes that the prior careers of central bankers influence their decisions on monetary policy, with appointees from the financial sector adopting lower inflationary policies than those central bankers with public sector or academic careers.

In sum, appointment and retention plans should provide judges with different motives. Renewable terms place judges in a potentially compromising situation, in which the desire for reappointment may lead judges to alter decision-making towards the interests of the reappointing body. Single terms could reduce some of this pressure to alter their decision-making, allowing judges to vote based on their sincere preferences, though this could result in outcomes not favoured by current majorities. Those with expected future post-court careers – younger judges, particularly – could face distinct pressures (real or perceived) from their appointing party to hew to the party line. And judges with past political or judicial experience could be more or less likely, respectively, to vote consistently with their appointers.

Data and testing

To examine these questions, I use a unique dataset of individual-level decisions for constitutional court judges in three countries: the Czech Republic (1998–2010), Poland (1998–2010), and Slovenia (2002–2010). As this data is slightly different than that in past chapters, it will be important to explain a few details. The data includes both case outcomes and individual vote choices, as well as individual judge characteristics and case characteristics. In total, this dataset comprises 5,470 individual decisions from sixty-four judges in 674 cases. The unit of analysis is the decision of the individual justice in each case.

The primary dependent variable tracks whether individual judicial decision-making aligns with the interests of their appointing party or actor. To operationalise whether judicial decisions align with the interests of an appointing party, I have created a variable called *Vote Proximity* that tracks whether an individual judge has voted in accordance with the expected wishes of his or her appointing party.[11]

---

11. Amaral Garcia et al. (2009) use a similar dependent variable in their own analysis of Portugal.

The variable works in the following manner: for each case, I determine the position (left or right) of the parliament that adopted the law under review, and the position (left or right) of each judge involved in deciding the case.[12] I then determine whether the law was overturned or upheld, and whether the individual judge voted with the majority to overturn or uphold or filed a dissent. From this information, I am able to determine whether a given judge voted in line with or in opposition to his or her appointing party's interests in the case.

Many studies of US courts use either 'liberal' or 'conservative' voting as the outcome of interest. The 'vote proximity' measure is similar to the liberal/conservative dichotomy, but allows for observation of changes in voting behaviour across multiple countries. In separate analysis for the Czech Republic, I use *conservative voting* as an additional dependent variable. Conservative voting simply measures whether the individual judicial vote is in favour of legislation adopted by rightist parties, or against legislation enacted by left-leaning coalitions or parties.

Similar to Helmke's studies of strategic end-of-term decision-making, I created variables, *Last Two Years* and *Last Year*, that isolate the decision-making of judges in their final two years and final year on the bench. To explore differences in outcomes among fixed term and reappointment-eligible judges, I created another dichotomous variable (*Reappointment*) that determines whether judges face the possibility of reappointment (Czech Republic) or are limited to a single, non-renewable term (Poland and Slovenia).

To capture any time-dependency in decision-making, the variable *Years on Court* determines, in every case decided, the number of years each respective judge has served on the court. This variable can help to gauge whether judges are more (or less) likely to engage in certain voting patterns as their careers on the court proceed. In fact, Poland and the Czech Republic each had six different governments during the period studied, while Slovenia had four, increasing the practical likelihood of such a divergence.

To examine whether younger judges are more in tune with future career concerns, the variable *Justice Age* tracks the age for each judge at the time the decision is announced, with the expectation that younger judges, who presumably have a greater probability of post-court employment, should rule in line with the interests of their appointing party. To account for the expected positive effect of younger judges on voting congruence with their appointing party, I also create a simpler variable (*Younger Judge*) that tracks, for each decision, whether each justice is younger than 55 when the court hears the case. Finally, I examine the backgrounds of judges using variables indicating whether that judge has a previous

---

12. The ideological positions of judges are determined by the ideology of their nominating actor. As noted in Chapter Four, I use several sources to determine President Havel's party affiliation, including the POLCON database (Henisz 2010), which affiliates Havel with the Civic Forum (OF). Notwithstanding, Havel always referred to himself as a political independent. Tests using 'conservative voting' as the dependent variable are then particularly valuable to determine whether Havel's appointees shifted their voting in a conservative direction during their final years in office.

background in elected office or governmental office, and whether judges have more than one year of past experience in the judiciary, either in the lower level or supreme courts. As in previous chapters, I also examine the effect of constitutional referrals from parliamentary groups.

Examining the data

Table 6.2 reports information on the variables used in this study. Overall, just over 30 per cent of all votes in the sample were recorded by judges in the reappointment system (the Czech Republic), and over one-third of all votes were recorded by judges with political backgrounds. Most judicial votes in the dataset are taken more than five years into a given judicial term. With the nine and ten year terms for the Slovenian, Polish, and Czech judges, this means there is a roughly even split between votes taken in the first half and second half of a judicial term. Twenty per cent are taken within two years of the end of their term. The longest serving constitutional court term in the dataset is eighteen years. The average age for judges in the dataset is fifty-nine years old, with the youngest judge at forty-five years of age and the oldest judge at seventy-nine years of age. Table 6.3 provides a breakdown of these numbers by individual country.

Table 6.2: Descriptive statistics

Variable	Mean	Std. dev.	Minimum	Maximum
Vote proximity	0.48	0.49	0	1
Reappointment	0.31	0.46	0	1
Last two years in office	0.20	0.40	0	1
Years into term	5.60	3.16	1	18
Age	59.25	7.03	45	79
Political background	0.36	0.47	0	1
Judicial background	0.41	0.49	0	1

Table 6.3: Descriptive statistics by country

Variable	Czech Republic	Poland	Slovenia
Vote outcomes	1,989	1,767	1,757
Reappointment	Yes	No	No
Last two years in office	0.20	0.20	0.21
Means years on court	7.31	4.96	4.67
Mean age	60.5	61.4	56.3
Political background	10 of 27 judges	9 of 21 judges	3 of 17 judges
Judicial background	13 of 27 judges	7 of 21 judges	7 of 17 judges
Vote proximity	0.42	0.50	0.53

Table 6.4: Logit regression models of vote proximity, errors clustered on case

	Model 1	Model 2	Model 3
Intercept	−0.04	−0.17	−0.05
	(0.14)	(0.14)	(0.14)
Reappointment	−0.43*	−0.38*	−0.46*
	(0.14)	(0.15)	(0.15)
Younger judge	−0.13*	−0.13*	−0.57*
	(0.05)	(0.06)	(0.13)
Political background	0.01	0.01	0.04
	(0.04)	(0.04)	(0.05)
Past judicial career	−0.14*	−0.12	−0.13
	(0.06)	(0.07)	(0.07)
Year in term	0.03	0.05*	0.03
	(0.02)	(0.02)	(0.02)
MP group referral	0.16	0.19	0.17
	(0.17)	(0.17)	(0.17)
Younger judge * year in term			0.09*
			(0.02)
Last two years in term		−0.23	−0.33
		(0.19)	(0.18)
Last two years in term * Reappointment		−0.26	
		(0.38)	
N	5303	5302	5302
Log L	−3637.46	−3624.59	−3617.46
AIC	7286.96	7269.17	7254.91
Chi^2	21.35	20.95	49.88

*indicates significance at $p < 0.05$. Standard errors in parentheses.

Table 6.4 reports the results from this consolidated data, with robust standard errors clustered by case. The first item to note is that the reappointment-eligible judges in the Czech Republic do exhibit different voting behaviours. Over the life of their term, they are much less likely to vote consistently with their appointing actors than the fixed term judges. One possible reason why this might be so is a need to look out for their future: judges subject to reappointment must be cognisant of the likelihood that parties or officials other than their appointing actor will be in power at the time of reappointment. Consequently, their voting behaviour appears less doctrinaire, or less beholden to one party. Another possibility, one explored later, is that judges change their voting behaviour over discrete periods of time. As discussed later, Czech judges, in fact do display different voting patterns in their final years before reappointment.

What about other career motivations? One key aspect of a 'career incentives' theory of judging is the ability or opportunity to have a post-court career.

Figure 6.1: Difference in anticipated voting, by age grouping

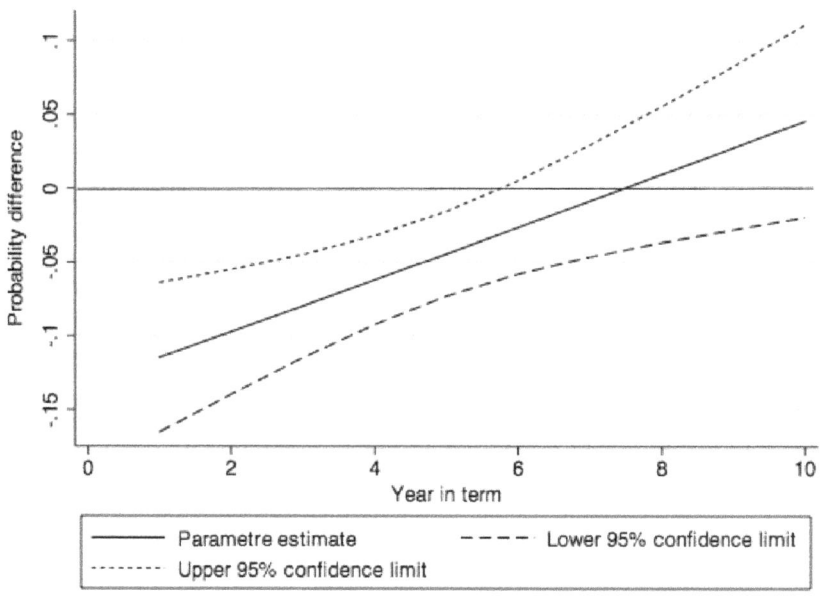

Regarding age, the data here points to several implications. Younger judges are, on balance, less likely to support their appointing party over the life of their term, which runs counter to my anticipated outcome. However, this trend changes in the final years of their term. As the end of their term approaches, younger judges have a higher probability of voting with their appointing party, which we see in the interaction included in model 3. This difference in voting patterns can be explained by the career motivations theory of judging: as younger judges near the end of their court career, the need for a future position off the court could lead these judges to move closer to the parties that appointed them to the bench. Figure 6.1 shows this trend visually, comparing the probability difference between younger judges (those under 55) and older judges as their terms in office progress. However, the graph illustrates an important limitation to the interaction results above: the strongest effect is actually seen earlier in their terms, when younger judges are much less likely to support their appointing party. Though increasingly likely to support their appointer late in the term, until year six in their term younger judges are significantly less likely to vote ideologically than older judges.

Other findings are equally important. Constitutional court judges with past judicial careers are markedly less likely to vote in accordance with their appointing actor. The distinct absence of loyalty to the interests of their appointing party could indicate greater interest in legal merits and jurisprudential principles. It could also indicate a stronger functional independence of these career judges while on the constitutional court (see Choi, Gulati and Posner 2009). Perhaps surprisingly, previous political experience has little effect on judicial decision-making among constitutional court judges.

Testing reappointment influences

Compared to the Polish and Slovenian judges, who have fixed, non-renewable terms in office, the Czech judges are less likely to vote in accord with their appointers. Less clear is why this variation exists. Table 6.5 below shows results from tests examining whether Czech judges voted in accord with his or her appointing actor's expected interests, and whether the vote outcome is conservative. In the approximately 2,000 individual decisions made by Czech judges, the results show evidence of a move away from anticipated voting in the final two years of their term, though the effect is stronger in their final year.

The voting behaviour of these judges in the final year of their term is particularly interesting due to the unique characteristics of many judges facing reappointment in this dataset – nearly all were appointed by President Vaclav Havel but faced reappointment by a conservative President Vaclav Klaus. As noted earlier, Klaus was appointed president by the parliament in March 2003, only a few months before most judges were subject to be reappointed. However, the president of the Czech Republic was at that time appointed by a joint session of parliament and the senate. From the late 1990s into the early 2000s, the overall composition of the lower house chamber and upper house senate was roughly split between left and right. Therefore, while it is unlikely that many justices directly feared Klaus himself in the years before reappointment, the move towards more conservative voting could serve as a way to gain reappointment in an uncertain environment.

In many ways this result makes intuitive sense. Similar to US state judges facing re-election, high court judges who can be reappointed must consider not only their own views on the legal and policy merits, but also the interests of potential reappointing agents. This alteration in voting patterns also supports Helmke's (2002) conclusion that judges who fear for their future on the court have strong incentives to move towards a possible future regime. Thus, even in more democratic regimes with stronger judicial independence protections, judges still face incentives to rule strategically in the interests of majoritarian actors.

Results from Table 6.5 indicate that judges subject to reappointment face a very real incentive to alter their decisions so they can remain on the court. A closer look at several judges who faced this reappointment pressure gives further corroboration to this outcome. Table 6.6, which shows the voting behaviour of recent Czech Constitutional Court judges up for reappointment over various points in time, provides further visual confirmation for the effect of reappointment uncertainty on judicial voting. Not all of these judges were successful in obtaining reappointment – only Justices Guttler, Hollander, and

Janu were reappointed – yet it is important to note that it is not the result but rather the incentive provided by reappointments that should lead to changes in voting behaviour.

Table 6.5: Logit models for judicial decisions by Czech judges, robust errors clustered on case

	Model 1	Model 2	Model 3
Dependent Variable	Vote proximity	Vote proximity	Vote conservative
Intercept	−0.93*	−0.85*	−0.83*
	(0.30)	(0.30)	(0.38)
Last two years in office	−0.50		
	(0.36)		
Last year in office		−1.12*	1.21*
		(0.54)	(0.54)
Age	0.00	0.00	0.01*
	(0.00)	(0.00)	(0.00)
Year in term	0.04	0.05	0.02
	(0.03)	(0.03)	(0.02)
Past judge	−0.04	−0.04	0.17
	(0.12)	(0.13)	(0.10)
Political background	0.11*	0.08	0.02
	(0.04)	(0.04)	(0.07)
MP group referrals	0.30	0.39	−0.24
	(0.26)	(0.26)	(0.35)
N	1989	1989	1985
Log L	−1335.59	−1332.69	−1338.12
AIC	2685.18	2659.37	2690.25
Chi^2	35.14	31.67	15.61

*indicates significance at $p < 0.05$. Standard errors in parentheses.

Table 6.6: Recent Czech judges subject to reappointment

Justice	Appointer	Reappointing actor	Reappoint year	% left, yrs. 1–8	% left, last 2 years
Guttler	Havel	Klaus (Right)	July 2003	51	34
Duchon	Havel	Klaus (Right)	June 2012	57	31*
Janu	Havel	Klaus (Right)	Sept 2004	53	26
Melenovsky	Havel	Klaus (Right)	May 2004	46	34
Zarembova	Havel	Klaus (Right)	Nov 2003	47	33

*voting outcomes only from June 2010 to January 2011.

Independence and Majoritarian Review

The implications of these findings for judicial independence are not unequivocal, and provide potential arguments for proponents of reappointment systems and fixed term appointment plans. If a goal of democratic society is to maximise the independence of judges in practice (i.e., *de facto* independence), then reappointment systems appear to perform very poorly, at least if we are to interpret the above results as evidence that high court judges who face reappointment shift their decision-making to be in accord with the party or actor that controls reappointment. Yet these results should assuage those in favour of stronger judicial accountability to majority preferences. If a goal of democratic society is to maximise the accountability of office-holders (including judges) to the will of the people, then reappointment systems appear to perform reasonably well: these judges do seem to respond to elected actors who control, or potentially control, their reappointment. And they engage in less 'party line' voting throughout their terms.

Conversely, the lack of accountability to current elected actors seen in fixed, single-term judges, while independence-enhancing, could threaten the integrity of the court, particularly if the decisions from those judges countermand the majority will. For example, twenty-four Polish judges served on the constitutional court at some point during the time period studied here, with 137 combined years served by these judges during this period. Of those 137 years, nearly 60 per cent of these judicial term-years were served during periods in which parties ideologically opposed to their appointing party ruled in government. Fully 56 per cent of votes by Polish Constitutional Tribunal judges over this time were made in cases in which that judge reviewed a law passed by a party ideologically opposite to the party that appointed that judge. Thus, most of the Polish court's decisions were made during periods and in cases in which the court's ideological balance did not match that of the legislature and government. And without an incentive, such as reappointment, there is little in the fixed term systems to keep judicial decisions in line with the will of the current majority.

Ultimately, reappointment rules appear to limit the independence of the judiciary, but they also may provide a link to public preferences. From a majoritarian perspective, this could be a suitable trade-off as long as the reappointment incentive actually provides a link to majority preferences. The reappointment process in the Czech Republic gives the president the ultimate authority to reappoint constitutional court judges. However, until 2012 the president was not directly elected by the people, but rather appointed by the Czech parliament. This doubly-indirect link to the public will is troubling for those who seek greater public accountability in the court system. Yet given the now-direct election of Czech presidents, it is a concern that is largely mitigated.

Finally, individual characteristics yield interesting, though mixed, conclusions. Younger judges – who presumably have a heightened need for future career opportunities – display a higher probability of party line voting as their judicial terms come to a close. Overall, though, these judges are less likely to support their appointers early- and mid-term, which dampens conclusions about career motivations for younger judges. Differences in voting outcomes can also be seen in constitutional court judges with past judicial backgrounds. These judges display a lower probability of voting with the expected wishes of their appointing party, and perhaps a greater amount of the 'principled independence' that Hamilton treasured in judges.

We have seen in previous chapters that politics matters to high court voting. Yet it is also apparent that other factors, institutional and personal, also contribute to judicial outcomes. Providing the opportunity for reappointment gives judges on constitutional courts incentives to rule in favour of the interests of parties in power, particularly when judges are at the end of their terms. To many scholars of courts and of politics, this will be seen as an inherent weakness of the reappointment systems: part of the legitimacy of judges and the larger judicial system is a result of the perception that rulings are made by relying on neutral principles of law and equity. This chapter provides additional evidence that different patterns of decision-making develop when judges are given incentives to remain on the court contingent on the approval of the current appointing actors. This is troubling for a definition of judicial independence that focuses on allowing judges to vote sincerely. Yet these results also demonstrate that courts do not need US-style judicial elections to be democratically accountable actors. Institutional incentives that exist in other environments can also help tie judicial decision-making to the will of current majorities.

In the end, this chapter provides some confirmation that institutional incentives may be able to tie judicial outcomes to majority preferences. Given the support seen in this and previous chapters for the majoritarian vision of judicial review, what role might the legalist vision play in judicial decision-making? This subject will be discussed in Chapter Seven.

The Use of Precedent in Constitutional Courts: Legalism in Action?

Introduction

Within the legalist vision, judicial review is a normatively desirable rule for democracies in that impartial judges are best placed to ensure fair processes and are best able to fairly and consistently apply legal obligations and rights in democratic society. Through the written judicial opinion, judges use established legal reasoning and principles of law, including case law, to reach the best outcomes to constitutional questions. Given this backdrop, it may seem both natural and unusual to examine the presence of the legalist vision within the civil law world. Natural in that the basis of the civil law is focused on a limited and separate role for the judiciary as legal interpreters: finders of law, not makers of law (Merryman 1986). Unusual in that, due to this same history, court decisions from the civil law tradition are often denigrated as mechanical and uninteresting. Scholars describe them variously as terse, formalist, and syllogistic, in contrast to the 'florid mosaics of [...] citations and comments about earlier judicial decisions' existing in common law opinions (Shapiro 1981: 135). One leading casebook on the civil law in the United States notes that, even in the modern era, 'the reader of a German or [...] a French opinion finds [little] to remind him of the nonmechanical nature of the judicial process' (Von Mehren and Gordley 1977: 1140). In fact, the idea that the creation of precedent differentiates the Anglo-American tradition from other legal systems has long been a theme in comparative law (e.g., Goodhart 1934; Cappalli 1998). With this unpropitious backdrop, the constitutional courts in civil law systems may seem a poor environment to test whether there is support for the legalist vision: if judges do not meaningfully engage with past cases and decisions, or engage in reasoned decision-making, then examining judicial outcomes for their presence will be meaningless. Yet the continued acceptance, in some corners, of this traditional view of civil law decision-making has masked the reality that constitutional courts in civil law systems make case law and rely on past decisions to justify the policies they establish in their decisions (Lasser 2004; MacCormack and Summers 1997; Del Luca 2006). In fact, the development and use of case law in this potentially difficult environment should provide a good test of the strength of the legalist vision for judicial review.

The use of case law, precedent, and reasoned decision-making by judges – even those in the civil law tradition – should not be surprising. More than any other governmental actor, judges depend on legitimacy and public acceptance to effectuate their decisions. Deliberation and transparency in the reasoning process provide the legitimacy that judges need to insulate their outcomes against political retaliation and societal disaffection (Lasser 2004). Maintaining (depending on one's perspective) either the perception or reality of apolitical decision-making is critical for judges, as decisions that 'depart too far from the principles and methods of law will invite direct political attack' (Burley and Mattli 1993: 73). Thus, regardless of whether a judge rules neutrally and apolitically, or with policy motives, judges must utilise the law and legally based decision-making practices to legitimise and effectuate their outcomes.

The use of precedent is one method to justify and legitimate outcomes. As scholars are increasingly discovering, reliance on neutral principles like case law and legal precedent can lead to greater acceptance of court outcomes – particularly among people who would otherwise be inclined to disagree with the court's outcome (Zink, Spriggs and Scott 2009). Public acceptance of court outcomes, in turn, can lead to increased court power (Stephenson 2004; Vanberg 2005). Accordingly, a growing body of research investigates how courts use precedent to reason, to bargain, to emphasise favoured policy, and otherwise direct and shape the path of the law (see, e.g., Corley and Wedeking 2014; Cross *et al.* 2010; Bartels 2009; Spriggs and Hansford 2001). Comparative scholars also have begun examining the emergence of judicial 'dialogues', which often can be seen through the development of 'networks' of citation and engagement among judges on different high courts, including constitutional courts (Groppi and Ponthoreau 2013; Bobek 2013; Lupu and Voeten 2012; Gelter and Siems 2012). These studies have, in fact, helped to demonstrate that civil law judges both provide reference to past cases and engage in sophisticated reasoning within opinions (Komarek 2012).

Using evidence from case citations and legal argumentation, in this final chapter I examine whether the legalist vision for judicial review can help to explain judicial outcomes. Those who adhere to a legalist justification view judicial review as normatively desirable in a democracy because impartial judges are best placed to ensure the rule of law and fair process within society. To Louis Favoreu, constitutional judging is the capture of the democratic political process by the law (Rousseau 2007). As outlined in Chapters One and Two, if the legalist vision holds true we should see an absence of incentives-based or ideology-based decision-making, as it is the neutrality of judges – their distance from partisan politics – that best places them to uphold the constitutional bargain. From past chapters it is apparent that some form of ideological voting does occur, and likely some form of incentives-based voting. The presence of either factor in judicial decisions should call into question the legalist vision in its strictest form. Yet, a softer version of legalism may yet survive. We may still be able to discern whether judges attempt, through their legal opinions, to come up with neutral interpretations that legitimate their judicial decisions as the best answers and that advance the rule of law within society. If judges do this without ideological or partisan bent, then the legalist vision should survive.

To examine the legalist vision, I focus on the decision-making of judges on Poland's Constitutional Tribunal, one of the first and most important of such courts in post-Communist Europe. Due to the constraints of creating a full multi-country case law database, I focus on one court in this chapter, supplemented with interviews with current and former tribunal judges and officials. There are many good reasons for studying the work of the Polish court, and Polish judges. First, many judges on the court were educated within a system of legal formalism, one in which the role of judges was severely limited. Thus, if we see discursive opinions with references to precedent even among judges raised in this non-fortuitous environment, then we will have even stronger evidence that legal argumentation matters. Second, the Polish court introduces novel factors that allow for full investigation of legal, strategic, and ideological factors that may influence judicial decision-making practices. Similar to US appellate courts, the Polish Tribunal only rarely meets as a fully plenary body of fifteen. Instead, most cases are decided by smaller three- and five-judge panels (typically five-judge panels). Panel compositions are chosen based on alphabetical order, with modifications to the order based on current judicial caseloads.[1] Thus, any given five-person panel hearing a case could include a majority of right-appointed judges, or a majority of left-appointed judges. Opinion writers are also chosen through the same modified alphabetical order formula, which leaves open the possibility of a divergence between the voting majority and the opinion writer. Notably, this means that opinion writers need not be a part of the panel's voting majority – a rule shared by several other constitutional courts, including Germany and Russia (Vanberg 2005; Trochev 2008) – but absent from current studies of judicial decision-making. This potential gulf between opinion writer and panel is not illimitable: conversations with tribunal staff indicate that when a justice who is given the opinion-writing assignment is unable to carry a majority, the panel president can give the opinion writing assignment to another justice.[2]

I begin this chapter with background on legal traditions and some preliminary evidence of decision-making on constitutional courts. I then examine, theoretically and empirically, two different ways of approaching the use of case law and citations on the constitutional courts, with various statistical tests investigating the ways in which judges use case law within judicial decisions.

Legal origins, legal convergence, and judicial decision-making

The historical differences between common law and civil law traditions – and the reasons behind those differences – have long fascinated legal and political scholars. The most distinct difference between these families relates to the role of the judge as decision-maker. It is often said that, through the creation of case law and precedent, the common law tradition permits greater independence and flexibility in judicial decision-making, while the civil law tradition has focused

---

1. Monitor Polski 720, 3 October 2006, pp. 2429–34. Confirmation of these rules obtained via personal correspondence with tribunal staff.
2. Interviews with Constitutional Tribunal staff (March 2015).

more on the judge as a mere mouthpiece of the legislature, an actor simply applying the law as established by the parliament. For many scholars, these differences between common law and civil law traditions can be traced back to two revolutions: England's Glorious Revolution and the 1789 French Revolution.

England's Glorious Revolution led to an expansion of court power. Facing chronic money shortages, the Stuart Kings in seventeenth century England used royal status to create forced loans and avoid payment on contracts, using the claim that royal privilege trumped the common law (Klerman and Mahoney 2007; North and Weingast 1989). Siding with an increasingly vocal parliament, many English judges refused to bow to royal pressure. Following a turbulent time of civil war that ultimately culminated in the Glorious Revolution of 1688, parliament won its long battle against royal privilege, and judges were rewarded with greater independence from the government. No longer would they be subject to removal by the king, and their power to create and interpret law was enhanced. This greater independence only increased the development of the common law and the use of precedent – judicially created law based on interpretation and application of past cases to present disputes.

French judges, on the other hand, lost considerable power following the 1789 French Revolution. Before the Revolution, French judicial offices (*parlements*) were 'part court, part legislature, and part administrative agency', with broad powers to adopt, implement, and modify rules (Mahoney 2001: 509). These judicial offices conferred nobility and were also heritable; often, judicial offices also were used by their holders to obtain bribes in return for favourable verdicts. After the Revolution, judges would no longer have discretion to create, interpret, or modify existing law. Instead, judges would be tasked with simply applying the civil code (the Napoleonic Code), a practice designed to subordinate judicial opinions to the majority will.

Zweigert and Kötz (2011) note that the post-Revolution Napoleonic Code was largely a response to this past history, but also was built from progressive enlightenment principles, which made it quite attractive to many elements within society. Though initially developed in France, Napoleonic conquests gradually spread the French-inspired civil code to most of continental Europe, thus increasing legislative control and decreasing judicial discretion. In some countries, like Italy and the Netherlands, the civil code was retained after the fall of Napoleon's empire. In the Germanic lands, a long battle played out between those, like Thibault, who sought to adopt a comprehensive and unified German civil code, and those who opposed the code, notably Savigny, Windscheid, and Puchta. Ultimately, by the end of the nineteenth century, comprehensive civil code adherents won out in the new unified German state. This new German code saw inspiration from the move towards exhaustively 'precise solutions and predictability' in law popular in the late nineteenth century (Gordley and von Mehren 2006: 60). In other parts of Central and Eastern Europe, the comprehensive Austrian civil code quickly became predominant during the 1800s (Kuhn 2011).

Thus, for many years the idea of parliamentary sovereignty prevailed throughout much of continental Europe, with parliaments having an absolute monopoly on law-making power. The prevailing view held that parliaments were both the voice and the expressed will of the people, and their legislative enactments should not be called into question, much less overturned, by judges. Instead, in Montesquieu's phrase judges were to be simply 'the mouth of the law', issuing discrete, and often terse, formalist solutions to legal conflicts within the Code's strictures (Cappelletti 1981: 21).

Case law in common law and civil law: the traditional dichotomy

This history has been problematic for judicial prestige and power, as case opinions emanating from the ordinary courts in civil code countries are not formally recognised as a source of law (Merryman and Perez-Perdomo 2007; Mahoney 2001). Instead, judges must look to the relevant section of the legislatively-created civil code (Novak 2003; Cappelletti 1970).[3] Because cases are not a formal source of law, the doctrine of *stare decisis* does not apply to decisions made by ordinary courts in civil law systems. However, in many jurisdictions past cases can serve a persuasive role. The doctrine of *jurisprudence constante* allows courts to take into account a past line of cases in their decision-making when that line of cases is sufficiently strong and at a high level of consistency (Fon and Parisi 2005; Algero 2004). Still, this past line of cases is not binding in any official sense.

Academics and lawyers comparing the two systems have often used case law and precedent as the primary concepts by which to differentiate the civil and common law systems (see discussions in Lasser 2004; Komarek 2012; Cappalli 1998). Some go even further: a prominent group of economists and political scientists found the common law tradition of precedent, case law, and dynamic interpretation to be a primary driver of the economic freedoms that lead to comparatively higher levels of economic growth in the common law world (La Porta *et al.* 2004). Law professor Paul Mahoney (2001) also uses the dynamism of the common law judiciaries to help explain why twentieth century economic growth rates were larger in common law countries than civil law countries.

Despite this traditional case law-based differentiation between civil law and common law, it is difficult to conceive of a well-functioning legal system without mechanisms to ensure some uniformity or certainty in outcomes. Lasser (2004) questions whether any modern system of law can develop legitimacy and trust in its outcomes if essentially every legal dispute starts anew, with no guarantee that past legal solutions and guidelines will be applied in present conflicts. The importance of this question should not be underestimated. Judges administer systems of law, with more or less concrete foundations but less stable structures and edifices that arise from it – even in the more comprehensive civil code. It is

---

3. Regulations and custom are the other acceptable sources of law. Despite this presumed historical difference, scholars have often acknowledged that judges and attorneys use past court opinions in civil law cases, despite the absence of true precedent or *stare decisis*. See later discussion, as well.

the role of the judicial system to fill in the cracks within the legal code, but also to require changes to the structure, when necessary, to keep the system in balance. This essentially requires both a detailed jurisprudence as well as the maintenance of a system in which the results of past cases can be used as authoritative reasons to continue – or perhaps change – legal pathways. As far back as 1820s Saxony, civilian judges recognised the need to develop legal rules and decide similar cases similarly, or else face erosion of social trust over the long-term (Dawson 1968: 442). Savigny ([1831] 1975: 28) wrote contemporaneously that the current fashion of developing complete codes 'must fail', as there are 'no limits' to permutations of cases created within the real world. This idea was later taken up in Europe by the German free law and Scandinavian legal realist scholars (Rytter and Wind 2011). Even Aubry and Rau's mid-nineteenth century exposition of the French civil code advocated for judicial examination of the 'spirit' or the 'consequences' of law, albeit in limited circumstances and with 'great reserve' ([1869] 1971: 40). In today's French Cour de Cassation, the archetype civil law court, cases still are rarely cited within judicial opinions, yet a detailed examination of past cases occurs both in private judicial chamber discussions and in the contemporaneously published official commentaries on the case written by leading law professors (Lasser 2004; Shapiro 1981: 137).[4]

Increasingly, the view of stultified civil law judging is changing. In particular, there is recognition that these courts, notably constitutional courts, do engage with past cases and give reasons with reference to past decisions (Komarek 2012; Stone Sweet 2000; McCormack and Summers 1997).[5] Lasser's (2004) textual analysis of the argumentative strategies within the decisions of the French Cour de Cassation – the highest court in the French ordinary court system – found that court does provide precedent-like guidance through supplementary materials, despite the unhelpful terseness and syllogistic reasoning style within the opinions themselves. Siems (2010) and Algero (2004) similarly find judges and attorneys in Germany and Louisiana, a civil code state, use case law and believe in its importance to overall court outcomes. Nowhere is this truer than in the constitutional courts in civil law countries, where case law and precedent have become important and meaningful decision-making devices. However, given the growing importance of constitutional courts in continental political life, surprisingly little is known about the jurisprudence of constitutional courts, and specifically the use of case law in constitutional courts. This absence is particularly striking, as there is little debate about the binding nature or precedential effect of constitutional court opinions (Peczenik 1997; Groppi and Ponthoreau 2013).[6]

---

4. The Cour de Cassation is the highest civil court in the French legal system.

5. However, as far back as 1968, Dawson described the tendency of the 1880s German *Reichsgericht* to discuss past cases.

6. Morawski and Zirk-Sadowski (1997: 224) note that the opinions of the Polish Constitutional Tribunal are 'predestined to become precedents'.

Those authors that have examined constitutional court jurisprudence – notably, the authors in the MacCormack and Summers (1997) collection – have found the use of case law to be quite important in civil law systems and widely used in the opinions of constitutional courts, though the evidence presented in that collection is largely anecdotal. More recently, Bobek (2013) and the authors in Groppi and Ponthoreau (2013) detail the increasing inter-court dialogues and the borrowing of foreign legal precedent by European constitutional court judges. Both works show generally increasing trends of dialogues by constitutional courts across national borders, as well as increasingly sophisticated legal argumentation. Still, the empirical question remains how these constitutional courts use the larger body of case law they create within their own opinions.

To examine this larger question, I created a unique dataset of Polish Constitutional Tribunal decisions from 2004 to 2010. Figure 7.1, which displays the number of citations provided within Polish Constitutional Tribunal cases, shows that judges on this court provide citations to past cases in nearly every opinion. We also see a significant increase over time in the use of case citations within the opinions of the Polish Tribunal. In 2004 the average number of citations per case stood at less than ten, while in 2010 the average number of citations increased to nearly twenty per opinion. Though this increase could be explained as the natural

Figure 7.1: Number of citations to precedent per opinion, by year

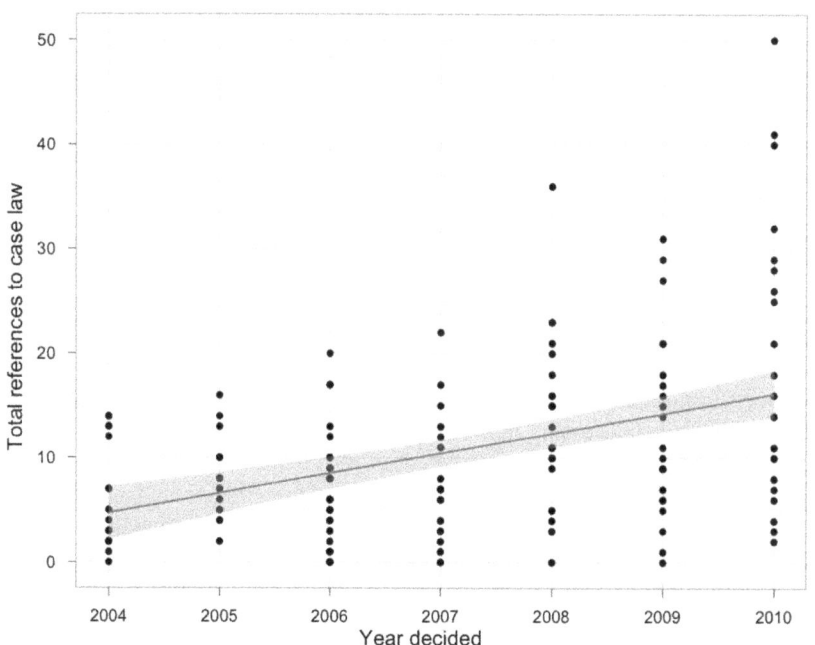

outcome of an increasing corpus of case law, it also indicates that the role of case law is growing more important and more central to judicial decision-making for judges on the Polish Constitutional Court.

Given that these judges are making decisions and justifying opinions based on previously decided cases, we must ask next the factors that contribute to this type of judicial reasoning. Do courts use precedent and other neutral legal sources in a 'legalist' manner to help legitimate and provide democratic sanction for their outcomes? Are there ideological or other strategic uses to case citation practices? In the next section I investigate these questions, and propose a general theory and set of testable hypotheses for the use of case law by civil law constitutional courts.

The use of precedent by constitutional court judges: theory and data

Why should judges use precedent, and why rely on past cases and past principles to justify current outcomes? Traditionally, two related reasons could drive the practice: the first is the lawmaking function of courts; the second is the need to legitimate those judicial opinions by showing they are the product of neutral legal factors – which also can defend them against partisan political attack. Notably, both reasons could fit within a legalist justification for judicial review. We shall see if these rationales find support.

Judges make law, yet unlike other actors in democratic government judges are not elected by the citizenry. How, then, can judicial decisions gain popular legitimacy? Blackstone ([1753] 1893: 74) believed that judge-made English common law flowed from societal customs, and thus ultimately from the people. The judicial decision was, then, an act in which the common law judge would determine the proper, socially correct (and thus legitimate) outcome to a distinct case while also setting the broader social principle to resolve similar disputes. To do this required reasoning, distinguishing between proper and improper arguments, explaining why the final outcome was the proper one, and relying on previous decisions to guide resolution of the current dispute.

In today's world, all courts with the power of judicial review have the capacity to make law and ratify norms of behaviour in society and among political actors. As Lasser (2004: 303) notes, '[w]hen a legal system posits that its judicial decisions carry [...] the force of *law*, the explanatory burden borne by those decisions changes dramatically'. Judges must not only decide an outcome, but must also explain why the chosen outcome is the correct outcome – particularly when overturning acts of elected actors. Thus, providing reasons within their decisions becomes a necessary part of the judicial law-making function. Creating reasoned opinions, including using past cases, also helps improve the democratic legitimacy of judicial review. By providing reasons, citizens and government officials alike can learn correct answers or solutions to constitutional questions. It can, according to Ferejohn and Pasquino (2002: 24), 'help to perfect the rule of law in light of experience'. We see evidence of this development in the elaboration of the Polish Constitutional Tribunal's principle of equality. In a

2000 case concerning the constitutionality of a law that set different retirement ages for men and women, the Tribunal noted:

> that regulations similar in content to [this law] already have been the subject of adjudication and were deemed unconstitutional. In the judgment of 24 September 1991 Kw 5/91 (OTK 1991, pp. 96 et seq.), the Court held unconstitutional a partial provision of the Higher Education Act, which provided that the employment relationship with an academic teacher expires at the end of the year academic in which the teacher has reached retirement age. (Case K 17/99 of 18 January 2000)

Similarly, in a 2006 case in which a public sector union challenges the constitutionality of a regulation that differentiates classes of workers, the Tribunal notes:

> According to the settled case-law of the Constitutional Tribunal, which has always emphasized the relative nature of the principle of equality before the law, equality does not prevent any differentiation among entities [or classes] … (see judgment of the Constitutional Tribunal of 24 January 2001, ref. SK 30/99, judgment K 8/97, OTK ZU No. 5-6/1997, pos. 70, 12 May 1998, ref. judgment K 17/97, OTK ZU No. 3/1998, pos. 34, 23 June 1999, ref. judgment K 30/98, OTK ZU No. 5/1999, pos. 101, 8 May 2001, ref. judgment P 15/00, OTK ZU No. 4/2001…). (Case K 36/03 of 4 October 2005)

In both cases, we see a conscious effort to elaborate and develop legal argumentation, particularly a desire to demonstrate a continuation of earlier lines of judicial decisions on a path towards proper interpretation of the constitution.

Constitutional court judges in civil law systems should be particularly mindful of the need to develop normative reasoning and coherent case law as a way to establish their own authority as the arbiter of law. As the only judicial body with the ability to overturn governmental acts and create law, constitutional courts face a unique explanatory burden within their countries – to develop legal principles and potentially constrain the political branches while also avoiding overt politicisation of their opinions. The use of precedent allows these judges to structure and legitimate outcomes by developing compelling, neutral rationales based in principles of law. In fact, from interviews with various current and former constitutional court staff members in Spain and Poland, it is apparent there is a common need on the part of the judges and their law clerks to show that the constitutional law being developed within the opinion is rooted within legal traditions and established constitutional principles.[7]

---

7. Interviews with current and former constitutional court assistants and judges in the Spanish Constitutional Court and Polish Constitutional Tribunal (November 2014 and March 2015).

The need to establish principled, facially neutral decision-making should be particularly important to constitutional courts in new democracies like Poland, given the general lack of legitimacy with which many courts began (see Schwartz 2000). Bobek (2013), Kuhn (2011, 2004), and Sadurski (1999) describe the low status held by post-communist judges in the ordinary court system, and the lack of public trust in their decisions. Giving reasons for their decisions, including by citing past decisions, could, then, be used to show a sceptical public the lawfulness, coherence, and fairness of constitutional court decision-making, as well as the self-imposed limits these judges place on their decision-making power. One former Tribunal justice noted the court was cognisant of the potential that their opinions could be attacked or criticised, and this fear led to development of stronger legal opinions.[8]

By relying on neutral legal principles to justify rulings, judges send a public signal that legal and constitutional considerations demand the outcome they pronounce. And by relying on legal considerations to legitimate their rulings as democratic necessities, judges place themselves on much firmer ground to withstand partisan attack. Thus, judges should be able to use precedent as a way to give legitimacy to judicial lawmaking; in effect, to use precedent as a *shield* to protect the court's opinions and even the court itself against political attack (Burley and Mattli 1993). The need to legitimate should be particularly important when courts engage in the 'negative' lawmaking of overturning existing laws. Accordingly, I propose as a first testable hypothesis (Hypothesis 1) that constitutional court decisions *overturning* laws should be supported by more case law and citations than cases upholding the constitutionality of a law.

To test this idea, I assembled a unique database of Polish Constitutional Tribunal opinions from 2004 to 2010. As in past chapters, I have limited the universe to decisions on the conformity of laws and regulations arising from abstract judicial review. Due to the overwhelming number of individual constitutional complaints filed each year, a full study of all cases decided would be unworkable at this time. Still, the large number of cases to be examined and the length of time to be studied will allow for a systematic examination of the factors influencing the use of precedent in civil law constitutional courts.

Overall, the dataset includes opinions from 148 cases decided between 2004 and 2010. The dataset comprises every unique citation within the 148 opinions – 2,408 total citations, including 1,627 citations to previous Polish Tribunal cases. The dataset also includes the name of all judges in the panel deciding the case, the opinion author (the case rapporteur), as well as the party affiliation of each judge in the panel. In addition, I also include the names and party affiliations of judges in every case that is cited within the opinions in the dataset, and the overall party-based composition of each panel cited.

For each case in the dataset, I determined the number of unique citations included in that case. These citations form the basis for two dependent variables: one is a count of the number of unique Polish Constitutional Tribunal decisions

---

8. Interview with former Tribunal justice (March 2015).

cited; the second is a count of the total number of unique citations, including cites to the Polish Tribunal, other Polish Courts, foreign courts (including the ECJ), legal articles, and books. The second formulation of the dependent variable should be a particularly important one for judges in the civil law tradition, which emphasises the authoritative role of scholarly legal doctrine to an extent not seen in the US judicial tradition (Lasser 2004; Alexy and Drier 1997; Shapiro 1981: 144). Using scholarly material also opens up the field of potentially authoritative reasons to justify a particular ruling.

The independent variable for this test indicates whether or not the judicial panel ruled unconstitutional all or part of the law under review. If my hypothesis is correct, there should be a positive effect of unconstitutional rulings on the number of citations included per opinion. I also test for other possible reasons why citation practices would differ within cases. First, judges may include higher numbers of citations in prominent or politically salient cases (e.g., Lupu and Voeten 2012). Cross et al. (2010) gauge case salience by newspaper coverage of court cases in *The New York Times*. In Poland, case importance can be determined in a different way. Relatively few cases are decided by the full bench of fifteen judges; instead, most cases are decided by smaller five member panels. The full fifteen-member court meets only for important cases, including cases initiated by the president of Poland, cases involving disputes between constitutional branches, and 'cases of notably complicated nature'.[9] Accordingly, I will use the size of the panel as a general proxy for case importance. Providing citations for these cases could be particularly important, as a significant number of cases heard by the plenum involve legal battles between political institutions, which should particularly invoke the need for courts to provide insulation from the perception of political decision-making.

In addition, cases in which a dissenting opinion is filed could potentially be harmful to the legitimacy of the majority opinion. Dissenting opinions indicate potential discord concerning the legal merits of the case. At a minimum, it indicates the legal conclusions reached in the opinion are not the only conclusions that reasonable judges could make. In these cases, there should also be a concern on the part of the majority to provide extra legal legitimation for their decision, and thus the possibility that recourse to precedent and past legal authority will be all the more necessary. I also include a control variable that accounts for certain types of issues the court hears: social welfare, property, and civil rights claims. From Chapter Four, we know that all three issues are commonly heard by constitutional courts; with the high number of cases heard, there could be larger numbers of cases cited.

Table 7.1 shows the results of these tests. Given that the dependent variable is a count of the number of citations within judicial opinions, I use a negative binomial model.[10] The first column shows results using only citations to

---

9.   Polish Constitutional Tribunal. http://www.trybunal.gov.pl/eng/index.htm [Accessed: 1 March 2015].

10. A negative binomial model is appropriate over a poisson model when using over-dispersed count data, as this data is. The variance of both dependent variables is significantly larger than their means. The alpha parameter estimates for the negative binomial models are far from zero, suggesting the negative binomial is appropriate.

Table 7.1: Use of precedent and legal citations in Polish Constitutional Tribunal opinions

	Tribunal citations	All citations (cases, books, etc.)
Intercept	2.09*	2.55*
	(0.16)	(0.16)
Unconstitutional ruling	0.43*	0.40*
	(0.14)	(0.14)
Dissenting opinion	0.02	0.12
	(0.09)	(0.10)
Panel size	0.01	0.00
	(0.02)	(0.02)
Prominent issue	−0.26	−0.21
	(0.15)	(0.15)
N	147	147
Alpha	0.52*	0.55*
Log L	−494.72	−545.78

*indicates significance at $p < 0.05$. Standard errors in parentheses.

Polish Constitutional Tribunal cases, while the second column shows results using the count of all citations, including mentions of other courts (national and international) and scholarly articles. In both models, the decision to rule a law unconstitutional results in a significantly larger number of citations, which supports the validity of a vision of judicial review in which judges use case law to legitimate outcomes. By providing a greater number of authoritative reasons why the majority answer is correct, we see the importance of legal argumentation to these constitutional court decisions and evidence that judges attempt to include greater legal corroboration when the legitimacy of the court's ruling may be put into question. The increased number of total citations in opinions overturning laws is also interesting in that it corroborates past work discussing the importance and influence of the legal academic world to judges and attorneys trained in the civil law tradition (Merryman and Perez-Perdomo 2007; Lasser 2004).

However, the size of the panel deciding the case has no real relationship to the number of citations, as does the presence of a dissenting opinion. This last finding is a bit surprising, as interviews with a former Tribunal justice indicated that dissenting opinions generally brought out stronger majority opinions.[11] It appears this need does not result in greater reference to precedent or other legal arguments.

---

11. Interview with former Tribunal justice (March 2015).

Distinguishing political from apolitical decision-making

The previous section has shown that the role of precedent and case law has steadily increased on the Polish Constitutional Tribunal over time. Judges on the court increasingly use citations as argumentation and legitimation devices in their opinions, and refer to precedent at higher rates when overturning laws. Both findings provide support for the legitimating capacity of precedent in constitutional courts – a legitimation that could help paint a portrait of principled, law-based judicial decision-making consistent with the legalist vision of judicial review. Given this, could there still be policy-based or strategic uses for precedent?

To illustrate the concern, imagine two courtrooms. In one, a dutiful and completely apolitical judge presides over a dispute between two parties. In a second courtroom, an intensely ideological judge hears a similar dispute between two separate litigants. After hearing the competing claims, both judges retire to their respective chambers to begin the process of creating an outcome. In deciding the case, each judge will have his own motives for reaching the final outcome. Yet, both judges are still limited by law. Specifically, both judges must utilise the methods of law and of legal decision-making when constructing outcomes and creating their opinions. As noted earlier, by Burley and Mattli (1993), overtly partisan political opinions will not be treated as legitimate, nor will they be respected in society. Thus, both the political and the apolitical judge must utilise the law and legally-based decision-making to gain acceptance for their outcomes. Yet, within this constraint comes the potential for opportunity – specifically, the opportunity to use this neutral process to gain ideological advantage.

Most previous political science theory regarding the use of precedent and citation practices comes from the US courts. Examining the decision-making process on the US Supreme Court, Maltzman *et al.* (2000) found that justices maintain wide latitude to shape both the direction and the content of judicial opinions. Notably, opinion writers are able to engage in strategic bargaining, changing the content of Court opinions – including the clarity of the language and the type of legal test used – in return for votes from other members of the court. Past research focusing on the use of precedent in the Supreme Court also has found that opinion authors use the norm of precedent to strategic advantage, citing to ideologically proximate cases over distant cases, for example (Hansford and Spriggs 2006). Both *stare decisis* and legal relevance are important considerations in the Court's interpretation of precedent. At the same time, ideologically proximate cases are more likely to be positively interpreted by opinion-writers than ideologically distant cases (Spriggs and Hansford 2001). If European constitutional court judges use precedent, too, perhaps they also may use the content of their opinions in ways that maximise their policy usefulness. If so, the strength of legalism argument would decline.

Opportunities for policy creation arise largely due to the discretion granted to judges in the opinion-writing process. Law, in the words of Israeli justice Aharon Barak, 'is not mathematics' (2003: 19) and *stare decisis*, in the words of Daniel

Farber, 'is not rocket science' (2005: 1176). There is inherent uncertainty within the law and within past decisions, and this uncertainty provides judges with a necessary amount of discretion. The judge as opinion writer is free to emphasise past cases and to develop and clarify existing interpretive strands, even insert their own judgments to create new visions for the direction of the law. This is particularly true in what have been termed the 'hard cases' – those cases which, due to indeterminacy of the law, require judicial discretion at the opinion stage (Hart 1961; Dworkin 1977). Such indeterminate cases – cases with competing narratives and competing rights – are just the type that often must be resolved by the supreme constitutional tribunals.

Whether in Poland, or Germany, or in the United States, control over the content of the opinion leaves room for judges to attempt to move the path of the law in their own preferred direction (within limits described above). Burley and Mattli (1993) describe the law as both a mask and shield for judicial decision-making. We have already seen that judges appear to use precedent as just such a shield to legitimate outcomes. However, in a policy-laden environment, this power to shape the opinion also may lead judges to use legal decision-making processes as a 'mask' to conceal policy motivations.

To examine whether opinion authors use precedent as just such a mask to advance partisan outcomes, we are aided by Poland's unique panel and cases assignment rules, in which opinion author assignments are created based on alphabetical order.[12] Thus, the opinion author need not be a part of the majority coalition – that is, the judge assigned to write the opinion may disagree with the basic outcome of the case, though it should be noted that if the gulf between the author and the majority is too great, the president can then ask a new justice to write the opinion. The original justice would then write the dissenting opinion.

As a result, opinion authors may, in an unusual way, have more freedom to write an opinion that advances their preferred policy. With opinion authors selected semi-randomly, justices need not have the same incentive to bargain or otherwise win over adherents to their preferred view. A judge appointed by the leftist SLD could be selected as the opinion writer for a panel dominated by judges appointed by the parties of the right (i.e. PiS, LRP, and AWS).[13] In reality, such practice occurs regularly: of the 231 cases decided from 2000 to 2010 which contain a majority of judges appointed by rightist parties, eighty-three of those cases – or 36 per cent of cases – have a left-appointed judge assigned as opinion writer. Given such an arrangement, where the opinion author need not necessarily agree with the ultimate decision, what should we expect within the court's opinion?

---

12. With some modifications based on current workloads. Thus, the system is not random, but could be described as arbitrary. This rule is partially described in the current governing by-laws for the Constitutional Tribunal. I obtained confirmation of this arrangement through the Tribunal's public affairs office (personal communication). However, it is also apparent from interviews that the Tribunal president is able, in certain cases, to change the composition of the panel. This appears to be a very infrequent practice, however.

13. Panel assignments are also chosen on the basis of alphabetical ordering.

As a second testable hypothesis (Hypothesis 2), we can examine whether, counter to the legalist vision, judges will seek to advance preferred outcomes by citing the decisions of ideologically similar panels over panels dominated by judges appointed from opposing parties.

If the above hypothesis is true, then strong indications exist that opinion authors use case citations and precedent to promote favoured policy directions over other directions. The citation of friendly courts does not necessarily mean that policy is the decisive factor, though it does provide strong suggestive evidence of such motivations, and would damage the legalist vision.

However, there are countervailing reasons to believe such ideological motivations will not exist on constitutional courts. First, many country scholars have noted that precedential or *stare decisis*-like effects occur in national civil court systems only after a series of courts have confirmed the validity of an initial judgment (Morawski and Zirk-Sadowski 1997: 247; Alexy and Drier 1997; Del Luca 2006; Fon and Parisi 2005). Though more frequent citations also indicate the strength of US Supreme Court precedent, the formal difference does indicate that case law in continental Europe may still operate differently from the Anglo-American model at the margins (Falcon y Tella 2011: 55).

Perhaps more important, constitutional court judges operate in different institutional environments than US Supreme Court justices. Notably, while constitutional courts are 'the only game in town' for constitutional adjudication, these courts still face potential competition for jurisprudential dominance from the supreme courts in the ordinary court system – a competition that has been seen directly in Spain and the Czech Republic, among other countries (Trochev 2008). This judicial competition for the minds of lower court judges could decrease any tendency towards advancing partisan or ideological interests within opinions. Additionally, judges trained in a traditional, mechanical civil law model of legal science may simply show little interest in advancing policy. Thus, we may see no evidence of judicial opinions advancing preferred outcomes.

To test these ideas, I use the same dataset of cases from the Polish Constitutional Tribunal decided from 2004 to 2010 used to test the earlier theory of opinion legitimation through case law. The dependent variable is a count of the number of citations to right-majority panels and left-majority panels. A right-majority panel is a judicial panel that contains a majority of judges appointed by parties placed on the right of the ideological spectrum.[14] In Poland, Solidarity Electoral Action (AWS), Law and Justice (PiS), and Civic Platform (PO) all are counted as parties of the right. A left-majority panel is a judicial panel that contains a majority of judges appointed by parties placed on the left of the ideological spectrum. The Democratic Left Alliance (SLD) is the only leftist party within the data period. The independent variable is the affiliation of the opinion author, based on the appointing party or coalition of the judge. Previous studies of

---

14. I employ Comparative Manifesto Project (CMP) scores, using Tavits and Letki's (2009) key variables for Eastern Europe to determine scores. The right-left dimension is confirmed by the Chapel Hill Expert Survey of political parties (Bakker *et al.* 2012).

US courts have relied on the ideological distance between the precedent cited and the ideological direction of the Court in the year the precedent was cited (Hansford and Spriggs 2006). I rely instead on the ideology of the judge writing the opinion, with ideology determined by the party or coalition that appointed that judge.

Results of empirical testing

One way of observing any ideological aspect to decision-making is to examine the rates of citation by judges, grouped according to appointing party. As seen in Figure 2, left-appointed judges cite to just under four cases with left panel majorities per opinion, on average, while right-appointed judges cite to approximately three per opinion.[15] Right-appointed judges cite to 5.5 cases with right panel majorities per opinion, on average, while left-appointed judges cite to three right cases per opinion.[16] As an initial matter, then, it appears there are differences in case law citation based on ideological values. However, these simple tests cannot account for possible alternative explanations. Could this simply be a product of more cases being cited over time, or the make-up of co-panelists? Further analysis is provided in Table 7.2. As the dependent variable is a count of the number of left and right citations within judicial opinions, I again use a negative binomial model.[17]

Model 1 shows the results with the number of right-majority citations serving as the outcome variable. In this model, we see an increase in the propensity of right-appointed judges to cite to opinions decided by right-leaning panels. Model 2 examines the number of left citations, and largely confirms the results seen in model 1: judges appointed by parties of the right cite to fewer cases decided by left-leaning panels.[18] Combined, models 1 and 2 show a clear difference in the manner of opinion justification between two distinct camps of judges: those appointed by rightist parties, and those appointed by the left. Right-appointed judges cite to more cases decided by their right-appointed colleagues, while left-appointed judges favour the decisions of their fellow leftist judges. Could this be a result of changing citation practices over time? To account for any temporal variation, I re-ran all models with control variables for the year in which the opinion was decided and the aggregate number of cases decided by the constitutional court at the end of the preceding year (not shown in the Table). The substantive results do not vary with this addition.

---

15. A difference of means test shows this difference to be significant at the 0.10 level.

16. A difference of means test confirms this result is significant at the .05 level.

17. This choice is appropriate when using over-dispersed count data. The variation for both dependent variables is roughly three times greater than their means. Alpha parameter estimates for negative binomial models in Table 7.2 are all significantly greater than zero, suggesting the negative binomial is more appropriate than the poisson.

18. Left-appointed opinion authors are the reference group for these statistical tests.

Figure 7.2: Citation choices, by ideology

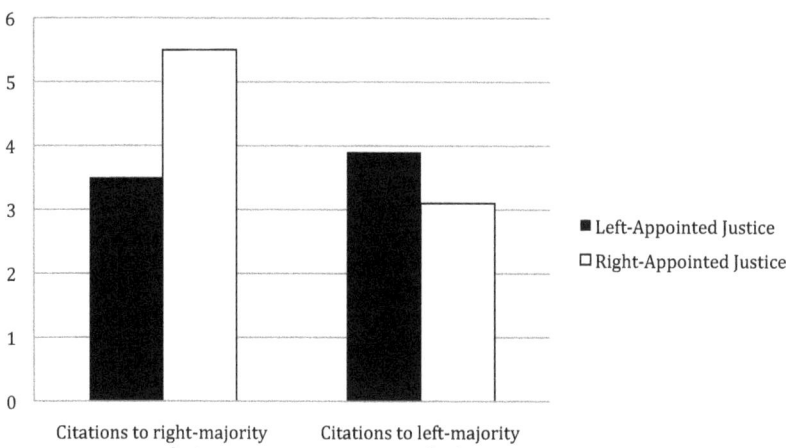

Table 7.2: Test of citation choice by opinion author appointing party

	Model 1	Model 2
Dependent variable:	Number of left cites	Number of right cites
Intercept	−183. 91*	−256.42*
	(78.11)	(69.53)
Opinion writer (Right)	−0.31	0.38*
	(0.16)	(0.15)
Panel composition (% Left)	−0.23	−0.29
	(0.46)	(0.41)
Year decided	0.09*	0.13*
	(0.04)	(0.03)
N	148	148
AIC	683.47	753.79
Log L	−321.73	−356.90

*indicates significance at $p < 0.05$. Standard errors in parentheses.

Conclusions

Constitutional courts both make case law and rely on precedent to resolve cases. Yet theoretical and empirical investigation of these courts' decision-making practices has been relatively rare. I try to address both aspects, using the Polish Constitutional Tribunal as a representative case. As a preliminary matter, we see some evidence of the vibrancy of legal decision-making on the Polish Constitutional Tribunal. Far from the civil court stereotype of terse formalism, the judges on the Polish court cite – regularly and increasingly – to past decisions as authority for current outcomes. This nuance extends to ideological and strategic uses of precedent. Much like past findings for US Supreme Court justices, constitutional court judges are guided in the opinion writing process by competing pressures of policy and jurisprudence. In their opinions, we see these judges care about the need to provide facially neutral justifications for their opinions, particularly when striking down legislative or executive acts, yet also cite regularly to the opinions of friendly panels over more distant panels.

The findings are suggestive of several important trends in constitutional court decision-making. Judges value the legitimacy of their legal decisions and opinions. When overturning legislative and executive decisions, judges on the Polish Constitutional Tribunal support their decisions with more frequent references to past decisions, and to other legal sources. Thus, these judges appear to use the law as a shield to protect and secure the validity of their judgments. This need to legitimate should be particularly important to constitutional courts, given the historical distrust of judicial lawmaking in the civil law tradition. Judges also appear to engage in at least some amount of ideological citation, favouring precedent decided by ideologically similar panels over those of distant panels. This result shows evidence that constitutional court opinion-writers also use precedent, at least in part, to move policy and jurisprudence towards their own favoured paths.

Though the legitimating use of precedent and language conforms with a looser interpretation of legalism, other behaviours are more at odds with a purely legalist vision of judicial review. Instead of adhering to neutral principles simply to find the best legal answer, judges also appear to use neutral legal principles to advance policy and institutional interests. Thus, while the evidence does not support a claim that the legalist vision dominates the operation of judicial review, neither can it be said that jurisprudence, legal language, and opinion writing are irrelevant factors in judicial decision-making. This mixed conclusion makes sense in the real world of constitutional judging. The need to provide internal and external coherency to outcomes, to legitimate decisions by referencing and giving reasons for the correctness of the outcome, is fundamental to the judicial role. This coherency also is fundamental to the development of the rule of law in democracies. At the same time, these institutions sit at the intersection of politics and law, with their rulings standing as important veto points for policy. This duality of policy and law is seen in the use of precedent: judges engage in some amount of legalism, but also use legal methods to subtly advance important interests.

Conclusion

The Visions of Judicial Review Considered

This book started with an apparent paradox of modern democracy: societies that organise on democratic principles of majority rule and the people's will increasingly establish courts with the power of judicial review – a seemingly non-majoritarian institution in which unelected actors review and potentially overturn the actions of the people's representatives. Though it is often seen as *de rigeur* today – by one count 128 countries have adopted the institution of judicial review (Romeau 2006) – establishing judicial review has real consequences for how governments operate and how policy is created. This is true everywhere, but perhaps most acutely felt in counties that have established centralised judicial review processes using specialised constitutional courts. Returning to the example in the introductory chapter, the organisers of Poland's Equality Parade were able to bypass political and administrative roadblocks by using constitutional court review to overturn the law that prevented them from organising their march. With the help of the Polish Ombudsman, this group was able to utilise the courts to nullify a valid law passed by a legislative majority and applied many times over the years by national and regional officials – often to prevent disfavoured groups from demonstrating. Similarly, legislative opposition groups in nearly all centralised judicial review systems can use the constitutional court to attempt a reversal of laws passed by the parliamentary majority, an effort that can 'instantaneously' reorder the power relationship between the political opposition and the political majority (Stone Sweet 2000: 198). Thus, modern rules for judicial review provide courts with *power* – the power to say what the law is, but also the power to change social outcomes, and alter social policy. With this power over social outcomes and policy, it is important to consider how the institution of judicial review fits into the larger goals of democratic governance. In a democracy, we expect government to represent the interest of its citizens. Yet, as Arendt Lijphart noted in 1991 when discussing the constitutional choices for new democracies, we also expect democratic governments to provide for equality among citizens, promote citizen participation, and create increased accountability of those in office (Lijphart 1991). Now that we have examined the outcomes of judicial review over time across multiple countries, we must next ask: does the institution of judicial review help to realise such democratic goals in practice?

To determine the value of judicial review, I have categorised several explanations that attempt to justify the institution of judicial review in democratic society, and reconcile the practice of judicial review with democratic principles. In large part, these explanations concentrate around three main visions for democracy and judicial review. In one view, courts exist to protect the rights of individual citizens. Liberal democratic government is limited government, one where elected leaders cannot infringe on the constitutional rights of its citizens. Majority rule electoral and governing processes may lead to majority tyranny, in which the rights of social and political minorities are marginalised or trampled by majority preferences. Accordingly, courts are needed to protect and safeguard individual constitutional rights, particularly the rights of disadvantaged and minority groups. Thus, judicial review maintains democratic legitimacy by acting to ensure the fundamental equality of citizens, particularly, against the predations of current majorities.

Another vision begins with democratic government as a government of rules – rules that apply to all within society. In societies governed by the rule of law, neutral and impartial courts are needed to apply those rules to real conflicts that develop within society. Within this 'legalist' view, the courts are not designed to enter the policy field, or seek out the protection of certain individual rights or certain groups. Instead, the role of the judge should be to seek out the best, or 'right', legal and constitutional answer, even if it contradicts the views of the current political majority. Thus, judicial review might protect rights, but only as part of a larger, neutral judicial role of administering the constitution.

A final vision directly questions whether judicial review truly is the counter-majoritarian, or anti-majoritarian institution that arouses so much concern among democratic theorists, and some judicial theorists. Rather than thwart majority outcomes, this vision advances the view that judicial review is often used in ways that advance the 'will of the people'. Courts that exercise judicial review might, then, serve a valuable role in participatory democracy.

Judicial review can be either majority-enhancing or majority-reinforcing under several circumstances. In the basic iteration of a majoritarian vision, it is assumed that judges on courts of constitutional review likely vote with ideological preferences. This behaviour is not problematic for democratic legitimacy, though, as appointment processes ensure that judicial ideologies will be in line with political majorities. Thus, judicial review has a beneficial, legitimating role in democratic government. Ultimately, evidence from the four countries examined in this study shows, as recent US studies have (Owens 2010; Hall 2012), an absence of this type of legitimating behaviour. Constitutional judges are not very deferential to the current government; instead, they are highly active in striking down legislation of all sorts, including laws enacted by current governments, former governments, and even affiliated political actors in parliament. From a normative standpoint, this absence of judicial deference should be vitalising for democratic rule. The political legitimacy of judicial review still rests largely on the traditional hallmarks of the courts – neutrality and impartiality. Overt partiality towards current majorities would bring up difficult questions regarding the desirability of judicial review in a separation of powers democratic system. As Jeff Staton (2010) notes, why would citizens ever turn to courts to resolve their problems if judges consistently take the side of the government? Though this type of policy legitimation is not seen in the data, judicial ideology is a consistently strong predictor of decision outcomes. While there is not deference to current majorities, we do see a fairly consistent pattern in which legislation and regulations are struck down when the median judge on the panel was appointed by a party on the opposite end of the ideological spectrum to the party whose law or regulation is under review. This result potentially calls into question the independent spirit we so often ask judges to carry within them in deciding cases and creating outcomes. If we view constitutional judges as neutral finders of truth and principle, then outcomes that advance the policy goals of appointers call into question the rationale for judicial review of legislative and executive acts. A better view of constitutional judging is more nuanced, though. To use the analogy in Chapter Seven, when the typical constitutional judge sits down to write his or her opinion, both law and policy should be weighed because they are so inextricably tied together. Law *is* policy, and when constitutional judges are asked to weigh law against the constitution, they are given an inherently policy-laden task. Thus, if we view judging, particularly constitutional judging, as a process in which policy must be considered, then we arguably have little to fear from decision-making driven, at least in part, by policy considerations.

Staton's above point raises a second possibility: that judges may understand the importance of public support to judicial legitimacy, and strive to create outcomes that are within the bounds, generally speaking, of public preferences. By following the bounds of public opinion, judicial review can be majority enhancing in a quite direct manner. Previous examination of the public's connection to the courts, almost exclusively drawn from the United States, has produced a host of inconsistent findings – perhaps judges follow public opinion, but perhaps in making opinions they are just shaped by the same forces that guide everyone else in society. Using public opinion data from Poland, this study provides additional confirmation of the value of public support to judicial outcomes. Higher levels of public support are associated with greater activism, while lower levels of the support are associated with times of greater restraint, suggesting that the courts do draw, even if unconsciously, a connection between the voting public and their own power.

Staton's above question also raises a third possibility: that constitutional court judges will recognise the importance of protecting the individual rights of citizens. An often-stated goal for courts is to protect the rights of all citizens, not just those who belong to the majority. Given the baseline goal in democratic society of equality among citizens, it is often seen as imperative that courts, the only major actors not directly beholden to the voting public, uphold this vision of rights protection for all. Anecdotally, there are many examples of such rights protecting behaviour, including Slovenia's 2009 decision on same-sex civil union inheritance laws and Poland's 2007 case striking down differences between men and women in retirement and pension standards.

When examining broad outcomes from these courts, though, there is limited evidence that a 'rights-protecting' vision of judicial review is realised in practice. This statement of only 'limited' confirmation must be qualified: these courts do, in fact, overturn laws involving individual civil rights claims at reasonably high rates, just not at the even higher rates seen in other areas of constitutional law.

And though these courts do not appear to take an overriding interest in promoting traditional civil rights claims (as was seen in Epp's (1998) study, for example), they do take strong interest in protecting certain socio-economic rights claims, including rights to pensions, social welfare, and other rights that ensure citizens live in dignity, free of basic deprivations. Therefore, in the Eastern European countries studied here, we may be seeing the protection of important rights, albeit in new areas of law and society.

Similarly, there is only partial confirmation for the existence of a 'legalist' vision of judicial review. Constitutional judges do engage in detailed public deliberation within their opinions, citing previous case law and scholarly works to support outcomes. In this sense, judges, through their opinions, do advance important democratic interests in the accountability of officials. Given that much more citation occurs when overturning laws, it appears judges do use precedent and other legal argumentation methods to show and to explain that the answer reached is the right answer. This need to legitimate decisions should be even more important for the judges in the newer Eastern European courts, where damaged communist-era judicial systems led to mistrust of judges (and other political actors) in the early transition period. However, strong adherents to the legalist vision for judicial review point to it as superior because it shuns the political decision-making that permeates other arguments in support of judicial review. Evidence from citation choices, however, point to distinct ideological effects within this ostensibly neutral process. The presence of ideological effects within the use of case law – favouring friendly precedent over ideologically distant cases – calls into question the larger arguments behind the legalist vision.

Stronger evidence exists for certain iterations of a majoritarian vision of judicial review. Chapter Six confirmed that career-based incentives lead to discernible changes in the voting patterns for some judges. Judges subject to reappointment have different voting patterns than fixed term judges, while younger judges move their voting closer to the interests of their appointers at the end of their terms. These differences in voting patterns show how elected actors can use appointment and retention schemes to potentially influence outcomes. These findings carry their own problems as such behaviour seemingly places the functional independence of courts in some jeopardy. However, other iterations of majoritarian review can be considered more beneficial for democratic government.

Notably, we see strong evidence in Chapter Five that courts are more activist when reviewing legislation that may be far from the majority will. Arguably, this type of 'majoritarian' behaviour is most in line with what we hope a majoritarian court could be. Rather than engage in partisanship, these courts are more willing to be active in overturning legislation produced by oversized governmental coalitions – coalitions that often include extreme or special interest parties, and that, due to their make-up, are more likely to produce pieces of legislation far from the median voter or legislator. By overturning laws from these oversized coalitions, constitutional courts can bring government policy back in line with majority preferences.

Ultimately, the evidence does support the idea that policy matters to court outcomes. Further, judges can be tied to majoritarian actors and processes in ways that may implicate the independence of the judiciary. At the same time, law is not an unimportant factor. This statement is not just faint praise. Major works in the field of public law have discounted the influence and meaning of law and methods of legal interpretation in constitutional judging. Others largely ignore the role of law, seeking instead the answers to questions of politics alone in constitutional court outcomes. In fact, few works have examined all potential influences on outcomes – law, politics, and rights protection. And though a vision of constitutional judges as pure seekers of impartial truth and 'right' answers is unsupported, we do see support for a view of judges as legal actors seeking to advance case law and develop compelling rationales to support their outcomes. Ultimately, there exists a tension between law and politics in constitutional judging, which is seen in constitutional outcomes. Examining this tension, it is apparent that law and politics both are important to constitutional court outputs. Judges seem cognisant of their job as judges, and judicial outcomes are supported by legal rationales. Yet even within the advancement of law, politics can intrude. We see the influence of politics not only in the basic outcomes of court cases, which are well predicted by ideology, but also in the advancement of jurisprudence and case law towards favoured pathways.

Apart from examining on a cross-national level multiple theories of judicial review, these chapters also have shown in a larger sense the importance of ideology and strategic interactions outside of the United States. These two factors are well established among scholars of the United States courts, yet relatively few studies have compared the importance of these factors to judicial decision-making across multiple countries. The cross-national perspective taken in this study does just that, and provides an important extension of past empirical work examining the judicial decision-making and the normative role of judicial review in democratic governance.

These findings can inform not only the literature in judicial politics but also other areas of comparative politics. The relationship between government coalition size and judicial outcomes speaks to larger structural interactions between judiciaries, legislatures, governments, and the mass public in parliamentary democracy. The overall activism of the constitutional courts in these newer democracies also should help advance theories of democratisation. To this day, one of the basic assumptions underlying the establishment and growth of judicial power is the need for judges to avoid confronting elected actors. Courts in new democracies around the world, from Ukraine to Honduras, are encouraged to tread delicately and focus on building trust, not courting conflict. The results from Chapter Four suggest constitutional courts can successfully be strong actors from an early time. However, we also saw that courts could be aided by government monitoring and oversight agencies – agencies that are designed to ensure that elected leaders stay within democratic bounds. Thus, empowering not only courts but also other outside institutions can help to improve compliance and build judicial power.

Finally, this study advances the field of comparative legal studies. The traditional story within comparative law – especially on the US side – holds that the use of precedent is a common law phenomenon. For many years, the subordinate role for the judiciary in civil law systems, viewed as either the mouth of the law, or the simple finder of law, allowed little explicit ability for judges to develop legal interpretation. This was all the more true in the Eastern European countries during the communist period, when the judiciary truly was subordinate to the interests of the party. Yet, the adoption of constitutional judicial review in these civil law systems allows judges new opportunities to develop case law and doctrine, and what we have seen is an embrace of that task. Judges, and their clerks, have developed in a short time a decision-making style based on the use of judicially created tests and the justification of current decisions in past outcomes.

In the end, judges matter to legal and policy outcomes in democratic societies. Given the important role judges play in creating these outcomes around the world, it is necessary to discover the pathways by which judges exercise judicial review, and the factors that lead to judicial outcomes broadly. This discovery is all the more important when considering the unrepresentative nature of most judiciaries around the world. Given that courts lack a direct connection to voters, conflicts between the judicial and the political branches of government raise important questions of democratic legitimacy. I have proposed several competing pathways through which courts can exercise judicial power within democratic norms, and achieve outcomes that advance democratic performance. In many ways, courts are responsive to democratic majorities, whether channeled through political actors or directly through the mass public. Courts also appear responsive to implied threats of overturn from the majoritarian legislative branch. Through career-based incentives, majoritarian actors also appear to hold some influence over judicial voting. Thus, while high courts often remain free from direct public or political pressures in their decision-making, the 'public will' often provides external boundaries on court action. And in democratic society, this is probably the most ideal outcome – a balance of formal judicial independence from the public or political actors in their decision-making combined with needed accountability to prevent unconstrained judicial power. Though judges play an increasingly important role in law and policy, the 'government of judges' that so worried many democratic thinkers has not materialised – largely due to the democratic bounds placed on court actions. Thus, in the end, the results of this study generally confirm that courts play an important, but properly limited, role in democratic government, one that is inherently policy-based, but not necessarily partisan or outside the bounds of the mainstream.

Bibliography

ABA Central and Eastern Europe Law Initiative (CEELI) (1993) *Report Submitted to the US Agency for International Development*. http://pdf. usaid.gov/pdf_docs/PNABZ142.pdf (accessed 30 November 2015).

Acemoglu, D. and Robinson, J. (2005) *The Economic Origins of Dictatorship and Democracy*, New York: Cambridge University Press.

Ackerman, B. (1992) *The Future of Liberal Revolution*. New Haven: Yale University Press.

Adolph, C. (2013) *Bankers, Bureaucrats, and Central Bank Politics*, New York: Cambridge University Press.

Alexander, L. and Schauer, F. (1997) 'On extrajudicial constitutional interpretation', *Harvard Law Review*, 110 (7): 1359–1387.

Alexy, R., and Drier, R. (1997) 'Precedent in the Federal Republic of Germany', in MacCormack, D.N., and Summers, R. (eds.) *Interpreting Precedents*, Brookfield: Ashgate, 17–64.

Algero, M.G. (2004) 'The sources and law and the value of precedent: A comparative and empirical study of a civil law state in a common law nation', *Louisiana Law Review*, 65: 775–822.

Amaral Garcia, S., Garoupa, N., and Grembi, V. (2009) 'Judicial independence and party politics in the Kelsenian Constitutional Courts: The case of Portugal', *Journal of Empirical Legal Studies*, 6(2): 381–404.

Applebaum, A. (2013) *Iron Curtain: The Crushing of Eastern Europe, 1944-1956*, New York: Anchor.

Arce, A. (2012), 'Honduran congress dismisses Supreme Court justices', *Associated Press*. 13 December. http://www.abcnews.com (accessed 18 March 2013).

Arsu, S. and Tavernise, S. (2009) 'Turkish media group fined $2.5 billion', *New York Times*, A11.

Ash, T.G. (1993) *The Magic Lantern*, New York: Vintage.

Aubry, C. and Rau, C. ([1869] 1971) *Droit civil francais*. St. Paul: West.

Barak, A. (2003) 'The nature of judicial discretion and its significance for the administration of justice', in Wiklund, O. (ed.) *Judicial Discretion in European Perspective*, Stockholm: Kluwer Law International, pp. 15–28.

Bawn, K. and Rosenbluth, F. (2006) 'Short versus long coalitions: Electoral accountability and the size of the public sector', *American Journal of Political Science*, 50(2): 251–265.

BBC Monitoring (2006) 'Latvian constitutional court chairman slams government over judge candidates', *LTV1 (Latvian Television)*. 8 December. www. lexisnexis.org (accessed 1 April 2015).

BBC (2006) 'Thousands stage gay rights parade in Polish capital', *BBC Worldwide*. 11 June. http://www.lexisnexis.org (accessed 8 March 2013).

— (2005a) 'Gay marchers ignore ban in Warsaw', *BBC Worldwide*. 11 June. http://news.bbc.co.uk/2/hi/europe/4084324.stm

— (2005b) 'Poland: Gay parade may go ahead despite ban', *BBC Worldwide*. 16 November. http://www.lexisnexis.org (accessed 10 March 2013).

— (2001) 'Polish Ombudsman Critical of State Bodies', *BBC Worldwide*. 16 May. http://www.lexisnexis.org (accessed 8 March 2013).

Beisner, F. (2011) *The German Historicist Tradition*, Oxford: Oxford University Press.

Bickel, A. (1962) *The Least Dangerous Branch*, Indianapolis: Bobb-Merrill.

Black, R. and Owens, R. (2015) 'Courting the President: How circuit court judges alter their behavior for promotion to the Supreme Court', *American Journal of Political Science*, forthcoming.

Black, Jr., C. L. (1960) *The People and the Court*, New York: Macmillan.

Blackstone, W. ([1753] 1893) *Commentaries on the Laws of England*, Philadelphia: J.B. Lippincott Co.

Bleich, E. (2011) *The Freedom to be Racist?*, New York: Oxford University Press.

Bloom, S. (2011) 'The 2010 Latvian parliamentary elections', *Electoral Studies*, 30: 366–383.

— (2008) 'Which minority is appeased? Coalition potential and redistribution in Latvia and Ukraine', *Europe-Asia Studies*, 60(9): 1575–1600.

Bobek, M. (2013) *Comparative Reasoning in European Supreme Courts*, Oxford: Oxford University Press.

Boix, C. (2003) *Democracy and Redistribution*, Princeton: Princeton University Press.

Boros, L. (2003) 'Social and political context of the transformation process in the Hungarian system of justice', in Priban, J., Roberts, P. and Young, J. (eds.) *Systems of Justice in Transition: Central European Experiences Since 1989*, Burlington, VT: Ashgate.

Brzezinski, M. (1998) *The Struggle for Constitutionalism in Poland*, New York: St. Martin's Press.

— (1991) 'Constitutional heritage and renewal: The case of Poland', *Virginia Law Review*, 77(1): 49–112.

Bugaric, B. (2001) 'Courts as policy-makers: Lessons from transition', *Harvard International Law Journal*, 42(1): 247–290.

Burley, A.M., and Mattli, W. (1993) 'Europe before the Court: A political theory of legal integration', *International Organization*, 47(1): 41–76.

Cappalli, R.B. (1998) 'At the point of decision: The common law's advantage over the civil law', *Temple International and Comparative Law Journal*, 12: 87–105.

Cappelletti, M. (1989) *The Judicial Process in Comparative Perspective*, Oxford: Oxford University Press.

— (1981) 'The doctrine of stare decisis and the civil law: A fundamental difference – or no difference at all?', in *Festschrift fur Konrad Zweigert zum 70. Geburtstag*. Tubingen: J.C.B. Mohr.

— (1980) 'The "mighty problem" of judicial review and the contribution of comparative analysis', *Southern California Law Review*, 53: 409–445.

— (1970) 'Judicial review in comparative perspective', *California Law Review*, 58(5): 1017–1053.

Cappelletti, M. and Adams, J.C. (1966) 'Judicial review of legislation: European antecedent and adaptions', *Harvard Law Review*, 79(6): 1207–1224.

Carothers, T. (1998) 'The rule of law revival', *Foreign Affairs*, 77: 95–108.

Carrubba, C. (2009) 'A model of the endogenous development of judicial institutions in federal and international systems', *Journal of Politics*, 71(1), p. 55–69.

Carrubba, C. and Gabel, M. (2014) *International Courts and the Performance of International Agreements*, Cambridge: Cambridge University Press.

Carrubba, C., Gabel, M. and Hankla, C. (2008) 'Judicial behavior under political constraints: Evidence from the European Court of Justice', *American Political Science Review*, 102(4): 435–452.

Casillas, C., Enns, P. and Wohlfarth, P. (2011) 'How public opinion constrains the U.S. Supreme Court', *American Journal of Political Science*, 55(1): 74–88.

Centrum Badania Opinii Spolecznej [Public Opinion Research Center] (CBOS) (2011) Research Reports. http://cbos.pl/EN/publications/reports.php (accessed 30 November 2015).

— (2007) Opinie Polakow o Trybunale Konstytucyjnym [Polish Opinion about the Constitutional Tribunal] http://cbos.pl/PL/publikacje/raporty.php (accessed 30 November 2015).

Cerar, M. (2002) 'Slovenia's Constitutional Court within the separation of powers', in Sadurski, W. (ed.) *Constitutional Justice, East and West*, The Hague: Kluwer, pp. 213–246.

Cichowski, R. (2007) *The European Court and Civil Society*, New York: Cambridge University Press.

Clark, T. (2011) *The Limits of Judicial Independence*, New York: Cambridge University Press.

— (2009) 'The separation of powers, court curbing, and judicial legitimacy', *American Journal of Political Science*, 53(4): 971–989.

Clark, W., Golder, M. and Golder, S. (2013) *Principles of Comparative Politics*, Washington: CQ Press.

Cook, L. (2013) *Post-Communist Welfare States: Reform Politics in Russia and Eastern Europe*, Ithaca: Cornell University Press.

Crombez, C. (1996) 'Minority governments, minimal winning coalitions and surplus majorities in parliamentary systems', *European Journal of Political Research*, 29(1): 1–29.

Cross, F., Spriggs II, J., Johnson, T. and Wahbeck, P. (2010) 'Citations in the U.S. Supreme Court: An empirical study of their use and significance', *University of Illinois Law Review*, 2010(1): 1–103.

CTK (2009a) 'Czech president wants powers of Constitutional Court changed', *Czech News Agency*, 10 September.

— (2009b) 'Czech president issues statement on court verdict, Lisbon treaty ratification', *Czech News Agency*. 3 November.

— (2006) 'Czech Constitutional Court overturns Supreme Court appointment', *Czech News Agency*. 19 December.

Czech Radio (2006) 'Czech Constitutional Court fails to deregulate rents', *Czech Radio 1*. 7 March. www.lexisnexis.org (accessed 12 April 2015).

Dahl, R. (1989) *Democracy and its Critics*, New Haven: Yale University Press.

— (1957) 'Decision-making in a democracy: The Supreme Court as a national policy-maker', *Journal of Public Law*, 6: 279–295.

Dainow, J. (1961) 'The constitutional and judicial organization of France and Germany and some comparisons of the civil law and common law systems', *Indiana Law Journal*, 37: 1–50.

Damaska, M. (1986) *The Faces of Justice and State Authority*, New Haven: Yale University Press.

Dawson, J. (1968) *The Oracles of the Law*, Ann Arbor: The University of Michigan Law School.

Del Luca, L. (2006) 'Developing global transnational harmonization procedures for the twenty-first century: The accelerating pace of common and civil law convergence', *Texas International Law Journal*, 42: 625–660.

Demokracija (2012) 'Nekdanji czef ZKS-SDP Ciril Ribicic ne bo lan Beneke komisije', *Demokracija*. 29 February. http://www.demokracija.si/v-fokusu/politika/10618-ciril-ribii-ne-bo-lan-beneke-komisije (accessed 2 February 2013).

Devroy, A. (1990) 'Bush backs E. Europe aid "corps": New program to seek money and volunteers from private sector', *Washington Post*. 13 May, p. A1.

Diena (2006) 'Government may be trying to destroy country's court system', *Diena*. 14 December. http://www.lexisnexis.org (accessed 2 March 2013).

Döring, H. and Manow, P. (2015) 'Parliament and government composition database (ParlGov): An infrastructure for empirical information on parties, elections and governments in modern democracies.' http://www. parlgov.org

Dworkin, R. (1996) *Freedom's Law: The moral reading of the american constitution*, Cambridge: Harvard University Press.

— (1977) *Taking Rights Seriously*, Cambridge: Harvard University Press.

Dyevre, A. (2010) 'Unifying the field of comparative judicial politics: Towards a general theory of judicial behaviour', *European Political Science Review*, 2(2): 297–327.

Dyevre, A. and Jakab, A. (2013) 'Foreword: Understanding constitutional reasoning', *German Law Journal*, 14: 983–1014.

Economist (2013) 'And then they came for the judges', *The Economist*, 19 January, p. 38.

— (2012) 'Messenger shot', *The Economist*, 1 December.

Edwards, H., and Livermore, M. (2009) 'Pitfalls of empirical studies that attempt to understand the factors affecting appellate decision-making', *Duke Law Journal*, 58: 1895–1989.

Elster, J. (1993) 'The necessity and impossibility of simultaneous economic and political reform', in Greenberg, D., Katz, S., Wheatley, S. and Oliviero, M. (eds.) *Constitutionalism and Democracy: Transitions in the contemporary world*, Oxford: Oxford University Press, pp. 267–274.

Ely, J.H. (1980) *Democracy and Distrust: A theory of judicial review*, Cambridge: Harvard University Press.

Enyedi, Z. (2005) 'The role of agency in cleavage formation', *European Journal of Political Research*, 44: 1–25.

Epp, C. (1998) *The Rights Revolution*, Chicago: University of Chicago Press.

Epstein, L. and Knight, J. (1998) *The Choices Justices Make*, Washington, DC: Congressional Quarterly Press.

Epstein, L. and George, T. (1992) 'On the nature of Supreme Court decision making', *American Political Science Review*, 86(2): 322–337.

Epstein, L., Posner, R. and Landes, W. (2013) *The Behavior of Federal Judges*, Cambridge: Harvard University Press.

Epstein, L., Knight, J. and Shvetsova, O. (2002) 'Selecting selection systems', in Burbank, S. and Friedman, B. (eds.) *Judicial Independence at the Crossroads*, Sage. pp. 190–226.

— (2001a) 'The role of constitutional courts in the establishment and maintenance of democratic systems of government', *Law and Society Review*, 35(1): 117–164.

— (2001b) 'Comparing judicial selection systems', *William and Mary Bill of Rights Law Journal*, 10(1): 7–36.

Epstein, L., Segal, J. and Spaeth, H. (2001) 'The norm of consensus on the U.S. Supreme Court', *American Journal of Political Science*, 45(2): 362–377

Eskridge, W. (1991) 'Overriding Supreme Court statutory interpretation decisions', *Yale Law Journal*, 101(November): 331–456.

Europa (2007) Phare programme. http://eur-lex.europa.eu/legal-content/EN/TXT/?uri=URISERV%3Ae50004 (accessed 30 November 2015).

Falcon y Tella, M.J. (2011) *Case Law in Roman, Anglo-Saxon, and Continental Law*. Leiden: Martinus Nijhoff Publishers.

Farber, D. (2006) 'The rule of law and the law of precedents', *Minnesota Law Review*, 90: 1173–1203.

Faiola, A. and Moura, P. 'Middle-class rage sparks protest movements in Turkey, Brazil, Bulgaria and beyond', *Washington Post*, 28 June, A1.

Favoreu, L. (1990) 'Le droit constitutionnel, droit de la constitution et constitution du droit', *Revue Française De Droit Constitutionnel*, 1: 71–89.

Febbrajo, A. (2010) 'Legal cultures in transition: A system-theory approach', in Febbrajo, A. and Sadurski, W. (eds.) *Central and Eastern Europe After Transition*, Surrey: Ashgate, pp. 35–72.

Ferejohn, J. and Pasquino, P. (2004) 'Constitutional adjudication: Lessons from Europe', *Texas Law Review*, 82(7): 1671–1704.

— (2002) 'Constitutional courts as deliberative institutions', in Sadurski, W. (ed.) *Constitutional Justice, East and West*, The Hague: Kluwer, pp. 21–36.

Ferreres Comella, V. (2009) *Constitutional Courts and Democratic Values. A European Perspective*, New Haven: Yale University Press.

Financial Times (2013) 'Editorial: Orban's threat to democratic values', *Financial Times*, 5 March, p. 12.

Fiss, O. (1994) 'Introductory remarks, judiciary panel, constitutionalism in the Post-Cold-War world', *Yale Journal of International Law*, 19(1): 219–254.

Fon, V. and Parisi, F. (2005) *Judicial Precedents in Civil Law Systems: A dynamic analysis*, American Law & Economics Association Annual Meetings, Working Paper 10.

Franck, R. (2009) 'Judicial independence under a divided polity: A study of the rulings of the French Constitutional Court, 1959–2006', *Journal of Law, Economics and Organization*, 25(1): 262–284.

Friedman, B. (2009) *The Will of the People: how public opinion has influenced the supreme court and shaped the meaning of the constitution* New York: Farrar, Straus and Giroux.

Galyas. V. (2014) 'The US cancels visas for Hungarians involved in corruption', *The Wall Street Journal*. 17 October. http://wsj.com (accessed 15 February 2015).

Garlicki, L.L. (2005) 'Constitutional law', in Frankowski, S. (ed.) *Introduction to Polish Law*, The Hague: Kluwer Law International.

— (2002) 'The experience of the Polish Constitutional Court', in Sadurski, W. (ed.), *Constitutional Justice, East and West*, London: Kluwer Law International, pp. 265–282.

Gelter, M. and Siems, M. (2012) 'Networks, dialogue, or one-way traffic? An empirical analysis of cross-citations between ten of Europe's highest courts', *Utrecht Law Review*, 8: 88–99.

Gibson, J. and Caldeira, G. (2009) *Citizens, Courts, and Confirmations: positivity theory and the judgments of the american people*, Princeton: Princeton University Press.

Giles, M., Blackstone, B. and Vining, R. (2008) 'The Supreme Court in American democracy: unraveling the linkages between public opinion and judicial decision making', *Journal of Politics*, 70(2): 293–306.

Ginsburg, T. (2003) *Judicial Review in New Democracies*, New York: Cambridge University Press.

Ginsburg, T. and Versteeg, M. (2014) 'Why do countries adopt constitutional review?', *Journal of Law, Economics and Organization*, 30: 587–605.

Glaeser, A. (2011) *Political Epistemics*. Chicago: University of Chicago Press.

Golder, M. and Stramksi, J. (2010) 'Ideological congruence and electoral institutions,' *American Journal of Political Science*, 54(1): 90–106.

Goodhart, A. (1934) 'Precedent in English and continental law', *Law Quarterly Review*, 50: 40–67.

Gordley, J. and von Mehren, A. (2006) *An Introduction to the Comparative Study of Private Law*, New York: Cambridge University Press.

Gordon, S., and Huber, G. (2007) 'The effect of electoral competitiveness on incumbent behavior', *Quarterly Journal of Political Science*, 2(2): 107–138.

Grijalva, A. (2010) *Courts and Political Parties: The politics of constitutional review in ecuador*, unpublished Ph.D. thesis, University of Pittsburgh.

Groppi, T. and Ponthoreau, M. C. (eds.) (2013) *The Use of Precedents by Constitutional Judges*, Oxford: Hart Publishing.

Grzymala-Busse, A. (2007) *Rebuilding Leviathan*, New York: Cambridge University Press.

— (2002) *Redeeming the Communist Past*, Cambridge: Cambridge University Press.

Guarnieri, C. and Pederzoli, P. (2002) *The Power of Judges: A comparative study of courts and democracy*, Oxford: Oxford University Press.

Hague, R. and Harrop, M. (2010) *Political Science: A Comparative Introduction*, London: Palgrave Macmillan.

Hall, M.G. (1992) 'Electoral politics and strategic voting in state supreme courts', *Journal of Politics*, 54(2): 427–446.

Hall, M.K. (2012) 'Rethinking regime politics', *Law & Social Inquiry*, 37(4): 878–907.

Hanretty, C. (2012) 'Dissent in Iberia: The ideal points of justices on the Spanish and Portuguese Constitutional Tribunals', *European Journal of Political Research*, 51: 671–692.

Hansford, T. and Spriggs II, J. (2006) *The Politics of Precedent on the U.S. Supreme Court*, Princeton: Princeton University Press.

Hamilton, A., Madison, J. and Jay, J. (1961). *The Federalist Papers*, New York: Penguin Press.

Hart, H.L.A. ([1961] 2012) *The Concept of Law*, 3rd edn. Oxford: Oxford University Press.

Hart, H.M., Jr. (1959) 'The Supreme Court, 1958 term, forward: The time chart of the justices', *Harvard Law Review*, 73: 84–125.

Harvey, A. (2013) *A Mere Machine*, New Haven: Yale University Press.

Harvey, A. and Friedman, B. (2006) 'Pulling punches: Congressional constraints on the Supreme Court's constitutional rulings, 1987–2000', *Legislative Studies Quarterly*, 31(4): 533–562.

Havel, V. (1992) *Open Letters: Selected writings*, New York: Vintage.

Helmke, G. (2005) *Courts Under Constraints*, New York: Cambridge University Press.

—— (2002) 'The logic of strategic defection: Court-executive relations in Argentina under dictatorship and democracy', *American Political Science Review*, 96(2): 291–303.

Helmke, G. and Staton, J. (2011) 'The puzzling judicial politics of Latin America', in Helmke, G. and Rios-Figueroa, J. (eds.) *Courts in Latin America*, New York: Cambridge University Press, pp. 306–320.

Henisz, W. (2010) *The Political Constraint (POLCON) Index*. https://mgmt. wharton.upenn.edu/profile/1327

Hilbink, L. (2008) 'Judicial independence in authoritarian regimes: insights from Chile', in Ginsburg, T. and Moustafa, T. (eds.) *Rule By Law*, New York: Cambridge University Press.

Holmes, O.W. (1881). *The Common Law*, Boston: Little, Brown and company.

Hondius, E. (2004) 'Precedent in East and West', *Penn State International Law Review*, 23: 521–535.

Hönnige. C. (2011). 'Beyond judicialization: Why we need more comparative research about constitutional courts,' *European Political Science*, 10: 346–357.

—— (2009) 'The electoral connection: How the pivotal judge affects oppositional success at European constitutional courts', *West European Politics*, 35(2): 963–984.

Huber, J. and Gordon, S. (2004) 'Accountability and coercion: Is justice blind when it runs for office?', *American Journal of Political Science*, 48(2): 247–263.

Hubner-Mendes, C. (2013) *Constitutional Courts and Deliberative Democracy*, Oxford: Oxford University Press.

Human Rights Watch (HRW) (2013) *Wrong Direction on Rights: Assessing the impact of hungary's new constitution and laws*, www.hrw.org (accessed 4 April 2015).

Iaryczower M., Spiller P. and Mariano, T. (2002) 'Judicial independence in unstable environments', *American Journal of Political Science*, 46: 699–716.

Jhering, R. von (1915) *The Struggle for Law*, trans. John J. Lalor, Chicago: Callaghan and Co.

Keleman, R.D. (2006) 'Suing for Europe: Adversarial legalism and European governance', *Comparative Political Studies*, 39(1): 101–127.

Kelsen, H. (1945) *General Theory of Law and State*, Cambridge: Harvard University Press.

Kennedy, D. (2010) 'Savigny's family/patrimony distinction and its place in the global genealogy of classical legal thought', *American Journal of Comparative Law*, 58: 811–841.

Keszthelyi, K. (2014) 'PM: There's democracy in Hungary – Period', *Budapest Business Journal*, 15 December. http://bbj.hu (accessed 15 February 2015).

King, G., Keohane, R. and Verba, S. (1994) *Designing Social Inquiry: Scientific inference in qualitative research*, Princeton: Princeton University Press.

Kischel, U. (2013) 'Party, pope, and politics? The election of German Constitutional Court Justices in comparative perspective', *International Journal of Constitutional Law*, 11(4): 962–979.

Klarman, M. (1997) 'Majoritarian judicial review: The entrenchment problem', *Georgetown Law Journal*, 85: 491–553.

Klerman, D. and Mahoney, P. (2007) 'Legal Origin' *Journal of Comparative Economics*, 35: 278–293.

Knight, J. and Epstein, L. (1996). 'The norm of stare decisis', *American Journal of Political Science*, 40(November): 1018–1035.

Komarek, J. (2012) *Reasoning with Past Decisions*, LSE Law, Society and Economy Working Papers 8/2012.

Kruma, K. (2009) 'Checks and balances in Latvian nationality policy', in Bauböck, R., Perchinig, B. and Sievers, W. (eds.) *Citizenship Policies in the New Europe*, Amsterdam: Amsterdam University Press, pp. 67–96.

Kuhn, Z. (2011) *The Judiciary in Central and Eastern Europe: Mechanical jurisprudence in transition?*, Leiden: Martinus Nijhoff.

— (2010) 'The democratization and modernization of post-communist judiciaries', in Febbrajo, A. and Sadurski, W. (eds.) *Central and Eastern Europe after Transition*, Brookfield: Ashgate.

— (2004) 'Worlds apart: Western and Central European judicial culture at the onset of the European enlargement', *American Journal of Comparative Law*, 52(3): 531–567.

Kulish, N. (2010) 'Gay parade in Warsaw meets jeers from some', *New York Times*, 18 July, p. A10.

Kurski, J. (2008) 'PiS violently refusing to let go', *Gazeta Wyborca*, 7 February. http://www.lexisnexis.org (accessed 28 March 2015).

— (2007) 'What has the PiS Government given us', *Gazeta Wyborcza*, 7 September. http://www.lexisnexis.org (accessed 28 March 2015).

La Porta, R., Lopez de Silanes, F., Pop-Eleches, C. and Schleifer, A. (2004) 'judicial checks and balances', *Journal of Political Economy*, 112(2): 445–470.

Lambert, E. (1921). *Le government des juges en la lute contre la legislation sociale aux Etats-Unis*, Paris: M. Giard and Cie.

Lasser, M. (2004) *Judicial Deliberations: A Comparative analysis of judicial transparency and legitimacy*, Oxford: Oxford University Press.

Law, D. (2009) 'A theory of judicial power and judicial review', *Georgetown Law Journal*, 97: 723–801.

Law, D. and Versteeg, M. (2012) 'The declining influence of the United States Constitution,' *NYU Law Review*, 87: 763–858.

Leiter, B. (2010) *Legal Formalism and Legal Realism: What is the issue?*, Working Paper.

Letowska, E. (1990) 'The Polish Ombudsman (The Commissioner for the Protection of Civil Rights)', *International and Comparative Law Quarterly*, 39(1): 206–217.

Letowska, E. (1994) 'The Polish Ombudsman and Human Rights', in Matscher, F. (ed.) *Ombudsmen in Europe: The institution*, N.P Engel: Strasbourg, pp. 57–103.

Levi E. (1949) *An Introduction to Legal Reasoning*, Chicago: University of Chicago Press.

Levine, A. (1993) *The General Will*, New York: Cambridge University Press.

Lijphart, A. (1999) *Patterns of Democracy: Government Forms and Performance in Thirty-Six Countries*, New Haven: Yale University Press.

— (1991) 'Constitutional choices for new democracies', *Journal of Democracy*, 2(1): pp. 72–84.

MacCormack, D.N. and Summers, R. (eds.) (1997) *Interpreting Precedents*, Brookfield: Ashgate.

Mattei, U. and Pes, L. (2008) 'Civil law and common law: Toward convergence?', in Whittington, K., Keleman, R.D. and Caldeira, G., (eds.) *Oxford Handbook of Law and Politics*, Oxford: Oxford University Press.

Magalhaes, P. (1999) 'The politics of judicial reform in Eastern Europe', *Comparative Politics*, 32(1): 43–62.

Mahoney, P. (2001) 'The common law and economic development: Hayek might be right', *Journal of Legal Studies*, 30: 503–527.

Maltzman, F., Spriggs II, J. and Wahlbeck, P. (2000) *Crafting Law on the Supreme Court: The collegial game*, New York: Cambridge University Press.

Manchin, R. (2004) 'Religion in Europe: Trust not filling the pews', *Gallup*. 21 September. http://www.gallup.com (accessed 10 March 2013).

Markovtis, I. (1996) 'Children of a lesser God: GDR lawyers in post-socialist Germany', *Michigan Law Review*, 94: 2270–2330.

— (1982) 'Law or order – constitutionalism and legality in Eastern Europe', *Stanford Law Review*, 34: 513–613.

Martin, L. and Vanberg, G. (2013) 'Multiparty government, fiscal institutions, and public spending,' *The Journal of Politics*, 75(4): 953–967.

Mavcic, A. (2009) *Slovenian Constitutional Review*, Postojna: MV.

Merryman, J.H. and Perez-Perdomo, R. (2007) *The Civil Law Tradition: An introduction to the legal systems of Europe and Latin America*, 3rd edn, Stanford: Stanford University Press.

Miasik, D. (2008) 'Application of general principles of EC law by Polish courts', in Bernitz, U., Nergelius, J. and Cardner, C. (eds.) *General Principles of EC Law in a Process of Development*, Alphen an den Rijn: Kluwer Law International.

Millard, F. (2010) *Democratic Elections in Poland*, Surrey: Ashgate.

Mishler, W. and Sheehan, R. (1993) 'The Supreme Court as a countermajoritarian institution? The impact of public opinion on Supreme Court decisions,' *American Political Science Review*, 87(1): 87–101.

Mitchell, P. and Nyblade, B. (2008) 'Government Formation and Cabinet Type in Parliamentary Democracies', in Strøm, K., Müller, W. and Bergman, T. (eds.), *Cabinets and Coalition Bargaining*, Oxford: Oxford University Press, pp. 201–236.

Moffett, J. (1998) 'Poland: Ex-communist constitutional courts face similar problems', *RFE/RL*. 30 September. http://www.rferl.org (accessed 15 January 2013).

Moraski, B. and Shipan, C. (1999) 'The Politics of Supreme Court Nominations: A Theory of Institutional Constraints', *American Journal of Political Science*, 43(4): 1069–1095.

Morawski, L. and Zirk-Sadowski, M. (1997) 'Precedent in Poland', in MacCormack, D.N. and Summers, R. (eds.), *Interpreting Precedents*, Brookfield: Ashgate, pp. 219–258.

Moser, R. (1999) 'Electoral systems and the number of parties in postcommunist states', *World Politics*, 51(3): 359–384.

Novak, M. (2003) 'The promising gift of precedents: Changes in the culture and techniques of judicial decision-making in Slovenia', in Priban, J., Roberts, P. and Young, J. (eds.) *Systems of Justice in Transition*, Aldershot: Ashgate, pp. 94–108.

North, D. and Weingast, B. (1989) 'Constitutions and commitment: The evolution of institutions governing public choice in seventeenth-century England', *Journal of Economic History*, 49(4): 803–832.

Open Society Institute (2001) *Monitoring the EU accession process: Judicial independence*, Budapest: Central European University Press.

Owens, R. (2010) 'The separation of powers, judicial independence, and strategic agenda setting', *American Journal of Political Science*, 54(2): 412–427.

Paiders, J. (2010) 'LB President: Nothing indicates second phase in global recession', *Neatkariga Rita Avize*. 24 February. http://www.lexisnexis. org (accessed 1 March 2013).

PAP (2005) 'Gay pride parade may go ahead despite ban', *PAP News Agency*. 16 November.

Pelc, R. (2001) *Polish Model of Relations Between Ombudsmen and Judicial Bodies*, Warsaw: Office for the Commissioner for Civil Rights Protection.

Pellegrina, L.D., and Garoupa, N. (2013) 'Choosing between the government and the regions: An empirical analysis of the Italian constitutional court decisions', *European Journal of Political Research*, 52(4): 558–580.

Peretti, T. (2002) 'Does judicial independence exist?', in Burbank, S. and Friedman, B. (eds.), *Judicial Independence at the Crossroads*, Thousand Oaks: Sage Press, pp. 103–133.

Peto, P. (2012) 'The limit of the rule of law', *Nepszabadsag*, 20 July. www.lexinexis.org (accessed 20 March 2013).

Pfander, J. (2007) 'Federal supremacy, state court inferiority, and the constitutionality of jurisdiction stripping', *Northwestern University Law Review*, 101: 191–238.

Piana, D. (2010) *Judicial Accountabilities in New Europe: From rule of law to quality of justice*, Surrey: Ashgate.

Posner, E. and Sunstein, C. (2006) *The Law of Other States*, Chicago Public Law and Legal Theory Working Paper no. 119.

Powell, G.B. (2000) *Elections as Instruments of Democracy*, New Haven: Yale University Press.

—   (2004) 'The chain of responsiveness', *Journal of Democracy*, 15(4): 91–105.

—   (1982) *Contemporary Democracies: Participation, stability and violence*, Cambridge: Harvard University Press.

Puchta, G.F. (1887) *Outlines of the Science of Jurisprudence*, trans. W. Hastie, Edinburgh: T&T Clark.

Rasmusen, E. and Ramseyer, J.M. (2001), 'Why are Japanese judges so conservative in politically charged cases?', *American Political Science Review*, 95(2): 331–344.

Riker, W. (1962) *The Theory of Political Coalitions*, New Haven: Yale University Press.

Rogers, J.R. (2001) 'Information and judicial review: A signaling game of legislative-judicial interaction', *American Journal of Political Science*, 45(January): 84–99.

Rogowski, R. (1989) *Materialism and Post-Materialism*, Ann Arbor: University of Michigan Press.

Romeau, F.R. (2006) 'The establishment of constitutional courts: A study of 128 democratic constitutions', *Review of Law and Economics*, 2(1): 103–105.

Rosenberg, G. (2008) *The Hollow Hope: Can courts bring about social change?*, 2nd edn, Chicago: University of Chicago Press.

Rothschild, J. and Wingfield, N. (2000) *Return to Diversity*, 2nd edn, New York: Oxford University Press.

Rozenkrantz, C. (2003) 'Against borrowing and other non-authoritative uses of foreign law', *International Journal of Constitutional Law (I-CON)*, 1(2): 259–295.

Rytter, J. and Wind, M. (2011) 'In need of juristocracy? The silence of Denmark in the development of European legal norms', *International Journal of Constitutional Law*, 9(2): 470–504.

Rzecznika Praw Obywatelskich [Commissioner for Citizens' Rights] (RPO) (2008) Summary of report on the activity of the commissioner for civil rights protection in 2008 with some remarks on observance of human and civil rights and freedoms. http://www.rpo.gov.pl/pliki/12785944960.pdf

Sadurski, W. (2014) *Rights Before Courts: A study of constitutional courts in postcommunist states of central and eastern europe*, 2nd edn, Dordrecht: Springer.

—   (2010) 'Constitutional courts and constitutional culture', in Febbrajo, A. and Sadurski, W. (eds.), *Central and Eastern Europe After Transition*, Surrey: Ashgate, pp. 99–118.

— (2009) 'Twenty years after the transition: Constitutional review in Central and Eastern Europe', *Sydney Law School Legal Studies Research Paper* No. 09/69.

— (2006) 'Solange, chapter 3: Constitutional courts in Central Europe', EIU Working Paper no. 2006/40.

— (1999) 'Postcommunist constitutional courts in search of political legitimacy', Working Paper.

Safjan, M. (2006) 'Let's not embroil the Constitutional Tribunal into PiS politics', *Gazeta Wyborcza*, 7 February.

Savigny, F.K. von ([1831] 1975). *Of the Vocation of our Age for Legislation and Jurisprudence*, trans. A. Hayward, New York: Arno Press.

Scalia, A. (1989a) 'Originalism: The lesser evil', *University of Cincinnati Law Review*, 57: 849–865.

— (1989b) 'The Rule of law as a law of rules', *University of Chicago Law Review*, 56(4): 1175–1188.

Scally, D. (2004a) 'Polish PM holds onto office by narrow margin', *Irish Times*, 25 June, p. 13.

— (2004b) 'Poland's interim PM may win vote today', *Irish Times*, 24 June, p. 10.

— (2004c) 'Poland says EU accession sure despite PM's fall', *Irish Times*, 29 March, p. 11.

Scheppele, K.L. (2013) 'Constitutional revenge', *New York Times*, 1 March. http://krugman.blogs.nytimes.com

— (2005) 'Democracy by judiciary. Or, why courts can be more democratic than parliaments', in Czarnota, A., Krygier, M. and Sadurski, W. (eds.) *Rethinking the Rule of Law after Communism*, Budapest: Central European University Press.

— (2002) 'Declarations of independence: Judicial responses to political Pressure', in Burbank, S. and Friedman, B. (eds.), *Judicial Independence at the Crossroads*. Thousand Oaks: Sage Press.

Schofield, N. (1993) 'Political competition and multiparty coalition governments', *European Journal of Political Research*, 23 (January): 1–33.

Schauer, F. (1987) 'Precedent', *Stanford Law Review*, 39: 571–605.

Schlink, B. (1992) 'German constitutional culture in transition', *Cardozo Law Review*, 14: 711–736.

Schwartz, H. (2000) *The Struggle for Constitutional Justice in Post-Communist Europe*, Chicago: University of Chicago Press.

Schwartz, B. (1996) *Decision*, New York: Oxford University Press.

Segal, J. and Spaeth, H. (2002) *The Supreme Court and the Attitudinal Model Revisited*, New York: Cambridge University Press.

Shambayati, H. (2008) 'Courts in a semi-democratic/authoritarian regime: The judicialization of Turkish and Iranian politics', in Ginsburg, T. and Moustafa, T. (eds.) *Rule By Law*, New York: Cambridge University Press, pp. 283–303.

Shapiro, M. (2008) 'Courts in authoritarian regimes', in Ginsburg, T. and Moustafa, T. (eds.) *Rule By Law*, New York: Cambridge University Press, pp. 326–336.

— (2003) 'Judicial review in developed democracies', *Democratization*, 10(4): 726–740.

— (1981) *Courts: A comparative and political analysis*, Chicago: University of Chicago Press.

Shapiro, M. and Stone Sweet, A. (eds.) (2002) *On Law, Politics and Judicialization*, New York: Oxford University Press.

Shepherd, J. (2009) 'The influence of retention politics on judges' voting', *Journal of Legal Studies*, 38(1): 169–206.

Siedlicka, E. (2008) 'The abortion debate: New chapter', *Gazeta Wyborca*. 7 January.

Siems, M. (2010) 'Citation patterns of the German Federal Supreme Court and of the Court of Appeal of England and Wales', *King's Law Journal*, 21(1): 152–171.

Sloga, G. (2006) 'Lawyers do not support change in ST functions', *Diena*. 18 October.

Sobczyk, M. (2010) 'Hungary approves controversial media law.' *Wall Street Journal*. 21 December. http://blogs.wsj.com/emergingeurope (accessed 5 February 2015).

Spaeth, H. and Segal, J. (1999) *Majority Rule or Minority Will: Adherence to Precedence on the U.S. Supreme Court*, New York: Cambridge University Press.

Spiliotopoulos, E. (1983) 'Judicial review of legislative acts in Greece', *Temple Law Quarterly*, 56(2): 26–54.

St Thomas Aquinas (1947) *Summa Theologica*, Boston: Benziger Bros.

Staton, J. (2010) *Judicial Power and Strategic Communication in Mexico*, New York: Cambridge University Press.

— (2006) 'Constitutional review and the selective promotion of case results', *American Journal of Political Science*, 50(1): 98–112.

Stephenson, M. (2004) 'Court of public opinion: Government accountability and judicial independence', *Journal of Law, Economics and Organization*, 20(2): 379–399.

Stern, S. and Wermiel, S. (2009) *Justice Brennan: Liberal champion*, New York: Basic Books.

Stone, H.F. (1936) 'The common law in the United States', *Harvard Law Review*, 50(1): 4–30.

Stone, A. (1992) *The Birth of Judicial Politics in France*, Oxford: Oxford University Press.

Stone Sweet, A (2007) 'The politics of constitutional review in France and Europe', *International Journal of Constitutional Law* (I-CON), 5(1): 69–92.

— (2000) *Governing with Judges*, New York: Oxford University Press.

Stone Sweet, A. and Mathews, J. (2008) 'Proportionality balancing and global constitutionalism', *Columbia Journal of Transnational Law*, 47: 72–164.

Stone Sweet, A. and McCown, M. (2003) 'Discretion and precedent in European law', in Wiklund, O. (ed.) *Judicial Discretion in European Perspective*, Stockholm: Kluwer Law International, pp. 84–115.

Strøm, K. (1990) *Minority Government and Majority Rule*, Cambridge: Cambridge University Press.

Sunstein, C. (1999) *One Case at a Time*, Cambridge: Harvard University Press.

Tate, C.N. (1981) 'Personal attribute models of voting behavior of U.S. Supreme Court justices', *American Political Science Review*, 75: 355–367.

Tavits, M. (2009) *Presidents with Prime Ministers*, New York: Oxford University Press.

Tavits, M. and Letki, N. (2009) 'When left is right: Party ideology and policy in post-communist Europe', *American Political Science Review*, 103(4): 555–569.

Tocqueville, A. de ([1838] 1966) *Democracy in America*, G. Lawrence, trans., New York: Harper Perennial.

Tokes, R.L. (1997) 'Party politics and political participation in postcommunist Hungary', in Dawisha, K. and Parrott, B. (eds.) *The consolidation of democracy in East-Central Europe*, Cambridge: Cambridge University Press.

Trochev, A. (2008) *Judging Russia*, New York: Cambridge University Press.

Troper, M. (2003) 'The logic of justification of judicial review', *International Journal of Constitutional Law*, 1(1): 99–121.

Tsebelis, G. (2002) *Veto-Players: How political institutions work*, Princeton: Princeton University Press.

Tsebelis, G. (1995) 'Veto players and law production in parliamentary democracies', in Doering, H. (ed.), *Parliaments and Majority Rule in Western Europe*, New York: St. Martin's Press, pp. 83–111.

Tushnet, M. (1999) *Taking the Constitution Away from the Courts*, Princeton: Princeton University Press.

Tyler, T. and Mitchell, G. (1994) 'Legitimacy and the empowerment of discretionary legal authority: The United States Supreme Court and abortion rights', *Duke Law Journal*, 43 (February): 703–815.

Uitz, R. (2007) 'Constitutional Courts in Central and Eastern Europe: What Makes a Question Too Political?', *Juridica International*, 2(1): 47–60.

US Supreme Court (2013) *Shelby County v Holder* Oral Arguments Transcript. http://www.supremecourt.gov/oral_arguments/argument_transcripts/12-96.pdf

Vanberg, G. (2005) *The Politics of Constitutional Review in Germany*, New York: Cambridge University Press.

Vanberg, G. (2001) 'Legislative-judicial relations: A game-theoretic approach to constitutional review', *American Journal of Political Science*, 45(2): 346–361.

Vermeule, A. (2010) *Second Opinions*, Harvard Law School Discussion Paper 673.

Volcansek, M. (2000). *Constitutional Politics in Italy*, New York: Palgrave Macmillan.

Volden, C. and Carrubba, C.J. (2004) 'The formation of oversized coalitions in parliamentary democracies', *American Journal of Political Science*, 48(3): 521–537.

Volkens, A., Lacewell, O., Lehmann, P., Regel, S., Schultze, H. and Werner, A. (2011) *The Manifesto Data Collection*, Manifesto Project (MRG/CMP/ MARPOR). Berlin: Wissenschaftszentrum Berlin fr Sozialforschung (WZB).

Von Mehren, A., and Gordley, J. (1977) *The Civil Law System*, Boston: Little, Brown.

Waldron, J. (2006) 'The core of the case against judicial review', *Yale Law Journal*, 115: 1346–1406.

Walencik, I. and Domagalski, M. (2011) 'Polish Constitutional Court Reviews EU Law', *Rzeczpospolita*, 17 November.

Waluchow, W. (2007) *A Common Law Theory of Judicial Review: The living tree*, Cambridge: Cambridge University Press.

Whittington, K. (2007) *Political Foundations of Judicial Supremacy: The presidency, the supreme court, and constitutional leadership in U.S. history*, Princeton: Princeton University Press.

— (2005) '"Interpose Your Friendly Hand": Political supports for the exercise of judicial review by the United States Supreme Court', *American Political Science Review*, 99(November): 583–596.

Zink, J., Spriggs II, J.F. and Scott, J. (2009) 'Courting the public: The influence of decision attributes on individuals' views of court opinions', *Journal of Politics*, 71(3): 909–925.

Zweigert, K. & Kötz, H. (2011) *An Introduction to Comparative Law*, 2nd edn, Oxford: Oxford University Press.

Cases

Czech Republic

Pl. US 9/01, 5 December 2001.
Pl. US 50/04, 3 March 2006.

Germany

Greece Bailout Case, 2 BVR 987/10, 129 BVerfGE 124, decision of 7 September 2011.
The Bavarian Crucifix Case, 1 BVR 1087/91, BVerfGE 93, decision of 16 May 1995.
Re Wuensche Handelsgesellschaft, 3 CMLR 225, BVerfGE decision of 22 October 1986.

Latvia

Judgment 2003–22–01, 26 March 2004.
Judgment 2009–76–01, 31 March 2010.
Judgment 2009–43, 21 December 2009.

Poland
Case P 10/07, 23 October 2007
Case K 2/07, 11 May 2007
Case K 21/05, 18 January 2006
Case K 4/05, 19 April 2005
Case K 32/03, 20 March 2004
Case K 48/01, 2 October 2002
Case K 5/01, 29 May 2001
Case K 11/00, 4 April 2001
Case P 11/98, 12 January 2000
Case K 23/98, 25 February 1999
Case K 39/97, 8 October 1997
Case K 15/97, 29 September 1997
Case P 2/87, 2 March 1987

Slovenia
Blazic and Kern v Slovenia, U-I-425/06–10, 2 July 2009
Decision U-I-298/96 of 11 November 1999
Case U-I-121/97 of 23 May 1997

South Africa
Government of the Republic of South Africa v Grootboom, 2000 11 BCLR
        1169 (CC).

United States
Baker v Carr 369 US 186 (1962)
Blodgett v Holden 275 US 142 (1927)
Brandenburg v Ohio 395 US 444 (1969)
Brown v Board of Education 347 US 483 (1954)
Buck v. Bell 274 US 200 (1927)
Calder v Bull 3 US 386 (1798)
Marbury v Madison 5 US 137 (1803)
RAV v St Paul 505 US 377 (1992)
Snyder v Phelps 562 US ___ (2011)
United States v Carolene Products Company 304 US 144 (1938)
United States v Windsor 570 US ___ (2013)

Index

Lightning Source UK Ltd.
Milton Keynes UK
UKHW02f0808280818
327907UK00005B/503/P